THE DEVELOPMENT OF
THE AMERICAN CONSTITUTION

THE NEW AMERICAN NATION SERIES

Edited by HENRY STEELE COMMAGER *and*

RICHARD B. MORRIS

William E. Leuchtenburg	FRANKLIN D. ROOSEVELT AND THE NEW DEAL, 1932-1940. TB/3025.
A. Russell Buchanan	THE UNITED STATES AND WORLD WAR II, Volume I. TB/3044.
A. Russell Buchanan	THE UNITED STATES AND WORLD WAR II, Volume II. TB/3045.
Alfred B. Rollins, Jr.	POST WORLD WAR II—Domestic Affairs.*
Kenneth W. Thompson	AMERICAN FOREIGN POLICY SINCE 1945.*
Allen J. Matusow	THE DOMESTIC POLICIES OF KENNEDY AND JOHNSON.*
Earl Pomeroy	THE WEST IN THE TWENTIETH CENTURY.*
David M. Potter	FROM SECTIONALISM TO SECESSION, 1856–1861.*
David M. Potter	THE MOUNTING SECTIONAL CRISIS, 1846-1856.*
Projected titles:	CULTURAL HISTORY, 1860-1865.
	AMERICAN CULTURE IN THE TWENTIETH CENTURY.
	THE NEW SOUTH.

* *In preparation*

THE DEVELOPMENT
OF THE AMERICAN
CONSTITUTION
1877 ★ 1917

By LOREN P. BETH

ILLUSTRATED

HARPER TORCHBOOKS
Harper & Row, Publishers
New York, Evanston, San Francisco, London

First HARPER TORCHBOOK edition published 1971

STANDARD BOOK NUMBER: 06-131597-4

LIBRARY OF CONGRESS CATALOG CARD NUMBER: 78-138707

Contents

*Illustrations, grouped in a seperate section,
will be found following page 130.*

Acknowledgments

THE ideas expressed in a work of this type come from so many different sources that one can hardly give credit to them all even if they can be identified. But certain people deserve particular thanks for special contributions. Henry Steele Commager should be especially complimented, for besides the patience and wise counsel he provided as editor, he also conceived the dangerous idea that a political scientist could write history. I hope the result is testimony to the wisdom of his decision. I should also like to thank David Mayhew, Philip B. Coulter, and Glen Gordon for discussions over a period of time which helped me greatly in clarifying some of the basic themes of the book; and William C. Havard, my long-time friend, colleague and department head, for counsel, the provision of facilities and time, and for providing a lift to my morale at various times during the process of the work. Finally, I should mention the typists who worked long hours providing readable copy: Mrs. Fred Goodrich and Mrs. John Kikoski.

Editors' Introduction

AT the outset of our national history judges, statesmen and administrators were confronted with the task of adapting to the needs of a new and rapidly changing nation a constitution based on seventeenth century notions of the relations of men to government and on a Newtonian concept of Natural Law that obtained in the political sphere as in the physical. Thanks to the wisdom of leaders like John Marshall, James Madison, Alexander Hamilton, Thomas Jefferson, Joseph Story, this task was triumphantly fulfilled. These statesmen, and others, managed to adapt the written Constitution to the needs of the new nation and—by interpretation, addition, and even imagination—to make it a flexible instrument for national growth. The problem that confronted statesmen and jurists almost a century later was on many respects the same: to adapt a constitution which had flourished in a simple rural society and among a people deeply committed to the principle that government was at best a necessary evil and that local government was always to be preferred to national, to the needs of an urban industrial society that implacably required political supervision and governmental activism. No great statesmen or jurists presided over the new adaptation that developed during the half century after the close of Reconstruction. The two great Presidents came towards the end of that era, and the two really distinguished jurists—Harlan and Holmes—rarely had their way on the bench. Yet so powerful were the forces making for adaptation, change, and growth—the forces of the war and Reconstruction, of the economy, technology, immigration, urban growth, imperialism, and of the new ideas associated with Darwinian evolution—that the Constitution responded—reluctantly, sluggishly, almost incoherently. Certainly the Constitution of 1917 was almost as different from that of 1877, as the Constitution of 1877 was from that of 1787.

This half century between Reconstruction and the First World War witnessed a constitutional revolution almost as important as was the revolution (if we may use that term) carried through by John Marshall or, more than a century later, by Chief Justice Earl Warren. It was a revolution implicit rather than explicit, tacit rather than articulate, and reluctant rather than bold. It was not primarily judicial, but advanced and expanded by every branch of government, state as well as national, and in a sense by society and the economy too. It involved the adaptation of an agrarian Constitution to the necessities of an industrial age; of a constitution designed to restrict government to one designed to enlarge the sphere and scope of government; from one concerned exclusively with domestic to one forced to interest itself in international concerns. It involved, too, a quantitative administrative change so vast that it took on qualitative dimensions, and with it the emergence of civil service reform and of a more scientific, or perhaps only more mechanical, approach to the problems of politics. It required an accommodation to the realities of great trusts and combinations in business and industry, and of national labor unions. Most important of all it speeded up the emergence of the supervisory state and, especially in the state domain, the beginnings of the welfare state.

It would be a mistake to suppose that the courts took the lead in bringing about these prodigious changes; it was—despite an impressive series of minority opinions which foreshadowed the future course of constitutional theory—but a reluctant accomplice in developments it usually disapproved and often regretted but could not resist. As Professor Beth concludes, "by 1917 Americans had produced almost in a fit of absent mindedness fundamental changes in their institutions."

There are two other features of constitutional revolution which command Professor Beth's attention. The first is the revolution in our constitutional thinking brought about by, perhaps necessitated by, our emergence as a world power. The impact of this was felt not only in such obvious areas as the Insular Cases; it was felt, too, in the shift of authority from the legislative to the executive branch, and in those centralizing and nationalizing developments which inevitably accompany either war or imperialism. The second—fundamental in a sense to this whole chapter of our history—is the revolution in political and constitutional thought associated with that larger intellectual change produced by the impact of evolution and of pragmatism in the social sciences.

Because Professor Beth has understood the importance of all of these factors his history does not suffer from the limitations of that legalism or that obsession with judicial decisions which so often stultifies the study of the Constitution. It is rather in the tradition of Tocqueville, Bagehot, Dicey, and Bryce, for it goes far to fulfil Mark Roefels' definition of a constitution as "an Aristotelian conception of the constituting idea or body of ideas which lies within the political system, and within the society generally, and which by its presence qualifies the society and its political system to become a cohesive entity."

The Development of the American Constitution 1877–1917 is a volume in the New American Nation Series, a comprehensive co-operative survey of the history of the area now embraced in the United States, from the days of discovery to our own time. It will be supplemented by four other volumes tracing the evolution of the American constitution.

HENRY STEELE COMMAGER
RICHARD B. MORRIS

Preface

IT is the purpose of this work to trace the evolution of American constitutional institutions and practices from 1877 to 1917 in some detail. But prior to this it seems desirable to survey the events and ideas which developed during these years and gave rise to the need or desire for constitutional change. We may assume that social and economic development, and social, economic, and political theories, are the forcing beds for constitutional change, and that in the main such change is a response to the environment. In addition a constitution has a continuing life of its own which may dictate or guide the exact nature of the change; but the change must come rapidly enough and be functional enough so that the political system continues to provide a satisfactory framework for the life of the nation. It seems wise to begin by looking at these underlying constitutional features, because in a sense they provide a *grundnorm* within which change takes place.

The concept of "constitution" that Lord Bryce, the great English commentator who wrote the finest description of late nineteenth-century American government, uses will furnish the guidelines for the commentary which follows. He saw the American constitution not merely as the document written in 1787, but as the whole set of written and unwritten rules and practices which govern the way our political system operates. Thus one writer can realistically assert that "it is doubtful whether any mature Constitution can be said to be wholly written in a legal and authoritative sense."[1] Many of

[1] S. B. Chrimes, *English Constitutional History* (London, 1948), p. 5.

the rules of the constitution are unenforceable at law—that is, they depend upon political custom, rather than upon law, for their durability: when President Roosevelt decided to run for a third term in 1940, he consulted his political oracle and not the Supreme Court. Yet until 1940 the third-term rule was a customary part of our constitution; after 1940 it was not; but in 1951 it was restored by an explicit constitutional amendment.[2]

This conception of the constitution does not permit this book to be a mere record of Supreme Court decisions, nor can its organization fall into the patterns dominated by the categories into which these decisions have fallen. Such a book cannot ignore the Supreme Court; neither can it ignore changes such as those in state government and the role of political parties. No one since Bryce has undertaken this task.

Superficially at least, the institutions of government were based on assumptions about the nature of man and of politics which had survived almost unchanged—down to 1900—since they were adumbrated by the Founding Fathers, especially Jefferson and Madison, but also to some degree John Adams, James Wilson, Franklin, and Hamilton. And the statesmen of 1787 were still working with ideas presented to them by Montesquieu and Locke. There are two explanations for the tenacity of these ideas: first, despite its great growth, the United States was still in 1877—or at least was still thought to be—a polity based on the yeoman farmer and the small merchant; thus the self-reliant, independent citizenry envisaged by the rationalist thinkers of the eighteenth century was still in existence, although even American optimists would concede that the great size of the nation in both population and territory made the institutionalization of Lockean republicanism more difficult than it had been earlier. This, however, simply proved that the framers had been prescient in their invention of the federal system, which (so the theory ran) was ideally suited to cope with problems of size.

[2] The best definition of "constitution" with which I am familiar is that of Roelofs: "The constitution here referred to cannot be simply the document. It can only be that Aristotelian conception of the constituting idea or body of ideas which lies within the political system and, indeed, within the society generally and which by its presence qualifies the society and its political system to become a cohesive entity. To 'define' the Constitution, understood in this sense, is to 'perceive' it hidden in the texture and traditions, the daily practices and great documents, of the society." H. Mark Roelofs, *The Language of Modern Politics* (Homewood, Ill., 1967), pp. 130–131.

Second, the rationalist assumption was maintained by the fortunate situation of the country. Prosperous, economically and physically expanding, psychologically optimistic, Americans needed government intervention less than the peoples of less fortunate nations. The result was that political controversy could—slavery always excepted—proceed within the rather narrow limits of the American consensus, and there was little need for radical criticism of the system. Certainly (whatever contemporaries thought about it, and they could get mightily exercised over such questions) campaigns fought over the tariff, free silver, paper money, and the more trivial questions of state and local policy hardly challenged the American's feeling that he held his political destiny in his own rationally controlled hands. The lack of formidable threats from abroad reinforced this feeling. The experience in the Mexican War, and later in the Spanish-American War, only fortified the feeling of hemispheric and omnicompetent hegemony, a feeling based primarily on the mythic efficacy of President Monroe's doctrine.

This is not to say that American political theory was wrong; its staying power, even today, indicates that it was based on some degree of validity. In retrospect, however, the myth was clearly inadequate, and by 1890 there were both existent problems and clouds on the horizon which were beginning to force some thoughtful Americans to question things which had theretofore been taken for granted. True, most of the questioning was, in its own way, superficial. Americans were inveterate gadgeteers. But by 1917 they had produced, almost in a fit of absent-mindedness, some fundamental changes in their institutions, some others that were more showy than basic, and still others that were more fictitious than real.

What was this American consensus? Put briefly, it was merely that the free individual (white and male) could solve most of the problems that confronted him in the course of his life. Most of those which he could not solve himself could be met by voluntary group action taken with his neighbors. Only a few problems were left with which town, state, or nation would have to deal. These few problems required the existence of government; they consisted largely of defense, the maintenance of public order, and the fostering of domestic and international commerce. In dealing with them, governments were assumed to rest upon the same individualistic rationality. They were to respond, largely through frequent elections but also through other devices, to the rational wishes of substantial majorities. It was usual to assume that the wishes would be rational and consequently that the majorities would be substantial. That all of these things could be almost unquestioningly accepted in a period of burgeoning capitalistic enterprise, low factory wages, frequent panics, agricultural depression, and "robber barons" is attributable partly to the elements named above; it has been called "the victory of American Whiggery under the Horatio Alger dispensation." [3] Even the Progressive reformers were Whigs in this sense: "the root of the matter was the dogmatic bourgeois orientation of a nation 'born equal.'" Thus, the theory was not entertained in the mood of pessimism about human nature of a William Graham Sumner, who reached many of the same laissez-faire conclusions about government based on a belief in a capable elite which would rise to the top naturally, leaving the irrational or ineffective many at the bottom. [4] It was, rather, based on the optimistic complacency of Jeffersonian rural individualism, which in the new age was blind to the implications of great extremes of wealth and poverty. The changes in American life and the rise of new problems made the unsophisticated acceptance of these theories increasingly difficult. As early as the nineties thoughtful students of American society were searching for new principles and new institutions which would express them. Let us note some of these changes, and the responses which they inspired.

The most important, because it foreshadowed a diametric change in the American way of living and thinking, was the growth of an urban-industrial complex which by 1900 made the United States the leading manufacturing nation of the world. Associated with this was a decline in the importance of farming. This change was to bring about a rethinking of the agrarian bases of the American consensus and shock liberals into concern with the problem of fitting a mass urban working class into their theories. By 1900 the industrial age had already revolutionized American life, especially in the cities, introducing electricity, bathtubs, indoor plumbing—in general making comfort possible for those unable to maintain servants. The automobile had been invented, as had the high-speed printing press,

[3] Louis Hartz, *The Liberal Tradition in America* (New York, 1955), pp. 204–205.
[4] William Graham Sumner, *What Social Classes Owe to Each Other* (Caldwell, Id., 1954).

although the changes to which they were to lead were not yet realized.

Science and the scientific mode of thought had not only produced material progress, but had gone a long way toward destroying the theological underpinnings of Victorian Protestantism and the philosophic foundations of nineteenth-century liberalism. Millions of immigrants were passing the Statue of Liberty, manufacturers were still sweating their labor, which consisted as often as not of women and children; Negroes were the forgotten men of America—in some ways worse off than as slaves a half-century earlier. The age of railroads had bound the nation together and made possible a tremendous growth of internal commerce. The divorce rate was rising, heralding possible changes in family life. Mass production had arrived and the assembly line was almost here, accompanied and made possible by the great wave of mergers and consolidations known variously as trusts or monopolies.

It was by now the age of organization: not only business organization as such, but organization for practically everything else, and especially for political objectives. The vanishing farmer, for instance, refused to vanish and, indeed, perpetuated his power by the adroit use of both private and political organization. Workers had caught the virus and were organizing, in some industries very successfully. By 1917 even the Negroes had begun to organize. Thus as early as 1910 Arthur Bentley could typify American politics as a struggle among competing groups, restating Madison's similar theory; by then it seemed new, and gained added significance because of changes in the scope and intensity of organization.

Crime flourished in the dark streets of large cities, fostered by ignorance, poverty, and the lack of adequate policing. The police forces that did exist were tainted by the corruption that seemed endemic to the age of the city bosses. Cities were often misgoverned or even nongoverned, since no one knew how to govern such vast and unruly groups in a system founded on Jeffersonian assumptions.

Preachers, doctors, lawyers, small businessmen—the traditional middle classes who had formed the backbone of the ruling elite for more than a century—saw their power and prestige decline.[5] Representatives of big business like Boies Penrose, working-class leaders

[5] Richard Hofstadter, *The Age of Reform: From Bryan to F.D.R.* (New York, 1955).

like Eugene V. Debs, bosses who could mobilize the immigrant vote like Boss Tweed, took their place. Since the old middle class had been almost entirely Protestant, its decline meant the decline of political Protestantism as well, for the new leaders and the new masses were more than likely to be Catholic—or perhaps worse, non-religious.

This random selection of important changes open to observation by any thoughtful American whose life spanned the period from the end of the Civil War to 1900 gives some impression of the increasing complexity of American life and problems, and the consequent bewilderment, fumbling, and false starts with which Americans faced them. The theoretical and political responses to the new America were as confused and confusing as the new America itself. Glorying, like the Connecticut Yankee visiting Camelot, in their newfound strength and progress, most Americans faced the future with an optimism that was yet, as in Mark Twain himself, not unmixed with dark foreboding.[6] Panaceas were as common as inventions, but often a great deal less sophisticated. Nevertheless, by 1917 the intellectual foundations of American life and politics had changed strikingly from those outlined earlier.

Naturally, there were those who wished to change the entire society. They normally proceeded on Rousseau's assumption that man is born free only to be enslaved by his society: therefore only the reconstruction of society could bring about his moral regeneration. Proposals varied from Utopias like that of Edward Bellamy to varied socialist and communist schemes. The preconditions of American intellectual and political life, however, were not hospitable to left-wing root-and-branch theories, and although some of their specific proposals were adopted, the theories themselves were of marginal importance.

There were those, too, whose prescriptions called for "more of the same." That strange blend of Jeffersonian do-nothingism with Hamiltonian paternalism which had been so strong in American history found its exponents around the turn of the century in men like William Graham Sumner—who, however, was not quite Hamiltonian enough to satisfy the businessmen who ran Yale University.[7]

[6] See Henry Nash Smith, *Mark Twain, the Development of a Writer* (Cambridge, 1962).

[7] Sumner was almost fired because of his advocacy of international free trade; see his *Protectionism: The Ism That Teaches That Waste Makes Wealth* (New York, 1885).

Social commentators and critics taking this line constituted the actual right wing of American politics. Given intellectual respectability by Sumner and the tremendously popular Herbert Spencer, laissez-faire ideas were spread and popularized by the speeches of an Andrew Carnegie, or a Russell H. Conwell (of *Acres of Diamonds* fame), inveighing against (as Sumner put it) "the absurd effort to make the world over." [8] Such ideas were in turn consciously represented in politics; Mark Hanna, though he was more flexible than some, may be taken as typical. In essence, the political position of the classical liberals was that the Constitution, as written in 1787 and as interpreted by the Supreme Court in such decisions as the Income Tax case, the Sugar Trust case and the New York bakery case, constituted a sufficient framework for the working out of natural law, which was beneficent in the end regardless of the hardships it might impose in the here-and-now.[9] To them the Constitution established a laissez-faire economic order, and all its provisions were to be viewed in this light. Thus, states' rights were fundamental whenever the national government tried to intervene (as with the income tax or the antitrust laws), and the Court could find an invasion of the powers reserved to states, but were strangely forgotten when the intervention was by a state (as in the bakery case). The Republican party, practically captured by business, became the political vehicle for the expression of these ideas, which helps to explain why so many Republicans viewed Theodore Roosevelt as "unsound."

Another type of extremist thought was more simplistic. Some individuals and social movements embraced the idea that a single sovereign reform was so fundamental that society could be remade by it alone. Thus, Henry George asserted that land reform was the key to all other social problems; and land reform was to be achieved by one measure—the single tax on the surplus value of real prop-

[8] See Andrew Carnegie, *The Gospel of Wealth and Other Timely Essays,* ed. by Edward C. Kirkland (Cambridge, 1962); Russell H. Conwell, *Acres of Diamonds* (New York, 1915).

[9] The income tax case, Pollock *v.* Farmers' Loan & Trust Co., 158 U.S. 601 (1895), saw the Court holding an income tax law unconstitutional; in the sugar trust case, U.S. *v.* E. C. Knight Co., 156 U.S. 1 (1895), the Court held that manufacturing and other forms of production were not interstate commerce and thus were not covered by the Sherman Anti-Trust Act; while in the bakery case, Lochner *v.* New York, 198 U.S. 45 (1905), it held that a maximum hours law for bakers was a violation of the "freedom of contract" implied by the due process clause of the Fourteenth Amendment.

erty.[10] While this theory had great popularity and many disciples, it does not seem to have had much specific impact on political or economic policy. This was not invariably true of "sovereign remedy" theories, however, particularly in the political realm. A good many of the Progressive reforms of the early years of this century were conceived originally as single palliatives for all the political ills, or at least all of those ills within the scope of the originator's interest. For instance, one group felt that the elimination of city bosses would magically cure the ills of the urban areas, and that this could be done by instituting primary elections. Similar objectives were sought by some organizations through the introduction of the city-manager system. Suffragettes seemed to feel that the purification of politics would result from the granting of women's suffrage. There was, in addition, a widespread feeling that democracy's faults could be cured by more democracy. Such ideas were not extremist in their prescriptive aspect: any number of them were introduced without pronounced results either for good or for ill. But they were extremist insofar as their proponents saw them as political cure-alls or universal panaceas. Obviously these individuals and groups were of tremendous importance, even if their importance did not quite conform to their vision of themselves and the roles in which they were involved. The real effect of what they did was to provide piecemeal answers to isolated problems, many of which had to be dealt with; the over-all picture we see of them is, strangely, one of pragmatic tinkering. Yet for many this was the furthest thing from their minds, as their fixation on particular remedies for general reform demonstrates.

This is not to imply that none of these people were pragmatists, or that some did not try to see American problems as a whole even while approaching their solution piecemeal. The conglomerate movement known as Progressivism had room for many approaches. Some progressives—Herbert Croly and the young Walter Lippmann, for instance—attempted to construct sophisticated theories based on a reasoned analysis of the condition of society and a reasoned set of prescriptions.[11] The American political system, being invincibly pragmatic in operation, absorbed only selective portions of such

[10] Henry George, *Progress and Poverty* (New York, 1887).
[11] W. Herbert Croly, *The Promise of American Life* (New York, 1909); Walter Lippmann, *Drift and Mastery* (New York, 1914).

systematic theories. The politicians themselves were often almost
consciously pragmatic, although the tendency to say they were facing
Armageddon revealed in their public papers would hardly suggest
this. The political careers of Theodore Roosevelt, Woodrow Wilson,
or even "Fighting Bob" La Follette reveal cautious and gradual
acceptance of reforms suggested here or there and often at first rejected. William James might develop a theory of pragmatism which
had little to do with politics directly, but the politicians beat him
to it in practice.[12] Typically, however, once an individual or a group
adopted a particular reform as its own, it was spoken of publicly as
a part of a grand salvationist scheme for American redemption, and
defended in tones of righteous wonder that anyone could possibly
disagree.

As one might expect from historical experience, the development
of constitutional law tended to reflect a number of these divergent
attitudes. The reigning legal philosophy was an Austinian positivism
which places heavy reliance on precedent; this, however, provided
a method rather than answers to substantive questions.[13] The latter
were filled in from the preconceptions of judges, lawyers, and
juristic thinkers. Sumnerian laissez-faire was well represented: see,
for instance, Justice Field's concurring opinion in the second Income
Tax case, or Justice Peckham's opinion in *Lochner* v. *New York*.[14]
Progressivism came to be represented in two ways: through legal
realism ("law is what the courts will do in fact") as exemplified in
Justice Holmes,[15] and sociological jurisprudence as expounded by
Dean Roscoe Pound.[16] These were pragmatic rather than Progressive,
but since they were developed during a Progressive era they came
to be identified with it. Both methods fostered the willingness of
judges to escape from the binding force of precedent; but either of
them could as well have been turned to conservative uses. In practice,
Holmesian realism was made to do service in judicial acceptance of

---

[12] William James, *Pragmatism: A New Name for Some Old Ways of Thinking*
(New York, 1907).

[13] John Austin, the British legal philosopher, believed in a law of pre-existing
concepts or categories, into which the actual decisions made by judges should be
fitted. John Austin, *The Province of Jurisprudence Determined* (3rd ed., London,
1869).

[14] Cases cited in fn. 9.

[15] See Oliver Wendell Holmes, Jr., *The Common Law* (Boston, 1881).

[16] Roscoe Pound, "The Scope and Purpose of Sociological Jurisprudence,"
Harvard Law Review, XXV (1911), 591.

legislative decisions, as demonstrated in his dissent in the Lochner case. And the sociological approach could do yeoman service in convincing even conservative judges that "objective" social conditions made certain laws necessary, as lawyer Brandeis demonstrated so brilliantly in his brief for *Muller* v. *Oregon*,[17] in which he convinced the Supreme Court that states ought to be able to regulate the working conditions of women. Both theories emphasized the creative role of law in meeting social problems, but at least until 1917 they both were applied primarily to legislative rather than to judicial creativity: that is, they were oriented to judicial acceptance of social legislation enacted by state or national representative bodies. Only in recent years have these approaches normally been used to justify *judicial* policy making.

The theme of this book is that social problems and the intellectual ferment which they generate produce constitutional change; and the greater part of it will be concerned with what these changes were and how they came about. Why was there a movement for the merit system and other changes in the civil service? What was the existing system and what were its perceived defects? What was the intellectual response? What ideas were suggested for reform? Who suggested them? What political forces shaped the solution, and what was that solution?

The world of 1900 is gone irretrievably, and no historian can resurrect it. Understanding it is made more difficult by the profound gap between us and the people of that period. While the citizens of the *fin de siècle* are basically recognizable as Americans, they are at the same time apt to appear naïve: overoptimistic, "fools rushing in," simplistic, and unaware of the frangibility of political reform. We live in a more pessimistic age; to us problems often appear intractable, and their solution seems only to give rise to other problems. We are more aware of the complexities of human nature and of social existence. Even though we may no longer have a theology to deal with it, we do have a lively sense of the potentialities for evil in the human breast—every human breast. We are thus not quite as given to devil theories as were our grandparents, and we are extremely doubtful that all progress is good or that human or social life is perfectible. Even though—or perhaps because—we are dealing

17 208 U.S. 412 (1908).

with many of the same problems, our attempts to solve them are tinctured by these changes in attitude. We are also more cynical: we tend to assume that self-interest is man's only political motive, and that reform thus is reform for someone's benefit. Our feelings about our late nineteenth century forebears are inevitably colored by our present world view, and it has become difficult to take them or their problems seriously: they become almost stock comic-opera characters in a Victor Herbert world. Generations which have lived through two world wars, a great depression, totalitarianism, genocide, and the Negro revolution are hard put to consider protectionism or even antitrust as great political issues, or Colonel Roosevelt's "bully little war" in Cuba as more than a filibustering expedition.

Nevertheless that world led to this one, and we ignore it at our peril. It needs, however, to be looked at in its own terms if it is to be understood at all. One advantage of a constitutional history is that the discontinuities do not seem to be as great as those characteristic of the larger social milieu, and less imagination is required to under-stand the changes in constitutional practice that have occurred than to grasp the entire movement of national history in the same period. Fundamental problems such as that of how nations shall be governed are much more timeless than the transient events which constitute much of what is called history. At the same time the failure to deal successfully with such problems is likely to permit them to return to haunt the future.

Despite some evidence to the contrary, such as the popular elec-tion of Senators, it is probably true that one could summarize the changes taking place between 1877 and 1917 as the beginnings of a transition back from a "democracy" to a "republic." The process by which political decision making moved upward was well under way by 1917; the increasingly functional or national (rather than state-politics oriented) character of representation was noticeable by the 1890's; the strengthening of the executives—with their attendant bureaucracies—at all levels of government was clearly recognizable in the presidency as early as 1904, as was the accompanying decline of legislative bodies. Some other manifestations of this change were the decreasing popular participation in politics,[18] an increased in-

[18] See Walter Dean Burnham, "The Changing Shape of the American Political Universe," *American Political Science Review*, LIX (1965), 7–28.

equality of income, and a decreased subjection of the civil liberties of minorities to the dominance of popular majorities.[19] One commentator sums up all of this: "In defiance of de Tocqueville, we survived Jacksonian democracy." [20]

[19] John P. Roche, *Quest for the Dream: The Development of Civil Rights and Human Relations in Modern America* (New York, 1963).
[20] Verbal comment by David Mayhew of Yale University.

CHAPTER 1

The National Government

THAT the United States changed greatly between 1877 and 1917 is a truism; in fact, it is a truism which applies with at least equal cogency to practically any forty-year period of American history. Henry Commager regards the 1890's as a "watershed," and Henry May calls the Progressive Era "the end of American innocence." [1] In their differing ways these evaluations are quite plausible, but similar statements could be—doubtless have been—made about various other eras in our history.

Yet the American constitution in 1917 was not only different from what it was in 1877, but the difference consisted of the development of many of the "modern" features of constitutional development: features which are still observable today. Most obviously, the presidency had "arrived" as the focus of public interest and constitutional power, at least in outline and potentiality if not entirely in fact. It is doubtful that in 1877 any American observer could have forecast this growth of the presidential role, yet by 1917 it was clearly discernible. What some scholars invidiously call "administrative government" was also well under way by the time of the First World War—a war which only made clearer a trend visible by the end of Wilson's first term. The same thing might be said about the general ascension of the locus of political power from local to state and from state to national government.

[1] Henry Steele Commager, *The American Mind: An Interpretation of American Thought and Character since the 1880's* (New Haven, 1950); Henry F. May, *The End of American Innocence* (New York, 1959).

These three changes are symbolic of many others that were taking place. When one reads Bryce's *American Commonwealth* [2]—still the best commentary on the Constitution as it existed in 1890—one is struck by two things: first, the obsolescence of Bryce's conclusions from the viewpoint of the man of the 1960's; and second, the fact that most of the features of this obsolescence were present at least in germinal form as early as 1917. In many respects the constitutional practices of 1890 were closer to those envisaged by the Founding Fathers a century earlier than to those of a mere generation later.

Part of the 1890 constitutional framework emerged from the political compromise which secured the election of Hayes in 1877. The various parties to the compromise tacitly assumed that the issues of the Civil War could now be laid to rest. The national government had made good its "sovereignty" and the states were considered to be in some respects subordinate units—but the Radicals agreed not to make further attempts to *use* the newly affirmed national power; and the Supreme Court, for its part, in 1873 and 1883 took away most of the practical meaning of the Fourteenth Amendment. The question of the rights of the freed slaves would thus be left to the mercy of the southern state governments now being restored to the control of the white man.[3]

While Lincoln had been, perhaps, a constitutional dictator, it was assumed in 1877 that Presidents were properly restricted to their traditional roles, preferably along the lines of Pierce and Buchanan rather than of Jackson and Polk. Congress had again become, and was to remain for some years, the dominant organ of the national government except when it ran afoul of a Supreme Court which was once more becoming aware of its Marshallian inheritance of the right to share in governmental policy. However, because of its in-

[2] James Bryce, *The American Commonwealth*, 2d ed., rev. (2 vols., London, 1891).

[3] The details of the compromise were: (1) the Republicans would recognize the election of the Democratic state tickets in South Carolina and Louisiana; (2) Hayes would end the stationing of federal troops in the South; (3) the new administration would aid in securing internal improvements for southern states, including an East-West railroad via a southern route; (4) Hayes would include some southern Republicans in his Cabinet; (5) Hayes would give more federal jobs to southerners. For their part, the southerners would (1) allow Hayes to become President; (2) allow the Republicans to organize the House of Representatives; (3) protect Negro rights in the South; (4) help to revive the Republican party in the South. Needless to say, many of these tacit agreements were never carried out. See C. V. Woodward, *Reunion and Reaction* (Boston, 1951).

ability to generate its own leadership consistently, Congress was usually in the position of being a rudder lacking a helmsman, and in a real sense the whole nation was without firm political leadership—especially since the state governments exhibited the same characteristics.

For practical purposes the states and their local subdivisions did most of the governing in 1877. But by comparison with today, "that which Europeans call the machinery of government" was often "conspicuous chiefly for its absence" at all levels.[4] Nevertheless a few states had begun to experiment with new legal and administrative apparatus for dealing with some of the problems posed by the rapid economic development of the country. One such arrangement was symbolically to confront the Supreme Court in the form of a group of so-called Granger laws in that very year.[5]

It was assumed that government at each level would be in the hands of one of the two major parties and that elections would be conducted along party lines, even though it was not customary for the parties to differ on very many points of great consequence, especially at the state and local campaign levels. It was further assumed that the dominant party was entitled to the spoils of office, and that so long as corruption was not too obvious and the public business was conducted with at least a minimum of efficiency, it was perfectly proper for public appointments to be made on the basis of party service.

Formally, government at all levels bore a marked resemblance to the national structure, although in practice this was often illusory. The states universally had tripartite separation of powers and bicameral legislatures; and the executives were, if anything, even weaker than their federal counterpart. Legislatures, especially in the more urbanized states, were likely to be boss-ridden. City government, too, displayed certain uniformities of structure. Mayors, it is true, were often stronger—especially in large cities—and the states generally provided the local judiciaries. The major exception to this catalogue of similarities was in the rural county governments. Here, typically, there was no real executive, legislature, or judiciary, and a single elected board performed whatever functions were entrusted

---

[4] Bryce, *American Commonwealth*, I, 15.

[5] *Munn v. Illinois*, 94 U.S. 113 (1877), involved an attempt by Illinois to regulate the rates charged by grain elevator companies for the storage of grain.

to the counties. Boards of selectmen in New England were not markedly different from county commissions in other parts of the country.

It was the heyday of the elected official; Americans probably went to the polls more often and voted for more officeholders than at any other time in their own history or anywhere else in the world. Terms of office were typically short—in some cases only a year—on the assumption that "where annual elections end, there tyranny begins." At the local and state levels this system was not notably successful in preventing (at the least) petty tyranny, and it certainly, when combined with the spoils system, did nothing to promote governmental efficiency.

Obviously public opinion and pressure groups played roles in the constitutional structure, but so little historical study has been made of them that one can only assume (perhaps erroneously) that they performed on a lesser scale but were not essentially different from what we know today.

Many of these characteristics of the 1877 constitution have not changed notably to this day. Accommodation to contemporary problems has usually been attempted within the constitutional norms, so that, with the exception of the great growth in presidential power, the assumptions on which the system is based are not greatly different now than they were then. There have been tremendous changes, but these have usually come within the old framework. At least the old rhetoric still serves in many instances to veil the very real and dramatic development of our constitutional structure.

The Presidents of the United States from Andrew Johnson to McKinley can hardly be called a distinguished group; Johnson and Grant, indeed, were pronounced failures. None of the rest were as utterly unsuccessful, yet they were mediocre at best, and the political conditions in which they operated were not calculated either to induct strong men or to create them after induction. The answer to James Bryce's question "why great men are not chosen President" lies in this: that the political system as it existed before 1900 did not allow it; it did not even allow the greatness which exists potentially in most men to emerge.

Having said this, it may appear strange to say that as of 1900 the American presidency was a stronger office, the President himself commanded greater power and respect, and the executive branch as a whole was more efficient, more honest, and more powerful than had been the case in 1876. How did a succession of such men manage to produce such a result? The answer seems to lie mostly in the pronounced incapacity of Congress to govern—an incapacity that became the more evident once the overriding problems of the Reconstruction were forgotten and the new issues posed by industrial growth came to the fore. The congressional party leaders could act as kingmakers—they could and did control the nomination process. But the kingmakers could not run the country. They were state and local party chieftains, generally more concerned with maintaining their local power bases than with formulating national policy. Nor did they, on the whole, consider national policy making as a very important part of government. Most important were power and jobs. As a result, policy making fell into the interstices of politics; Congress could only with great difficulty concentrate its attention on the great policy issues long enough to accomplish anything. The two houses were usually at odds with each other and often were controlled by opposing parties anyway. And decisions on the issues that did come to a final vote were often in effect dictated by the balance of pressure groups almost without the intervention of political authority. This seems especially true of decisions on tariff questions, and on the free silver issue. It accounts for the fact that several times bills to reduce the level of protection ended by raising it instead.

In all this the Presidents at first played little part. While it is not precisely true that Presidents had no opinions on issues facing Congress, at least their opinions were not considered important, even by themselves. None of them, except to a limited extent Cleveland, thought in terms of presenting to Congress a suggestion and then using pressure to get it enacted into law. Annual messages would, it is true, contain suggestions as to desirable policies. These were treated by Congress merely *as* suggestions. In fact, it seems to be true that no single individual played a great role in policy making. Power was, instead, split into innumerable fractions. The result is that the great names of the eighties and nineties—Presidents, congressional leaders like John Sherman, James G. Blaine, Roscoe Conkling, and Thomas C. Platt, Cabinet ministers like Carl Schurz and John Hay, governors of great states like John Peter Altgeld of Illinois—have receded into history as almost faceless parts of a mass. No one held enough power, for long enough, to make a really personal impress upon history—except, perhaps, J. Pierpont Morgan.

The nadir of presidential power was reached in the time of Reconstruction, actually before our story proper begins, and instructively enough it came directly following the tenure of the strongest President up to that time. Congress had always been restive under Lincoln, but the exigencies of the Civil War had made it possible for him to exercise great power even so. Even before the conflict was over, the legislature took the bit in its teeth; witness the Wade-Davis bill of 1864.[6] The roots of the matter were twofold: one was that Congress fell into the hands of the (so-called) Radical Reconstructionists; the second was that in order to achieve their purposes these men had to oppose the President or to secure a President who would acquiesce in their policies. For the only time in our history, Congress—over a span of no more than seven or eight years—proved capable of evolving its own program and pushing it through to fruition. In order to do this against the opposition of President Johnson, however, congressional leaders had to, in effect, turn the Constitution on its head.

There is still a tendency to impugn the motives of the Radicals.[7] They were for the most part old abolitionists, sincere within their narrow limits, who were determined that the great objects of the war be achieved, and (humanly enough) also that the party which won the war be continued in power. There were, it is true, venal men among them, but no party or faction in that period had a monopoly on venality. The Radicals never had a majority in Congress, so that it was only the excesses of Johnson which, by alienating the Republican moderates, enabled the Radicals to gain control. The Radicals—or some of them—had three aims: to consolidate the position of American industrial capitalism ("doubtless a striking success"); to establish the Republican party as a majority in the nation ("also a success"); and to "make southern society more democratic" ("in the short run this was their greatest failure").

But, Stampp concludes:

The Fourteenth and Fifteenth Amendments, which could have been adopted only under the conditions of radical reconstruction, make the

[6] The Wade-Davis bill was an attempt by the nascent Radical group in Congress to impose upon Lincoln a harsher peace policy than he wished. Lincoln subjected it to a pocket veto.

[7] As in Rexford G. Tugwell, *The Enlargement of the Presidency* (Garden City, 1960).

blunders of that era, tragic though they were, dwindle into insignificance. For if it was worth four years of civil war to save the Union, it was worth a few years of radical reconstruction to give the American Negro the ultimate promise of equal civil and political rights.[8]

Constitutionally, Reconstruction meant the creation of a new federal-state relationship, accomplished through the three Reconstruction amendments to the Constitution; it meant using congressional majorities to override presidential vetoes on a scale unprecedented; it meant the only attempt in American history to turn a President out of power through the impeachment procedure; most of all it meant a determined effort by Congress to ensure presidential subservience to its will, through the Tenure of Office Act and other means, and through the development of a clear theory that Congress is the dominant partner in the government. As Thaddeus Stevens said:

He [the President] is the servant of the people as they shall speak through Congress. . . . Andrew Johnson must learn that he is your servant and that as Congress shall order he must obey. There is no escape from it. God forbid that he should have one title of power except what he derives through Congress and the Constitution.[9]

Stevens' actual words are unexceptionable enough: it was the tone that mattered. In action, the theory meant taking advantage of every opportunity to cut the presidency down to size. For instance, in 1865 James A. Garfield sponsored in the House of Representatives a rider to an appropriations bill. The attempt was obviously to take advantage of the need for appropriations to force the President to accept, without veto, laws with which he did not agree.[10] When the shoe was on the other foot, Garfield as Republican floor leader in 1879 led the fight against a rider imposed by the Democratic majority, and he used the constitutional argument that such devices violated the principle of the separation of powers.[11]

[8] Kenneth M. Stampp, *The Era of Reconstruction, 1865–1877* (New York, 1965), p. 215 and *passim;* see also Avery Craven, *Reconstruction: The Ending of the Civil War* (New York, 1969).

[9] Quoted in Wilfred E. Binkley, *President and Congress* (New York, 1947), p. 136.

[10] Robert G. Caldwell, *James A. Garfield, Party Chieftain* (Hamden, Conn., 1965), p. 268. See also Leonard D. White, *The Republican Era: 1869–1901* (New York, 1958), pp. 35–38; Tugwell, *Enlargement,* pp. 213–214.

[11] *Ibid.*

By the time Hayes assumed office in 1877, then, the powers of the President had been diminished greatly; on the other hand, the unity and control of Congress in the hands of the Radicals had disappeared, and the result was a weak presidency combined with a leaderless Congress.

Almost imperceptibly, and certainly without conscious design, a succession of Presidents brought the presidency gradually back to the position it had held with Jackson—a point from which in quite short order Theodore Roosevelt and Woodrow Wilson could raise it to undreamed-of power. Back of it was the growing demand of the American people—or of groups within it—for governmental aid or protection. The process of presidential aggrandizement really began in the summer of 1877, when a spreading railroad strike threatened to bring the national transportation system to a complete halt.

This was the first "general" strike in American history. It came as a result of wage cuts by some railroads and the firing of the members of a grievance committee which had protested the cuts. Once the strikes had begun, the use of nonunion labor by the companies both caused them to spread and led to resistance by the strikers. Resistance bred violence, and violence justified several state governors in calling out the militia—which led to more violence. Clashes and casualties spread from West Virginia to Maryland, to Pittsburgh, Columbus, Chicago. There was a wave of sympathy strikes.

In such conditions, partly since they were unprecedented in our history, conservatives and businessmen reacted in fright. In some quarters it was felt that the workers were about to revolt. State militiamen proved unable to stem the spreading crisis, and four governors appealed to President Hayes to call out federal troops. The national strike, of course, was the child of the developing national economy: such a thing was not only unheard of earlier, but until very nearly 1877 it would have been literally impossible. Then as now the moral was clear, federal system or no federal system: national problems must be dealt with nationally. Hayes called out the troops and suppressed not only the violence but the strike itself.[12]

---

[12] One story of the strike, although biased in favor of the workers, is Matthew Josephson, *The Politicos, 1865–1896* (New York, 1938), pp. 252–255; a more balanced account appears in John A. Garraty, *The New Commonwealth, 1877–1890* (New York, 1968), pp. 158–160, 311–312.

Thus began the long, sad, but in some ways necessary history of federal strikebreaking. It was sad not because federal power was used, but because that power was almost invariably exerted one-sidedly against labor rather than with mediating intent or effect. As Hayes himself admitted, once the strike was ended the problem causing it was still unsolved: but, significantly, he did not regard it as part of the President's function to help in the solution.[13] Later labor crises—as industrialism hurried on and strikes became more common—brought similar responses. Cleveland, it is true, suggested that the government assume some mediating function on a purely voluntary basis, but his proposal was a long time in bearing fruit.[14] The famous Pullman strike in Chicago in 1894 brought a typically Hayesian response from Cleveland rather than an offer to mediate: while Governor Altgeld called out the militia merely to maintain order, Cleveland at Attorney General Olney's insistence ordered federal troops into Chicago and other points—in express violation of Altgeld's request—explicitly to break the strike. The troops, aided by a court injunction, succeeded in doing just that.[15]

The constitutional power to use troops in such situations was always rather hazy. Hayes presumably based it on the President's power to suppress insurrection; Cleveland, primarily on the government's control of the mails, and secondarily on an application of the Sherman Anti-Trust Act. Tugwell's comments on this action are instructive:

[The Constitution] indicates the circumstances in which the President may intervene in domestic crises; these did not exist when Cleveland moved troops into the riotous area. He did not wait for a request, because he thought the disorders had reached a dangerous intensity and because Federal interests were involved. The evidence seems to indicate that there would have been no serious consequences if he had not intervened. . . . [H]owever, this is less important than that he exceeded the constitutional limits for presidential action and that he not only succeeded but was widely praised.[16]

[13] Harry Barnard, *Rutherford B. Hayes and His America* (Indianapolis, 1954), p. 447.

[14] See Josephson, *Politicos*, p. 510, for Harrison's actions; on Cleveland, see Allan Nevins, *Grover Cleveland: A Study in Courage* (New York, 1933), p. 349.

[15] A good brief treatment of the Pullman strike is given in Harold U. Faulkner, *Politics, Reform and Expansion, 1890–1900* (New York, 1959), pp. 169–181.

[16] Tugwell, *Enlargement*, p. 228.

Theodore Roosevelt, in this as in so many other areas, expanded the executive power to something like its present status. Not only did he use federal troops in strike situations—usually, it should be stressed, merely to maintain order rather than to end the strikes. In addition, however, he established the precedent for using troops to take over and run industries immobilized by strike action. It is true that in the anthracite coal strike of 1902 he did not actually call out the troops: he merely in a typically Rooseveltian gesture threatened to do so. The threat was enough to bring George F. Baer, the leader of the mining companies, to accept arbitration. It was also, incidentally, probably the first time that a President had sponsored arbitration, and TR even appointed the arbitrators.[17] Later Presidents—Wilson, Franklin Roosevelt, and Truman—have made the industrial take-over familiar enough, although as Truman's experience with the steel seizure in 1952 indicates, there is still doubt as to the constitutional validity of the practice. The action was, of course, part and parcel of Roosevelt's new concept of the presidency, particularly in his feeling that the President was empowered by the Constitution to do anything that was not actually forbidden by that document. He did not ask, nor even think of asking, for congressional authorization, which he could probably not have obtained in any case. "My belief was," he later wrote in what was possibly a piece of ex post facto rationalization, "that it was not only [the President's] right but his duty to do anything that the needs of the nation demanded unless such action was forbidden by the Constitution or by the laws. . . . I did not usurp power, but I did greatly broaden the use of executive power." [18] It is perhaps not too much to say that the modern conception of the peacetime powers of the President was first made explicit in TR's treatment of the anthracite strike.

Another facet of Rutherford B. Hayes' contribution to the rebuilding of presidential prestige lay in his reassertion of presidential control over appointments. The President's power had declined so drastically that Congress could pass a Tenure of Office Act designed to deprive Johnson of the effective power of appointment; and President Grant described the practice thus: "The President very rarely appoints, he merely registers the appointments of members of Con-

---

[17] The coal strike and Roosevelt's handling of it are well summarized in George E. Mowry, *The Era of Theodore Roosevelt* (New York, 1958), pp. 134–142.

[18] Theodore Roosevelt, *An Autobiography* (New York, 1916), p. 372.

gress. In a country as vast as ours the advice of Congressmen as to persons to be appointed is useful, and generally for the best interests of the country." [19] This was a practice which even the future President, Congressman Garfield, condemned as "seriously crippling the just powers of the executive," and Hayes was not going to put up with it.

He began by refusing to consult with the senatorial oligarchy on the appointment of the Cabinet. Senate leaders reacted by refusing the usual automatic approval, sending the nominations to committee instead; but public condemnation shortly forced approval of the appointments.

Hayes' great battle, however, and perhaps the most famous event of his presidency, resulted from his attempt to eliminate jobbery and corruption from the New York customhouse, which was the focal point of the New York Republican machine under the collector, Chester A. Arthur, and the naval officer, Alonzo B. Cornell. Both refused to resign at Hayes' request, so in the summer of 1878, after Congress' adjournment, the President dismissed them. Again, the Senate was eventually forced to accept his nominees for the vacant posts.[20]

This battle was concluded, probably for all time, when the next President, Garfield, nominated a foe of Roscoe Conkling for the collectorship. The New York boss fought to save his empire; he and his colleague, Tom Platt, even took the drastic step of resigning their Senate seats in the expectation that the New York legislature would vindicate them by re-electing them. The legislators, in a rare show of independence, refused to do so, and Conkling was almost finished as a political boss.[21]

Never since then has the Senate seriously contested the President's right to use his own discretion in nominations for posts in the executive branch; Senators may suggest, they may object, they may even reject an occasional appointment: but the initiative has since Hayes' time remained in the President's hands.

Another item in the low estate reached by the presidential office was the fairly common practice, apparently begun by Garfield him-

[19] Quoted in White, *Republican Era,* p. 24.

[20] See Binkley, *President and Congress,* pp. 152–158; Garraty, *New Commonwealth,* pp. 261–262; Tugwell, *Enlargement,* pp. 211–212; Barnard, *Hayes,* pp. 450–457.

[21] See references in fn. 20; Caldwell, *Garfield,* pp. 341–348.

self in 1865, of using riders to appropriations bills to force Presidents to accept legislation which they would otherwise veto. The strategy was obvious. Presidents are not given the power to veto parts of any bill; they must instead either accept or reject each bill in toto. The rider therefore was a usable device whenever both houses of Congress were opposed to a sitting President, and it was used with great effect against Johnson. President Hayes' second Congress was controlled by the Democrats, but they did not have the strength to override a veto. Consequently they resorted to the rider technique. First they forced a special session by blocking the army appropriation bill. Then, in the special session of March, 1879, they attempted to secure the repeal of the Reconstruction election laws (which, it seems, were by this time ineffective anyway), putting the repeal provision in a rider to the appropriation for the army.

Hayes met this stratagem by vetoing the entire bill, declaring that to sign it would deprive his office of its "equal and independent" status. Garfield, too, now minority leader in Congress, turned against his own previous practice and fought the rider technique.[22]

It makes no difference, Mr. Chairman, what the issue is. If it were the simplest and most inoffensive proposition in the world, yet if you demand, as a measure of coercion, that it shall be adopted against the free consent prescribed in the Constitution, every fair-minded man in America is bound to resist you. . . . [the rider] is revolutionary to the core and is destructive of the fundamental principle of American liberty, the free consent of all the powers that unite to make laws.[23]

Unable to override Hayes' veto, the Democrats were forced to give in, although they returned to the attack in several other appropriations bills during the same session and in the succeeding regular session. Each time Congress was forced to pass the appropriation without the rider.

The moral of this story is not that Congress may not attach riders to appropriation bills, but that any strong President—indeed, he need not even be strong—may defeat the technique if he is willing to exert his strength.

This battle over congressional riders also illustrates the possibilities of the veto power by which a President can at least prevent legis-

[22] Caldwell, *Garfield*, p. 268; White, *Republican Era*, pp. 35–38; Tugwell, *Enlargement*, pp. 213–214.
[23] Quoted in Caldwell, *Garfield*, p. 268.

lation which he dislikes. Although it was true that at least since the time of President Polk it had been finally conceded that the "executive" view of the veto power rather than the "legislative" view was the proper one, nevertheless weak Presidents were still somewhat hesitant to use it unless they felt very strongly about the legislative issue. In Johnson's case Congress could usually override vetoes anyway; Grant usually agreed with Congress, although he did veto about thirty private relief or pension bills. Hayes, although reluctant, did, as we have seen, veto seven bills carrying riders, but this was a defense of his executive power rather than a disapproval of the content of the riders. He also vetoed a Chinese exclusion bill and another on silver coinage. Arthur did little with the veto, as did Harrison. McKinley had little need of it, since he had fairly firm party control in Congress. The lone Democratic President before 1900—Grover Cleveland—sent in more vetoes in each of his two terms than all the Republicans combined. This was owing partly to the party situation, in which Cleveland was often faced with Republican-dominated legislatures; partly to the fact that he did not get along well with his own party; and partly to his own stubborn tenacity. The chief change in the veto was not in the nature of its use but in its frequency, which had the effect of producing a public which was accustomed to, and indeed expected and applauded, the "courage" of a President standing out against the political satraps inhabiting the halls of Congress. By the time of "Teddy" Roosevelt the policy use of the veto was so customary that all he could really do that was new was to dramatize it or to use it as a threat.[24]

Popularly elected Presidents have, since Jackson, always tended to use the veto to appeal to what they consider their own particular constituencies as opposed to the constituencies represented by members of the Congress, in an effort to secure the re-election of themselves or their party successors. Nevertheless, it is also true that the veto power is one of the ways in which the President shares in the legislative process. Indeed, during the 1880's, when Woodrow Wilson published his *Congressional Government*, he could realistically declare that (so far as legislation is concerned) "the President is no

[24] The development of the veto power is summarized in White, *Republican Era*, pp. 39–40; Joseph E. Kallenbach, *The American Chief Executive* (New York, 1966), pp. 345–361, includes a chart (p. 355) showing the frequency with which American Presidents have used the veto.

greater than his prerogative of veto makes him." Lord Bryce agreed.[25]

Such judgments were based on the experience of the country with Presidents from Johnson to Harrison. While Hayes and Garfield, as we have seen, were able to protect and restore the "negative" status of the presidency—its independence from and equality with Congress—later Presidents, starting with Cleveland, began to work from this base to create an affirmative power in their office. This would appear in various ways, but primarily in the development of executive initiative and influence in legislation. In picking out the origins of this development Wilson gave the credit to Cleveland. It is true that, in 1897, he regarded Cleveland's performance as exceptional; but McKinley's striking success as a party leader with a fairly united party majority behind him in Congress (almost the first time this had happened since Grant) convinced him that real changes were being made in the office. He attributed this to the effects of the Spanish-American War, an event which in retrospect seems unimportant, though there is some validity to his notion that the President will be more powerful in periods when foreign affairs command the nation's attention.[26]

By 1907, when he published *Constitutional Government in the United States,* the future President's ideas about the office had changed diametrically from those expressed twenty years before. Theodore Roosevelt's unparalleled ability to concentrate public attention in the presidency, and his ingenuity in developing means by which to influence Congress, had brought home to Wilson the potentialities inherent in a popular executive who could speak directly to the people. Wilson saw this as a healthy development, since he had earlier criticized our form of government for having no effective policy-formulating leadership. It was clear by 1907 that the President's office "is anything he has the sagacity and force to make it." [27] It goes without saying that this kind of a change in the powers

[25] Woodrow Wilson, *Congressional Government* (Boston, 1885), p. 266; Bryce, *American Commonwealth,* I, 55.

[26] A. J. Wann, "The Development of Woodrow Wilson's Theory of the Presidency," in Earl Latham (ed.), *The Philosophy and Policies of Woodrow Wilson* (Chicago, 1958), pp. 46–66.

[27] *Ibid.;* the quotation is from Woodrow Wilson, *Constitutional Government in the United States* (New York, 1907), p. 69.

of the executive came about with no formal constitutional revision; it was the informal constitution which changed.

The "enlargement" of the presidency thus perceived by Wilson—and later participated in by him—was the result of many forces of which Wilson himself was only half-conscious. Changes in party organization were made possible by McKinley's command of his solid congressional majority, so that Presidents, even weak ones, became party leaders to an extent unknown since the days of Jackson and Van Buren. Cleveland and McKinley, but to a far greater extent Theodore Roosevelt, were able to command attention sometimes even without consciously trying to, so that the office became the real center of American government so far as the average citizen was concerned. Congress' own ability to generate consistent leadership from within its ranks had practically disappeared when the Radicals lost control in Grant's first term, and the nation had been largely drifting since that time, incapable of discussing—let alone acting upon—most of the problems which were crowding upon the scene. Fortunately for the nation, her growth and progress were so prodigious that they overwhelmed the economic panics and the agricultural depressions which recurred during the period from 1870 to 1900. Nevertheless by 1896 there was widespread demand, unspoken and largely unconscious, for changes in government which would enable it to meet real problems rather than merely haggling over the spoils of office and handing out favors to the great interests.

But none of these "political" factors would, in itself, have brought about the great changes in the presidency which had occurred by 1900, let alone those which the twentieth century would see. In the background were the fundamental changes in American society which are generally referred to, categorically, as the Industrial Revolution. The result of these was the desire for, indeed the necessity of, government which could respond to, but in addition control and even shape, the economic and social conditions which actually existed. Such government had to have two major essentials: the power to formulate and adopt new policy—that is, effective legislative leadership; and the executive tools with which policies once adopted could be efficiently and effectively carried out—that is, a strong bureaucracy controlled by a powerful President.

These needs were clearly seen by some of the leaders of opinion after the turn of the century. The *New Republic,* for instance, established to express the views of people like Herbert Croly and Walter Lippmann, was in its early days calling for government ownership of railroads, economic regulation, a pro-labor policy, affirmative action to prevent or end depressions, technocracy, and Negro rights.[28] It is true that the publicists who evolved this program did not always see the moral; they talked of a Hamiltonian concentration of power in the national government, but they saw it as being combined with Jeffersonian democratic political institutions. Politicians did not clearly know better; but they did know that the laws are not self-enforcing, and thus half-consciously they developed political instruments to fit the new role that was being thrust upon government. While talking Jefferson they acted Hamilton.

Grover Cleveland may properly serve as a starting point in considering this growth of presidential leadership. Cleveland had some of the essentials for effective legislative leadership—tenacity, strength of character, a clear view of what he wanted. The effective instruments for leadership were still largely lacking, however. Not only was party organization inadequate—Presidents in those days were not even theoretically regarded as the head of the party—but Cleveland had the further difficulty that he alienated many of the Democratic leaders in Congress by his stubbornness, his want of tact, and his refusal to pay attention to their views when his own were different. The depression of 1893, among other factors, led to sweeping gains for the Republicans in the 1894 midterm elections, so that Cleveland was faced for the latter half of his second term with a large Republican majority in the House of Representatives and only nominal Democratic control in the Senate.

As though these handicaps to presidential leadership were not great enough, Cleveland contributed further to them by his own ideas of the presidency and (perhaps more significant under the circumstances) of proper governmental policy. One major item in this was Cleveland's persistent refusal to view himself as a "politician" or to make any concessions to political necessity. He thought he had risen entirely by his own merits to the White House. Thus he felt himself under no political obligations. In the American

[28] See Charles Forcey, *The Crossroads of Liberalism: Croly, Weyl, Lippmann and the Progressive Era, 1900–1925* (New York, 1961).

system of separation of powers this is a fatal handicap. Legislative leadership by a President is difficult enough at best in such a system. Cleveland made it worse by refusing to indulge in coalition politics or any of the other practices which later Presidents found helpful. Indeed, it is doubtful that he had any clear conception that the President could serve as a real initiating force in legislation.

Added to this was his conservatism and the consequent adoption of a policy of "do-nothing." A fervent admirer of the successful businessmen and financiers of the day, he was of the conviction that depressions were acts of God which governments could and should do little about. His "program" for dealing with the terrible depression of the mid-nineties consisted almost entirely of currency and banking reforms, which could have been accomplished without government entrance into new areas of activity. His major specific proposals were the repeal of the Sherman Silver Purchase Act and a lower tariff. On the other hand, he was perfectly willing to use governmental power to suppress strikes and control immigration. He was willing to see the relief of hungry unemployed workers and their families left to the "friendliness and charity" of private sources. Consequently there was really little, of an affirmative nature, that he wanted Congress to do, and leadership is dependent not only on someone to lead but on somewhere to go. Cleveland did not want to go anywhere.[29]

Nevertheless, he was willing to use his powers in the attempt to secure legislation in which he deeply believed, and he was perhaps the first President after the Civil War to do so. Such a measure was the silver purchase repeal:

Patronage power was withheld from Senators and Congressmen until the contest was decided. Enormous pressure was brought to bear upon wavering Representatives, who were given the darkest reports of business prostration, while each man who could be reached was reminded of his responsibility to provide relief to the embarrassed Treasury and aid to commercial revival. On the other hand, an influential old spoilsman like Senator Daniel Voorhees of Indiana, who had formerly been an opponent of Cleveland and

[29] For assessments—sometimes conflicting—of Cleveland, see Tugwell, *Enlargement*, pp. 242–251; Binkley, *President and Congress*, pp. 180–182; Josephson, *Politicos*, pp. 374 ff., 519 ff. A good view of Cleveland as a party politician is given in J. Rogers Hollingsworth, *The Whirligig of Politics: The Democracy of Cleveland and Bryan* (Chicago, 1963). And of course, see Allan Nevins, *Grover Cleveland: A Study in Courage* (New York, 1932).

a lifelong inflationist, was completely won over by being given all the organization patronage of his region. . . .[30]

This fight, with its implication that a President's wishes as to policy could be more than mere moral adjurations to a reluctant Congress, was Cleveland's major, and only, contribution to the development of presidential policy leadership. Even this was an important advance over the situation Henry Adams described in 1870: ". . . So far as the President's initiative was concerned, the President and his cabinet might equally well have departed separately or together to distant lands. Their recommendations were uniformly disregarded."[31]

The situation was far different with William McKinley. He had party majorities in both Houses; he was a thorough party man; he was friendly with party leaders in and out of Congress; he knew the value of party organization. Perhaps most of all on the political level, he had the advantage which none of his predecessors could boast, a party organization which had a fairly united leadership so that it could get him nominated, get him elected, and deliver the congressional votes to support executive initiative in policy making. His contemporaries described him as the most effective party and legislative leader since Jackson. Unlike Cleveland, he was courteous, patient, sometimes witty, and friendly. He also came into the presidency at a time when the House of Representatives was under the domination of its Speaker—and he was on friendly terms with Boss Reed. He had the affectionate support of the first effective national party organizer in many years, Marcus A. Hanna. By the time of his accession the depression had ended and prosperity stared America in the face, so that the old questions of tariff and money seemed less important and were certainly less divisive.

McKinley, in other words, had almost everything going for him. He is not, it is true, generally considered a great President despite all these factors. The reason seems to be that while he could lead, and was on occasion willing to, he was on the whole fairly conservative and had, like Cleveland, no great affirmative goals in mind. He was by temperament a conciliator rather than a creator, lacking "the vigor and imagination to perform bold new feats."[32]

[30] Josephson, *Politicos*, pp. 533–534.
[31] Henry Adams, "The Session," *North American Review*, CXI (1870), 41.
[32] H. Wayne Morgan, *William McKinley and His America* (Syracuse, 1963), p. 529.

Nevertheless, McKinley regarded himself as being properly a public, party, and policy leader. He used his skills of conciliation to unify his party and to create an executive base from which his successors could move into more effective and creative leadership. "He stood not as the last old-fashioned chief executive nor as the first modern one, but as something in between." [33] In addition, he unconsciously contributed to the increasing centralization of both power and attention in the national government and specifically in the White House. By fighting a war and acquiring an empire, however unintentionally, which had to be governed from Washington he inevitably added to the size of that burgeoning bureaucracy which is the executive branch. If this created problems it also created possibilities, which the dynamic "Teddy" was not loath to seize.

Roosevelt, whose famous motto might be more accurately rendered as "speak loudly and don't use the stick," used the propagandistic potentialities of the presidential office to the fullest. His mark on the presidency therefore lies in his successful conversion of his job from that of an administrative manager to that of a leader of public (and consequently of congressional) opinion. He was probably the first of the modern Presidents, too, in acting on the belief that he, alone of all elected officials, "is or ought to be peculiarly the representative of the people as a whole." He gained the cooperation of the powerful Speaker, "Uncle Joe" Cannon, who in effect became a floor manager for the President—a function fairly common among Speakers since that time, but perhaps in later days more commonly exercised by the majority leader.

Not only did the brash Rough Rider organize the liaison between the White House and Congress and outdo his predecessors (and most of his successors as well) in reaching and holding public affection and attention, but he was the first of our modern Presidents to conceive of his policy leadership in programmatic terms. Roosevelt's annual messages were full of "suggestions" to the legislators as to their proper duties in the coming sessions. While these were not always, by any means, converted into legislation, it is nevertheless true that TR often got what he really wanted, and that he so accustomed Congress and the people to this custom that no succeeding President has entirely given up the practice, though obviously there

[33] *Ibid.*, p. 527; an assessment of the quality of McKinley as President is given in the last chapter of Morgan, but see also Binkley, *President and Congress*, pp. 188–191.

have been great variations in the effectiveness with which they have used it.

The most famous Rooseveltian invention was probably his "stewardship theory" of the presidency. This was merely an inversion of the previously held concept. Before Roosevelt it was assumed that a peacetime President could do only those things which the Constitution empowered him to do. TR, however, seized upon the obvious fact that "the executive power" which Article II bestows upon the President is nowhere specifically limited. He consequently took the position that he was constitutionally permitted to perform any act which was not forbidden by the Constitution or allotted to some other agency. If this seems obvious to us today it was not so to Roosevelt's contemporaries, many of whom (including his immediate successor) thought of it as revolutionary. Many of his accomplishments in the conservation field fall into this category.

Another of the areas in which this dynamic man put the stewardship theory to work was that of foreign relations. Among other things, he developed the practice, common today, of avoiding the possibility of a Senate veto of treaties by embodying many of his agreements with other nations in documents which did not have to go to the Senate because they were not technically "treaties." This was possible provided the matters involved were not too important—it could hardly be done with a peace treaty, for instance—and provided money was not necessary to carry out the pact. These "executive agreements" have since become an accepted and useful, yet controversial, agency in the conduct of our foreign policy. Needless to say, they also constitute a major step in the aggrandizement of presidential power.

Despite the fact that in many areas Roosevelt's tenure contained more bluff than actual accomplishment, the outlines of the modern presidency were clearly discernible by the time he left office. As to the greatness of the man—much debated by historians, some of whom award him only the rank of "Near Great"—one must conclude that he was perhaps our greatest peacetime President in seeing and seizing upon the potentialities of the office. That later Presidents found more effective ways of securing what they wanted from Congress should not blind us to this accomplishment.[34]

[34] See Mowry, *Roosevelt*; Henry F. Pringle, *Theodore Roosevelt, A Biography* (New York, 1931); John M. Blum, *The Republican Roosevelt* (Boston, 1954), for assessment of Roosevelt's character and career.

William Howard Taft must have seemed to contemporaries like a reversion to an earlier day. Following Roosevelt was no easy job, especially for the relaxed and somewhat indolent Taft. In some ways—trust-busting, for instance—historians point out that he talked less and did more than Roosevelt. But in a constitutional sense he had little to contribute. His major contribution (one wonders how Roosevelt had slipped up on it) was to use the executive branch actually to draft legislative bills. This was done at least twice: for a corporation tax bill and for an expansion of the powers of the Interstate Commerce Commission; the latter evolved into the Mann-Elkins Act. As in so many instances, this practice proved so useful that later Presidents adopted it, and we no longer regard it as in the least unusual.[35]

With Woodrow Wilson the presidency reached essentially its present status. Wilson improved upon Roosevelt primarily by refining and perfecting the techniques already developed. Thus, in public leadership he developed the modern press conference; in legislative leadership he revived Washington's early practice of delivering his messages in person (the jealous Roosevelt exploded, "Now why didn't I think of that!"). He further developed the organization of the "President's party" in Congress. Coming into office with the crest of Progressivism, he was able to mobilize public support by the use of highly moralistic rather than ebullient pronouncements, and thus achieved the most remarkable legislative record during his first term that had yet been recorded by any President since Washington. His leadership was, in fact, so effective that he was able to mobilize every single Democratic Senator in support of the Federal Reserve Act, which in view of its controversial nature was a masterly feat.[36]

Behind the growth of presidential power after 1900 lay not only industrialization and urbanization and the increasing tendency of party organization to center in the President, but also the push given by the great reform wave known as the Progressive Era. Roosevelt, Wilson, even Taft, used this popular pressure, rode it into office, and sponsored the specific policies developed by various Progressivist publicists. The substantive achievements of Progressivism are debatable: they were in many cases superficial, partly because the iden-

[35] See Henry F. Pringle, *The Life and Times of William Howard Taft* (2 vols., New York, 1939).

[36] See Arthur S. Link, *Woodrow Wilson and the Progressive Era, 1910–1917* (New York, 1954); Latham, *Philosophy and Policies*; Arthur S. Link, *Wilson* (5 vols., Princeton, 1947–65).

tification of the root problems was difficult, and in any case most of them came at the state or local level. But without Progressivism the modern presidency could not have been created. Major changes in American constitutional institutions do not come about except when the combination of pressure of events, ideas, and personalities is sufficient to overcome the usual inertia of the system. The events were provided by the Industrial Revolution, the ideas by the Progressive thinkers, the personality—the charisma—by Roosevelt and Wilson.

Whether the development of the American presidency into the most powerful single office in any democracy is a good thing we need not decide.[37] Now, almost a century after Bryce, many English publicists argue that our system is actually superior to theirs—that the cabinet system is too responsive to public opinion to provide strong enough leadership to take and carry through difficult decisions. And whatever the difficulties and dangers of the American presidential system, it takes remarkable historical imagination to conceive how the United States could have survived the travail of two world wars, a great depression, and the alarums and excursions of the Truman-to-Johnson years without the leadership provided by strong—if dangerously fallible—Presidents. It is a dangerous world we live in, and the methods we adopt for coping with the dangers are inevitably not the least of the danger.

That magisterial student of American administrative history, Leonard White, gives a vivid picture of congressional dominance and presidential weakness during the Grant administration, a picture which was not to change drastically for some years:

. . . Both House and Senate were deeply involved in matters primarily administrative in character. Patronage deals with Presidents and heads of departments flourished on a greater scale than ever; appropriations committees toiled over the detail of constantly more voluminous estimates; investigations were frequent and partisan; members surged in and out of executive offices on constituents' business and in several fields Congress acted in effect as an appeal body to review the decisions of official agencies in particular cases. The consequences were bad both for Congress and for administration.[38]

[37] Marcus Cunliffe, "A Defective Institution?" *Commentary,* 45 (Feb., 1968), 27–33, points out dangers inherent in a powerful popular executive.
[38] White, *Republican Era,* p. 45.

The degree to which Congress made administrative decisions by legislation, and "the President was a mere onlooker," were also pronounced. The decline of Radical control left Congress a faction-ridden body in which neither party nor individual had the strength to provide effective leadership. The situation was made even worse by the frequent alternation of party majorities and the rapid turnover in membership. The lack of political leadership anywhere in the system may have resulted, however, from a lack of urgently felt national issues, and there is great danger that one may read back into the period problems which were not perceived by the citizens of the day (at least most of them).

What is clear is that this "system" contributed both to the absence of leadership and to the widespread corruption which pervaded the politics of the gilded age. Administration, constitutionally the President's responsibility, had gravitated into the hands of a Congress which was almost completely unable to control it effectively.

The President had no staff agencies through which control could be exercised. Not only was there no budget bureau, but no President even interested himself in the budget: the President "was not consulted on the preparation of the estimates; he was not consulted except sporadically on their disposition by the committees handling appropriations; and the Secretary of the Treasury was merely a compiler, not a minister of finance." [39]

Congress wandered freely in and out of administrative decision making. It specified, for instance, specific rural mail routes and the location of land offices by law. These two examples may be sufficient illustration of the situation. Under the spoils system it was unlikely that even a legislative body would do a worse job on these matters than the relevant administrative agency; either way, such matters were typically treated as spoils themselves, to be parceled out in ways that would benefit politicians and their followers.

The numerous private pension acts vetoed by Grover Cleveland were not exceptional. Congress was in the habit of treating private claims as legislative matters—again, part of the spoils of office, and the wonder is that earlier Presidents accepted them. Federal jobs were also perquisites of office, and every Congressman found it part of his duty to secure positions for his constituents.

Congress was not entirely without desire to improve the adminis-

[39] *Ibid.*, pp. 66–67.

trative process. Indeed, much time and effort were expended in committees and investigations aimed at such betterment. But in such conditions it was unlikely that Congress would be able often to rise above details; Congressmen might act "as amateur organization and methods analysts," but they were both unable and unwilling to view the system as a whole, because their own privileges and powers were too intimately involved.[40]

Until 1900 the only fundamental change in the administrative arrangements of the executive branch came with the adoption of the Civil Service Act in 1883. The immediate impetus for this was Garfield's assassination by a disappointed office seeker in 1881, but the corruption and inefficiency of the service had become so notorious that it would probably have come soon anyway. The educational and pressure activities of the newly formed Civil Service Reform League and the earlier activities of Representative Thomas Allen Jenckes of Rhode Island played an important part in preparing opinion for the law.[41]

In fact there had been since 1871 a law giving the President the power to prescribe entrance rules, and for a few years a commission had existed to administer such rules. After a good start, the agency withered owing to lack of support from Congress and from President Grant, and the rules disappeared with it. Hayes repeatedly stated his desire for reform, but did not think it important enough even to use the power given to him in the 1871 act. Like Grant, Hayes had a lively sense of political realities and was unwilling to proceed unless he had full support from Congress. His Secretary of the Interior, Carl Schurz, provided an illustration of both what could be done by a strong executive and how independent of the President the Cabinet departments were by instituting his own competitive examination system, which, within limits, worked well.[42]

The 1883 act set up a bipartisan commission the tenure of which was at the pleasure of the President. It had the power to establish rules of operation, require entrance examinations and the appointment of the applicants with the highest grades, and devise means of protecting jobholders from political pressures. Thus the patronage

[40] *Ibid.*, p. 84.
[41] *Ibid.*, pp. 279–281.
[42] *Ibid.*, pp. 289–290.

power was taken from both President and Congress provided they were willing to act to implement the new law. Although it is customary to speak of patronage as a presidential tool for securing favorable legislation from otherwise reluctant Congressmen, it was seldom so used before 1900; effectively the patronage was a prerogative of individual legislators.[43]

Under the circumstances one could hardly expect either Congress or the President to blanket the entire existing federal service into the merit system thus established. Substantial amounts of patronage existed on into the middle years of the twentieth century. The President was given the power to "cover in" new classifications as he pleased—a power which proved an irresistible temptation to Presidents to protect their party's appointees from losing jobs at the end of their terms. Nevertheless, the merit system included 30,000 employees by the end of Cleveland's tenure in 1897. McKinley thought Cleveland had gone too far up in the service by including many persons who were part of the "political high command," and he promptly withdrew 10,000 of these. Meantime, the federal bureaucracy grew faster for many years than did the part of it which was covered by merit rules. In 1883, out of about 132,000 positions, 118,000 were not covered; by 1901, while there were 106,000 covered positions, there were 150,000 still left to patronage.[44] Nevertheless, by the turn of the century the merit system was beyond effective challenge. And strangely, the more "partisan" presidential leadership of the twentieth century proved more reform minded than the relatively "unpartisan" Presidents of the nineteenth.

The major constitutional effect of this new approach to the administrative service was to make the President, for the first time, the effective head of the civil service. Temporary Cabinet appointees were more and more faced by relatively permanent subordinates, a fact which rendered the Secretaries less autonomous, more dependent on the President. Nevertheless, it was startlingly evident in Wilson's administration that the over-all administrative machinery was still a hindrance to effective leadership. One of the missing essentials was an executive budget: Taft had tried to submit a budget, but Congress had ignored it, and in any case it was obvious that if it were to be

43 *Ibid.*, pp. 301–302.
44 *Ibid.*, pp. 317–319.

done properly such a thing required a then nonexistent planning agency. Wilson proposed such a system, but Congress did not enact it during his presidency.[45]

At the same time the development of a permanent trained civil service led to the actuality of a permanent bureaucracy with vested interests and powers of its own, a semiautonomous and self-moved "fourth branch" of government which many recent writers have claimed is the real (and often arbitrary, unjust, and irresponsible) moving force of American policy making. One need not subscribe to the more extreme statements of the prophets of doom to realize that there are serious problems of control when a permanent bureaucracy arises within a governmental system supposedly democratic. The Civil Service Act of 1883 thus provides an excellent illustration of legislation which, like British acts reforming the House of Lords, are of constitutional significance because they change fundamentally the balance of powers in the political system. Another example, of hardly less importance, was the Interstate Commerce Act of 1887.

As a result of the growth of modern industry—particularly the building of railroads—public demand for some type of regulation became an important factor in American politics. This demand was of varying strength depending on where it was located, who was posing it, and what the current economic conditions were. Nevertheless, by 1885, stimulated mostly by agrarian agitation, most of the states had set up various types of regulatory programs.[46] These were of uncertain effectiveness, since national business corporations were too powerful to be amenable to local control. In addition, the Supreme Court made rate regulation difficult by various decisions including that in the Wabash case of 1886 which held the interstate aspects of railroad rates beyond the state's constitutional power.[47] This left only Congress to regulate railroads and any other business that was "in interstate commerce," to protect the farmer, shipper, consumer, exporter, etc. Despite all the furore over silver purchase and tariff laws which typified the era, the most important legislative acts of the

[45] Arthur W. Macmahon, "Woodrow Wilson: Political Leader and Administrator," in Latham, *Philosophy and Policies*, pp. 120–122.

[46] Robert E. Cushman, *The Independent Regulatory Commissions* (New York, 1941), pp. 19–36; Lee Benson, *Merchants, Farmers, and Railroads: Railroad Regulation and New York Politics, 1850–1887* (Cambridge, 1955). This subject will be dealt with in somewhat greater detail in Chapter 2.

[47] Wabash, St. Louis & Pacific Ry. *v.* Illinois, 118 U.S. 557 (1886).

years from 1875 to 1900 were the two great regulatory statutes: the Interstate Commerce Act of 1887 and the Sherman Anti-Trust Act of 1890. It is an instructive lesson concerning the nature of politics in those days that these two fundamental laws should have been passed with relatively little controversy and practically no campaign oratory. Neither, incidentally, was there any significant presidential influence in the passage of either law. Cleveland, indeed, was so little interested that he did not even protest the encroachment on his executive power represented by the setting up of the ICC as an "independent" agency, a device which was to be used frequently by Congress, usually without presidential objection, and partly in the belief that independence would keep the regulatory agency "out of politics."

The ICC and the Anti-Trust Act may be viewed also as representing two of the major possible ways by which regulation could be accomplished. In the first, a bipartisan commission was created, appointed by the President but with a specific tenure so that its members were largely uncontrollable by the President. The commission was vested with delegated legislative power in the form of rule- and order-making authority; it was also given executive enforcement power and the power to adjudicate violations of its rules.[48] Thus Congress was creating, in essence, a fourth branch of government, bypassing the separation of powers. How remarkable, too, that a laissez-faire-oriented Supreme Court should have upheld such a departure from traditional American practice: perhaps the fact that such agencies were by 1887 fairly common in the states had habituated the judges to the idea. Constitutionally, the ICC and its successors (several more such agencies were created during Wilson's first term) are of great importance, since they occupy an anomalous position beyond effective control either by the President or by Congress, while only negative control is ordinarily possible by the courts. At the same time their functions are, at least potentially, of extreme importance in regulation or planning.

The Anti-Trust Act of 1890 was, by contrast, relatively simple and traditional both in concept and in operation. It did not, for one thing, envisage a complex, continuous regulatory program; rather it continued the traditional idea of the mere enforcement of a law which was assumed to be fairly clear on its face. Then, too, the en-

[48] Cushman, *Regulatory Commissions*, p. 39.

forcement function was entrusted to an agency under the President's control: no *new* agency was created at all; the Department of Justice was assumed to be capable of carrying out the purposes of the law.[49] The adoption of this method of enforcement may have reflected Congress' hope that the law would not be enforced, and to a large extent this was the actual effect for some years. The antitrust law was thus not a constitutional departure from the norm except that it added to the power of the presidency. Like the independent regulatory commission, it was a device to be used frequently in the future, many times even for statutes of the same general nature as the Interstate Commerce Act For instance, the Pure Food and Drug Act of 1906— a major regulatory statute—is enforced by a Cabinet agency.[50] Still other laws follow the pattern of the Civil Service Act, being entrusted to commissions or boards which, while under presidential control, are yet outside the regular departmental structure of the executive branch.

By 1890, at least in principle, the United States had thus departed in three major instances from the civics textbook version of the separation of powers. Legislative power is given to executive or independent agencies; executive power is vested in organizations uncontrollable by the chief executive; judicial power is handed to agencies to enable them to enforce their own decisions. The constitutional ramifications of all this are still being worked out today.

It is an enigmatic fact that in one decade, generally known for legislative inactivity in Washington, Congress appropriated regulatory and administrative powers for the national government which profoundly changed the American constitution. When one recalls that at about the same time the regulation of immigration—hitherto left to the states [51]—was entrusted by Congress to a national agency, one realizes that the "nationalizing" trend associated with the powerful Presidents of the twentieth century in reality was begun (unintentionally but clearly) under congressional auspices (also recall that the Reconstruction amendments and statutes had the same

[49] Garraty, *New Commonwealth*, pp. 121–127; Carl Brent Swisher, *American Constitutional Development*, 2d ed. (Boston, 1954), pp. 420–426.

[50] Swisher, *Amer. Const. Devel.*, pp. 828–830.

[51] While the Supreme Court ruled as early as 1849 that immigration was a subject exclusively for congressional action, Congress did not take up the invitation with any actual regulations until 1882. See Passenger cases, 7 How. 283 (1849); Chinese Exclusion Act (1882); Foran Act (1885).

effect) and long before we have usually thought. It is fairly clear, however, that this was done more or less in fits of absence of mind, in the sense that neither Congress nor the Presidents seemingly viewed these developments as constitutionally suspect or revolutionary. Their concern was with the "radical" nature of the idea of regulation itself. This was so radical that some effective powers were not granted by Congress; Presidents were uninterested in enforcement; and courts in effect emasculated the laws. Not until Roosevelt, Taft, and Wilson was effective enforcement to be made possible—if indeed it ever has been.

No one now knows what the shape of American government would be had the Congress been able successfully to assume the role of policy initiation in the system. The opportunity arose, certainly, in the 1870's and 1880's. The response of Congress in the absence of an overriding sectional issue such as Reconstruction was one of failure, however, until the decade of the nineties; and despite some success after that, the President rather than Congress was riding the wave of the future.

The failure, which enveloped, as we have already seen, both President and Congress, can be put in statistical form, although to do so runs the risk of reading back into the nineteenth century the needs and expectations of a later age. From 1877, when Hayes became President, to the assassination of McKinley in 1901, only twenty-one major pieces of legislation cleared the Congress: an average of fewer than one per year; and, indeed, from 1877 to 1887 there were only five.[52] These statistics—which exclude appropriations bills and pork-

[52] Such lists are, of course, extremely subjective: one man's major legislation is another man's minor. For what it is worth, here is my own list through Cleveland's second term; it excludes pork-barrel acts, pensions, and appropriations.

Hayes	45th Congress	1. Bland-Allison Silver Purchase Act	1878
		2. Refunding of National Debt	1878
	46th Congress	(None)	
Garfield and Arthur	47th Congress	3. Restriction of Chinese Immigration	1882
		4. Pendleton Civil Service Act	1883
	48th Congress	(None)	
	49th Congress	5. Presidential Succession Act	1885
		6. Interstate Commerce Act	1887
		7. Hatch Act (Experiment Stations)	1887
Cleveland		8. Anti-Polygamy Law for Territories	1887
		9. Repeal of Tenure of Office Act	1887
	50th Congress	10. Creation of Department of Agriculture	1889

barrel legislation—serve to some extent to highlight the incapacity of the American system under congressional domination.

Of course, we do not know how much or what kinds of legislation were needed or desired; and the political "philosophy" current during the period was not helpful in providing an ideological structure for action by the national government. The agricultural depression which was more or less endemic in the United States for two decades provides an apt illustration of this. While the farmers' troubles produced political revolts such as the Granger movement and later the Populist party, for the most part (at least until the nineties) the demands were aimed primarily at the state governments, some of which tried in various ways to respond. The farmers turned to federal action only after it was clear that the states would not, or could not, provide relief, because the scope of the problem was beyond them. Through 1892, at least, federal activity was confined to indirect measures such as currency reform, tariff legislation, and, finally, railroad regulation. It is true that until the nineties few seem to have thought that the government should do anything more; the first important attempt to have it act directly and affirmatively came with the Populist party's national platforms of 1892 and 1896.[53]

Nevertheless, in terms of problems which were obvious even then—in terms even of the legislation which was passed—Congress showed a pronounced incapacity to deal with them promptly or effectively. It took years of effort to get a bill through the tortuous procedures of the legislature, which gave every advantage to those who wanted to block action. Why?

For one thing, the written Constitution was no help. The system of bicameralism is ideally adapted to stalling legislation; the poorly defined role of the President muddies the waters further. It seems, indeed, that the Founding Fathers had tried to make legislating as

Harrison	51st Congress	11. McKinley Tariff Act	1890
		12. Sherman Silver Purchase Act	1890
		13. Sherman Anti-Trust Act	1890
	52d Congress	(None)	
	53d Congress	14. Extension of powers of ICC	1893
		15. Repeal of Silver Purchase Act	1893
Cleveland		16. Wilson-Gorman Tariff Act with Income Tax	1894
	54th Congress	(None)	

[53] Faulkner, *Politics, Reform and Expansion,* pp. 128–131; and see John D. Hicks, *The Populist Revolt* (Minneapolis, 1931).

difficult as possible. They were, of course, interested in avoiding the possibility of tyranny: but in so doing they built a government with no well-defined driving force. Such a force was to be constructed, one which would serve moderately well, but it had not yet been developed in the nineteenth century.

Adequate leadership by Congress would, further, have required disciplined party organizations committed to known policies. Instead we had loose alliances of political satraps who were more interested in patronage than in policy. In Congress, these men, whose power base was in the states and who were often rather insecurely seated on that base, tended to spend most of their time fighting one another and attempting to improve their positions at home.[54] Leadership, therefore, had to come from outside; but the party organism which made internal leadership impossible also made external leadership most difficult. Senators, wrote Woodrow Wilson, act as individuals, "deriving little . . . gravity from connection with the designs of a purposeful party." [55] The remark could as well have been applied to the House of Representatives.

In the 1890's both the House and the Senate developed more effective leadership; this proved to be a passing phenomenon. It lasted for about twenty years and fell before the combined onslaughts of determined presidential leaders and an apparently equally determined group of party mavericks. While never sliding back into the depths of incapacity shown in the post-Reconstruction era, Congress by the First World War was again showing a pronounced inability to generate its own initiative. Congress, it must be said, was usually in the position of a fireman, whose usefulness seldom is obvious except in crises and who often arrives too late with too little. The American public, however, seldom seemed to expect more, and perhaps received the kind of government it deserved, or at least what it wanted. The prevailing ideas of government were inhospitable to national intervention, and the general theory that "that government is best which governs least" still had a strong hold on the American people. Sharing such assumptions, Congressmen (whether leaders or rank and file) were not likely to think in programmatic terms.

[54] David J. Rothman, *Politics and Power: The United States Senate, 1869–1901* (Cambridge, 1966), p. 6. Garraty, *New Commonwealth*, pp. 220–258, gives an excellent picture of the national politics of the period, but like most writers he ignores state and local politics and their influence on congressional leaders.

[55] Wilson, *Congressional Government*, quoted in Rothman, *Politics*, p. 11.

The details of this rise and fall of congressional leadership are instructive. The House of Representatives after Reconstruction was at the mercy of its minorities. Its rules were so constructed that obstruction was easier than action. The "filibuster" which we now identify with the Senate apparently had its origins in the House. Dilatory motions were used commonly and effectively by minorities to delay or prevent action. The Speaker was by custom expected to allow this kind of parliamentary tactics, and any attempt on his part to assert authority was condemned as dictatorship. While Speakers were always expected to act in a partisan manner, the partisanship was expected to be more personally than party oriented.[56]

The growth of effective leadership in the House was largely due to a gradual increase in the power of the Speaker. Speaker Samuel J. Randall began this process in 1881 when he successfully asserted his power to use complete discretion in recognition. It needs little imagination to see how important such a power could be in the hands of a Speaker who was willing to use it either for partisan or for personal ends. John Griffin Carlisle, Speaker from 1883 to 1889, took a further step by self-consciously departing from the "presiding officer" concept; he considered it his duty to take positions on policy questions and to use his authority to advance these positions. He "sought . . . to impose his will on the House and to be the real source of the legislation of the United States." [57] Carlisle, however, did not have the means at his disposal to make such an ambition come true.

It was Representative Thomas Brackett Reed of Maine who, by instituting the famous "Reed rules," became the real power in the House, so much so that he was accused of "sitting in the chair with his feet on the neck of the Republican party." Reed broke the back of the filibuster by refusing to entertain dilatory motions, by using his power of committee appointment deliberately to reinforce his own position, and most of all, by forcing the Democratic minority to accede to his practice of refusing to allow abstainers to prevent a quorum. His ruling in 1890 that all Representatives present but not voting were to be counted in quorum calls rendered nugatory one of the most effective obstructive devices that had been developed. After a few wild days of confusion the House settled down and even

---

[56] See Mary Parker Follett, *The Speaker of the House of Representatives* (New York, 1896).

[57] *Ibid.*, pp. 112–116.

formalized his positions by writing them into the rules. Under Reed and his immediate successors effective leadership was possible. The House took on a more orderly aspect, business proceeded with some dispatch, and an oligarchy centering on the Speaker and largely based on party became the real power.[58]

Charles F. Crisp, Speaker from 1891 to 1895, increased the effective powers of the Speaker still further by increasing the powers of the Committee on Rules, of which the Speaker was a member. This committee, which still retains a large measure of its power, was at the time composed of five men. Three were from the majority party, and they were invariably the ruling triumvirate: the Speaker, the Chairman of Ways and Means, and the Chairman of Appropriations. Mary Parker Follett, writing in 1895, could say, with some exaggeration, that the "House of Representatives is no longer the legislative power . . . it is not even the maker of the legislative power which is in the committees; it is but the maker of the real maker, the Speaker. . . ."[59]

That this was a revolutionary change in the character of the House was fully recognized by contemporaries; its party character was equally clear. Listen to a leading political scientist of the day, Albert Bushnell Hart of Harvard University:

> The power now exercised by the Speaker will probably be exercised by each succeeding Speaker and will somewhat increase. Since the legislative department in every Republic constantly tends to gain ground at the expense of the executive, the Speaker is likely to become, and perhaps is already, more powerful, both for good and for evil, than the President of the United States. He is Premier in legislation; it is the business of his party that he be also Premier in character, in ability, in leadership, and in statesmanship.[60]

Hart was a capable analyst but a poor prophet. Although "Uncle Joe" Cannon again increased the Speaker's power, he was the last to do so, and his exercise of these powers was such that he brought about the revolt which ended the possibility of legislative dominance of the government. Cannon used his power of committee appointment especially judiciously: the seniority rule was not yet unbreakable, and

[58] *Ibid.*, pp. 116–120.
[59] *Ibid.*, p. 247.
[60] Quoted in Chang-Wei Ch'iu, *The Speakers of the House of Representatives since 1896* (New York, 1928), p. 311.

he broke it often, always with a view to securing committee chairmen who were congenial to his own views of proper policy. Like Crisp, he gave large powers to the Rules Committee, which he controlled. By 1905 it was clear that the rules which had been adopted to end minority rule had fallen under the control of a smaller, more cohesive, and even more powerful minority.[61]

The end of this situation was not, however, merely a matter of internal revolt against a dictator. More important was the resurgence of party irregularity. The party control which Reed could exercise in the nineties was no longer possible, at least to the Republicans, by 1910. The Progressives were largely Republicans; but when they arrived in the House in increasing numbers they found their proposals blocked by a conservative oligarchy dominated by members of their own party. Democrats were nothing loath to abet a revolt. The Speaker was stripped of his control of the Rules Committee and of the power to appoint committees. The Rules Committee and the majority floor leader became co-equal with the Speaker; and although the control was still in a measure oligarchical, the oligarchy largely lost its unity because of the rise of the strict seniority rule, which meant that even the chairman of Rules rose to his position automatically and thus did not necessarily represent any important segment of his party. What was true of Rules was true of the other committees.[62]

The power of Speakers like Reed and Cannon, viewed in retrospect, does not seem as great as was thought by their contemporaries. The potential was there, but as remarked about President Cleveland, power needs an objective on which to feed. The power of these Speakers was largely exercised to prevent legislation which they did not like: they seldom had affirmative ends which they sought through legislation, and when they did they were not as successful unless they were in coalition with President McKinley or Roosevelt. The Speaker was a party leader, not a policy leader: and since the party, although now more disciplined, was yet not policy oriented, Speakers did not function often as initiators or sponsors of legislation.

[61] Charles R. Atkinson, *The Committee on Rules and the Overthrow of Speaker Cannon* (New York, 1911); Ch'iu, *Speakers*, p. 146. And see Michael Abram and Joseph Cooper, "The Rise of Seniority in the House of Representatives," *Polity*, I (Sept., 1968), 52–85.

[62] *Ibid.*

The so-called revolution of 1910 made even more certain the continuing ascendancy of the President in directing the course of policy making. Yet it does not seem to have been unpopular; on the contrary, clipping Czar Cannon's wings seems to have satisfied a pronounced public feeling that the Speaker's power "had grown so great as to upset the balance of power in the American constitutional system." [63] And, too, the revolt was led by liberals who resented a system of party discipline which operated to prevent liberal legislation. It was, in a sense, Cannon's increasing estrangement from Theodore Roosevelt which led eventually to his downfall. Over the years it has become plain that the House leadership leads most effectively when it leads in directions desired by the President: in fact, it is now often true that the Speaker and the majority floor leader are regarded as responsible for getting the President's legislative program enacted. This could not be clearly seen by 1917, but the events of 1910 were a step on the way.

Meanwhile the Senate was going through a progression remarkably similar. It is true that the upper house generally enjoyed greater prestige, and that its members were more likely to be leaders or bosses in their state party organizations; nevertheless, giving due allowance to its smaller size and to the fact that its presiding officer occupied a much different power position, events in the Senate were not notably different from those in the House.

There was, to begin with, much the same disintegration of leadership in the years from 1877 to 1890. The party caucuses and the committee on committees had a good deal of influence, especially in organizational questions; but legislative committees seem to have been made up in a haphazard manner, without much attention to party factions. The caucuses were unsuccessful in controlling Senators' votes on substantive issues. The majority caucus rather early gained control of the order of business, but although this was potentially important, it does not seem to have been used so as to make it so. In the 1870's and 1880's Roscoe Conkling, the Senator from New York, was probably the leading single figure in the chamber; but he used his power to reward his friends rather than to advance legislation, and the actual extent of his power was probably not very great

[63] George B. Galloway, *History of the House of Representatives* (New York, 1961), p. 54.

in any case—certainly the Blaine faction fought him on fairly equal terms. Party was important in organizing the Senate, but cohesion on votes was conspicuously absent.[64]

As in the House, however, this situation was markedly transformed in a few short years, again beginning around 1890, and by 1902 the Senate was criticized for excessive party control.[65] The change dated from a seemingly irrelevant incident which occurred in 1889: the organization of an informal poker group at the home of Senator James McMillan.[66] Somewhat accidentally, this group included William Allison, who as the senior Republican was the chairman of the Republican caucus. It also included Allison's close friend Nelson Aldrich of Rhode Island; the pair were to dominate the Senate for some years. Using McMillan's poker sessions as an informal policy committee, and taking advantage of Allison's position (he was also chairman of the Steering Committee, to which he regularly reappointed the same men), these effective leaders succeeded in stabilizing factional control in their hands.

Allison headed the caucus, the Steering Committee, and the Appropriations Committee; friends such as Orville Platt and John Spooner served on Finance and Judiciary; Spooner also chaired the Rules Committee. Eugene Hale and a few other members of the "junta" occupied other important positions. And it was understood that to rise to such positions one had to "go along."

Unlike Reed, the Senate leaders, especially Aldrich, were policy oriented and controlled Senate business with some success. As the young Senator from Indiana, Albert Beveridge, found, "this committee [the Republican Steering Committee] absolutely determines what shall and shall not be done in national legislation." [67] The Republican caucus, under strong leadership, functioned to compromise differences of opinion before matters went to the floor, and once the caucus had decided it could enforce party discipline.

The Democrats in the Senate underwent much the same transition, although the leadership was never as strong: Arthur P. Gorman, the caucus chairman, had to resort to compromise in order to keep them in line.

---

[64] Rothman, *Politics and Power*, pp. 26–29.
[65] M. Ostrogorski, *Democracy and the Organization of Political Parties*, Vol. II, *The United States* (Chicago, 1964), pp. 278–281.
[66] Rothman, *Politics and Power*, pp. 44–46.
[67] *Ibid.*, p. 59.

Thus, by 1900 "the prospects of particular measures depended upon caucus decisions and the course of legislation could no longer be considered apart from party considerations." By the 1890's "party unity on key roll calls became typical." [68]

By 1900 the Senate, like the House, was well on the way to a system of effective party leadership which could control organizational matters almost completely, and policy questions with a good deal of success. But as with the House, this system proved to be temporary.

The decline of Senate leadership can be traced to a complex of factors in which it is impossible to distinguish any single predominant feature. The negativism of the leadership in the face of the Progressive pressures for "radical" legislation undoubtedly had a good deal to do with it. The Senate leaders fought Roosevelt as did those of the House, and if they won some of the battles they lost the war, although Roosevelt was no longer President to crow over his victory. The power of Aldrich and his colleagues was to a marked extent personal rather than institutional; and as they died or retired from the Senate they were not replaced by men possessing the same kinds of leadership skills. This change was accentuated by the enactment of the Seventeenth Amendment, which by introducing direct election of Senators had the eventual effect of changing the type of person elected.[69] No longer could a state party boss have himself selected by a compliant legislature: he had to campaign and take his chances with the fickle public. This was a response to public pressure, which plainly rejected the kind of party-oligarchical rule which men like Aldrich typified. Even before the adoption of the amendment, in 1912, many states had secured the effective right of direct election through the primaries or other devices, so that the change in character of the Senate was a gradual one.

In the end, the beneficiary of these unsuccessful attempts to erect effective systems of party leadership in Congress was, of course, the President. Both Houses retained enough of the new disciplinary structure to ease the task of presidential leadership, but not enough for either House to act effectively in its own right as an originator of legislation—particularly of programs of legislation. But powerful

[68] *Ibid.*, pp. 73, 90.

[69] See Robert and Leona Train Rienow, *Of Snuff, Sin and the Senate* (Chicago, 1965), pp. 287–299.

personalities in the White House, who had legislative aims, could use the mechanisms of caucuses, floor leaders, and Speaker—if not the committee chairmanships—to advance these aims. If this was not clear by 1909 when Roosevelt retired from office it was amply evident by the end of Wilson's first term in 1917.

Despite the weakness of individual Presidents, the effective control of foreign affairs remained in executive hands throughout the period from 1877 to 1917. The only essential difference, which is perhaps of only indirect constitutional interest, seems to have been that the weaker Presidents tended to leave the conduct of American relations with the rest of the world in the hands of the Department of State. Grover Cleveland's conduct of the Venezuela dispute, in which Great Britain at length decided to submit to arbitration, strengthened the presidency by making it a more popular office: Cleveland, in effect, touched a popular chord, with the result that

. . . he advanced the Presidency immensely by foreclosing the leadership in foreign affairs which might have escaped him if he had temporized. . . . [H]e acted in one of those moments of intense understanding, a presidential moment, when he was at one with the people whose representative he was. He understood what was required of him and proceeded with appropriate energy to do it. That the sentiment he personified was belligerent and meretricious and that the risk he incurred was not worth any possible gains from it are historical conclusions. His resolution, however unjustified by the circumstances, was of immense use to the office he held.[70]

It is nevertheless true that the Venezuela crisis was precipitated partly by Cleveland's concentration on domestic affairs—a concentration typical of all the Presidents of this period except Theodore Roosevelt. It was this lack of interest which allowed Cleveland's Secretary of State, Richard Olney, to issue the bellicose statement which, by demanding arbitration, made a crisis out of a minor boundary dispute between Venezuela and British Guiana by making it difficult for the United States to back down. The President then felt that he must support his Secretary: and this does not necessarily imply that he would have wished to do differently in any case. The fact that the British decided to submit to arbitration gave a color of wisdom to a rash and precipitate act.

[70] Tugwell, *Enlargement*, p. 238.

But to say that the Secretaries of State conducted foreign relations tells us little of the constitution: in fact, it was clearly understood that in so doing, the Secretaries were acting for the President, and that in any instance he could supplant them and act on his own, as Cleveland finally did, as McKinley did in deciding to declare war with Spain, as Roosevelt did continuously, and as Wilson was forced increasingly to do after the outbreak of the First World War. Delegation to the State Department was a matter of preference and inclination, not a judgment that the Department was better fitted to conduct affairs, and certainly not an admission of constitutional incapacity to act.

It is one of the significant aspects of the rise of a strong President that it coincided with an increased American interest in the outside world. Americans by 1890 had filled out the continent: the frontier was said to have disappeared. Americans were both psychologically and materially prepared to take a more active role in the affairs of the world. Harrison was prepared to annex Hawaii, but Cleveland delayed the act until 1898; despite his moral tergiversations, McKinley was willing to be led into the Spanish war. And whatever the "warhawk" influence in Congress, the President made the decision, without which there could have been no war.

What this means in terms of the presidency is clear. The control of foreign affairs gives Presidents an opportunity to focus public attention on themselves with little competition from Congress and none from the Supreme Court. "Teddy" Roosevelt was very much aware of this, and was perhaps the first—indeed perhaps the only—President consciously to see and take advantage of it. Earlier Presidents, and even Wilson and Franklin Roosevelt, seem to have been forced by events into the foreign policy leadership which TR assumed by choice. To a public ready to hear it, Roosevelt announced, "I wish to see the United States the dominant power on the shores of the Pacific Ocean." He embarked upon a naval expansion program; sent the fleet around the world in a grandiose gesture which both declared his independence of Congress and forced that body to support his action; initiated—by measures of dubious ethics—the Panama Canal; announced and implemented the "Roosevelt corollary" to the Monroe Doctrine, which made the United States the policeman of the Western Hemisphere; settled the troubled finances of the Dominican Republic; mediated the Russo-Japanese War; and initiated the long era of friendly relations with Great Britain. Along with these accomplishments, naturally, went immoderate amounts of "bluster and brag," which actually exacerbated the relations of the country with other nations, but at the same time kept the general public enthralled.[71]

More than any other one man, Theodore Roosevelt taught the American people to watch, and listen to, the man in the White House. This habit has been perhaps more significant in the "enlargement of the presidency" than any specifically constitutional power or practice. It was reinforced by the lofty moralism of Wilson's pronouncements and by that President's trip to Paris and his attempt to settle the affairs of the world there. Even Americans who disapproved what was being done had a sneaking pride that America, in the person of her Presidents, was now taking her proper place on the world stage. Showmanship, it is clear, has had much to do with presidential power.

No treatment of the development of the constitution at the national level can ignore the role of the courts. This is not, however, the place to look at those court actions which defined national power as distinct from that of the states, or which developed theories of limitations on power. We are now merely concerned with the shareholders in national power, not with the modes by which that power was exercised or limited. What place did the Supreme Court hold in the tripartite constitutional system?

In brief, the Court fulfilled what might be regarded as the "promise" of *Marbury* v. *Madison* [72] and the Dred Scott case [73] (that is, the promise of a court willing to use judicial review to affect public policy), and rose to such an estate by 1900 that it could be attacked as being a third house of the legislature. As late as 1930, indeed, the American system was regarded—with some exaggeration, it is true—by some critics as "government by judiciary."

One might guess that this development came about mostly through the Court's increasing use of judicial review in such a way as to lay it open to the charge that it was substituting its own version of political wisdom for that of Congress. Formally, in other words, the Court ruled that Congress could not enact this or that law; but in effect

---

[71] Mowry, *Roosevelt*, pp. 143–164, 181–196.
[72] Marbury v. Madison, 1 Cranch 137 (1803).
[73] Dred Scott v. Sanford, 19 How. 393 (1857).

this might really be the judges' way of saying: "We disapprove of what you are doing and therefore will find some constitutional provision which we can interpret so as to prevent you from doing it." Considering the nature of nineteenth-century Presidents, it is not surprising that such activity was largely confined to restricting Congress rather than the President. In view of the wide possibilities for varied interpretations of the Constitution, moreover, it should occasion no surprise that commentators have never been able to agree whether the Supreme Court was claiming a new power, essentially legislative in nature, or whether it was merely carrying out in a legitimate manner the implications of judicial review. Either way, the Court was without doubt taking part in the policy making process for national affairs to a degree unrivaled earlier in our history. For in the long period between the adoption of the Constitution and 1870 the judges had only sporadically concerned themselves with federal legislation: most likely because there was usually little of it and what there was raised few constitutional issues.

The growth of industry and the accompanying growth of the large corporation as the typical form of business organization, as we have seen earlier, brought new demands on the federal government. Some came from the business corporations themselves, while others came from groups disadvantaged by industrial civilization. Slowly and reluctantly the government responded to such demands, and the whole political system was rebuilt. Part of the new system which emerged—in this case, clearly in the 1890's—was the new activism of the Supreme Court.

Historians once conceived of this development in terms of a laissez-faire court invalidating all legislation which interfered with the normal course of economic events, merely because the judges disapproved.[74] The actual picture was a good deal more complex: for oftentimes laws were upheld even though they did involve economic regulation in one form or another. There is enough validity in the old view, however, so that it cannot be entirely discarded, and some "revisionist" historians have gone too far in their eagerness to absolve the Court of all blame.[75] Nevertheless, it is easy to exaggerate the degree to which the Court's decisions were out of step with

[74] See, for instance, Louis Boudin, *Government by Judiciary* (2 vols., New York, 1932); Benjamin Twiss, *Lawyers and the Constitution* (Princeton, 1942).

[75] See Albert S. Mavrinac, "From *Lochner* to *Brown* v. *Topeka:* the Court and Conflicting Concepts of the Political Process," *American Political Science Review,* LII (1958), 641–664.

public opinion. Even such obviously pro-business decisions as the Sugar Trust and Income Tax cases of 1895 may not have been too far from the actual desires of the public. We may easily overestimate the degree to which a nineteenth-century public expected or wanted federal legislation in the manner of the 1930's. The results of elections would seem to show no such pronounced desire: the Democratic majority of 1892 was dramatically converted into a Republican one in 1894 in a vote which looked like a landslide and which was confirmed by McKinley's rout of Bryan in the presidential race of 1896, just after the Supreme Court's great "free enterprise" decisions in the above cases and *In re* Debs.[76]

Most of the judges during the entire period under review were Republicans, and by 1890 most were ideologically convinced of the wisdom of laissez-faire: some were convinced that any reasonable version of natural law would include it and that the Constitution makers must have intended to do so also. But as the revisionists have discovered, in many of the judges these feelings were not as simple as we have heretofore thought. John Marshall Harlan, whose judicial career comes the closest to spanning the entire period—he was Hayes' first appointee in 1877 and remained on the bench until his death in 1911—was in some ways typical both of the belief in individualistic free enterprise and of the complexities involved.

Harlan brought out of his Kentucky-based Civil War Unionism a firm belief in national supremacy, so that he was distinctly untypical in some matters; but despite his frequent disagreements with his brethren on the bench, he did believe that business should be allowed to operate largely without governmental interference. Like most of his colleagues, however, he could be convinced, and sometimes voted to uphold even *state* power to regulate.[77] While there were judges who rode the laissez-faire line without deviation, even Stephen J. Field (who is often regarded as the leading figure in business protection) was not always to be found on that side.[78]

Basically, what the Supreme Court accomplished during the period under review in regard to national power was to convert a

---

[76] U.S. *v.* E. C. Knight Co., 156 U.S. 1 (1895); Pollock *v.* Farmers' Loan and Trust Co., 157 U.S. 429 (1895); *In re* Debs, 158 U.S. 564 (1895).

[77] Loren P. Beth, "Justice Harlan and the Uses of Dissent," *American Political Science Review*, XLIX (1955), 1085–1104.

[78] Carl Brent Swisher, *Stephen J. Field, Craftsman of the Law* (Washington, 1930).

charter of powers (primarily in Article I, Section 8, of the Constitution) into a bill of limitations—in fact, practically into a new
bill of rights designed for the protection of American business.
This was done through the normal processes of judicial definition and case-by-case inclusion and exclusion. The effect was far from
normal, however, for much of the time decisions which denied power
to Congress at the same time in practice arrogated it to the Court.
The result was that the federal judiciary achieved a position in the
governing process which it had not previously held. A brief look at
the major cases will illustrate the point.

Perhaps the most significant area of limitation was found in the
commerce clause. This clause, like most of the great provisions of
the Constitution, is more notable for its Delphic ambiguity than for
the clarity which supposedly characterized it. Congress, it says, shall
have power "to regulate commerce among the several states." Marshall had found in these words a broad grant of power; now, however, under pressure from the business world which wished to avoid
effective regulation, the Court found that it limited power. This was
done by defining the term "among the several states" so that much
commerce was found to be the constitutional province of the states,
and by redefining "commerce" so that it was more or less (never
entirely) restricted to the physical transportation of goods across
state lines. So, in the Sugar Trust case in 1895 the Court majority
held that sugar refining—as a form of manufacturing—was not commerce and therefore could not be regulated by Congress under the
Sherman act.[79] And in the First Employers' Liability case it decided
that although railroads were undoubtedly interstate commerce, Congress could regulate their labor practices only for those workers who
physically crossed state lines in the normal course of their employment.[80] But it is also important to note that such decisions left it to
the Court itself to decide what would and what would not be regulated: a point that was highlighted in the Swift case in 1905, for the
Court there found that stockyards (and by extension packing houses)
were part of a "flow" of commerce across state lines and therefore
could be regulated by Congress.[81] Holmes, who wrote the opinion,
was a new judge who did not feel the need to explain why a sugar

[79] U.S. v. E. C. Knight Co., 156 U.S. 1 (1895).
[80] Employers' Liability Cases, 207 U.S. 463 (1908).
[81] Swift & Co. v. U.S., 196 U.S. 375 (1905).

refinery was not part of a similar flow. But it can at least be speculated that in *Swift* the Court was aware of the power of the American farmer whose interests Congress was trying to protect, whereas sugar cane growers were not as powerful and the business interests therefore could be allowed to have their way, especially since the antitrust laws were designed not to protect the growers but the consumers—an even less powerful interest. In any case it was the Court which decided whether or not a business was covered by the act.

In the interpretation of laws the Supreme Court sometimes found a similar role for itself. The interpretation of the antitrust law, for instance, after a period of uncertainty came to be governed by the view that the law was designed only—as Theodore Roosevelt himself had urged—to prevent the growth of "bad" trusts.[82] Therefore, the job the Court took upon itself was that of determining whether a specific combination was good or bad. This so-called rule of reason was first applied in 1911 in the Standard Oil case (the Court found Standard to be a "bad" trust) and the American Tobacco case (also bad).[83] But in 1920 U.S. Steel was found to be a "good" trust.[84] The power of Congress, in effect, was held to extend only to the regulation of bad things.

Strikingly similar was the "noxious articles doctrine," developed by the Court as a guide in both commerce and tax power cases. This doctrine held in essence that Congress could regulate interstate commerce in "bad" articles such as liquor or lottery tickets, or that it could impose a prohibitory tax on them—oleomargarine was putatively "bad"—but if the items were not found to be bad *by the judges,* regulations or taxes could not be imposed.[85] Thus, child labor, somewhat later, was found to be beyond the regulatory power of Congress, not indeed because the judges found it good, but because the products of such labor were harmless, and it was the product rather than the labor which was in interstate commerce.[86] Again the important point for the moment is the essentially legislative nature of the Court in making such decisions.

The point could be emphasized by discussion of numerous other

---

[82] Swisher, *Amer. Const. Devel.*, pp. 507–508.

[83] Standard Oil Co. *v.* U.S., 221 U.S. 1 (1911); U.S. *v.* American Tobacco Co., 221 U.S. 106 (1911).

[84] U.S. *v.* United States Steel Corp., 251 U.S. 417 (1920).

[85] The cases are dealt with in more detail in Chapter 5.

[86] Hammer *v.* Dagenhart, 247 U.S. 251 (1918).

areas of decision: the powers of the ICC were whittled away in some respects and broadened in others by judicial decision; [87] the power of Congress to carry out by affirmative legislation the protection of Negroes envisaged by the Fourteenth Amendment was denied, which meant in practice that the protection would be only such as the Court provided through its *ad hoc* decision-making process; [88] congressional power to investigate and the government's power to make treaties were also brought at least potentially within the control of the judges during the Court's conservative phase, which lasted, with ups and downs, until 1937.[89] But it hardly needs additional emphasis. It bears repetition, however, that in no simple sense could the Court at any stage be called liberal or conservative in the pattern of its decisions: cases can always be found to illustrate either side. What was important was that no law of any great significance could be enacted by Congress without having to run the gantlet of judicial review; the nine men possessed a kind of collective veto which they were not reluctant to exercise. No single judge during this period was immune from the tendency. Even Oliver Wendell Holmes, the apostle of judicial self-restraint, joined his brethren in clipping the wings of the ICC and in applying the rule of reason to antitrust decisions. One judge, as might be expected, would draw his lines at a different point than another, but the power to govern was held by all.

Nor was this necessarily a bad thing. If the Supreme Court, as Mr. Dooley thought, "follows the election returns," it was not very obvious (at least up to 1917) that it was following very far behind them. The American public was as ambivalent about big business as was the Court. And there is really little evidence of any great public outcry against the assumption of power by the Court; indeed, the people if anything seemed to expect it. The lip service which political leaders have always paid to the separation of powers (even while striving to find ways to govern despite it) has trained Americans to regard the Supreme Court as co-equal with the executive and the legislature, and thus to feel that the active use of judicial power is but an incident of equality. In any case, it is evident that by 1917—

[87] Counselman *v.* Hitchcock, 142 U.S. 547 (1892); Brown *v.* Walker, 161 U.S. 591 (1896); Cincinnati, New Orleans & Texas Pacific Ry. Co. *v.* ICC, 162 U.S. 184 (1896).

[88] See Chapter 5.

[89] Kilbourn *v.* Thompson, 103 U.S. 168 (1881); Geoffrey *v.* Riggs, 133 U.S. 258 (1890).

indeed by 1900—the Court had assumed the powerful position in the American polity which it still possesses, even though that power is in recent times exercised in quite different areas than it was before 1937.

We have thus seen the modern American national government take shape in the period between 1877 and 1917. Several aspects of this process may be mentioned by way of summary. The rise of presidential leadership did not, for instance, in any clear sense bring about a corresponding decline of Congress. In typical pragmatic fashion, the presidency became the agency to fill a gap which existed in our political institutions. For the framers had not included in their system any locus for domestic policy leadership. Indeed, it is to be doubted that they even realized the need for such a thing. Nor before the Industrial Revolution was the need very great. In areas in which the need was clear, such as foreign affairs and war, they found a perfectly definite place for the lodgment of power. As a legislative body—that is, as a place to deliberate and pass upon national policy—Congress actually became more effective and more powerful than it had ever been. In our system, in other words, Congress functions best when it is supplied with policy initiative from the outside, which means from the President. This lesson was taught by the work of Washington, Hamilton, and Jefferson early in our national history; it had, however, to be relearned when conditions again made programmatic legislation a necessity. A period of fumbling in the 1890's was a normal accompaniment of the learning process, but by the end of TR's tenure as President it had been learned, and it has not since been forgotten.

Increased regulatory action through legislation, in turn, forced the development of administrative techniques and institutions by which the new laws could be enforced. These techniques were largely developed and in use by 1917 except in the area of financial and budgetary control. We have not yet improved upon the regulatory commission, within old-line departments or independent, although the policy-planning deficiencies of independence have become increasingly obvious. Nor have we basically changed the approach to the means of achieving an effective and nonpartisan civil service.

An incident in the growth of presidential power was the entrance of the United States on the world stage as a great power. This development occasioned, at least before 1917, no great constitutional change, for it could be accommodated within the traditional conceptions of the President as foreign affairs chief, treaty maker, and commander in chief. Theodore Roosevelt may have dramatized these powers and used them more frequently and strikingly; he did not change their basic nature. It is true that two great wars and the recent tendency to use money as an element in foreign policy have both added to the President's power and at the same time, paradoxically, increased the influence of Congress. These developments lie outside our story.

Finally, we have seen the Supreme Court assuming its modern place in the threefold constellation. This was fully achieved by 1917, and though observers immediately after 1937 freely predicted that the Court would return to its pre-Civil War role as an occasional participant only, their prognostications have by now been proved obviously premature. Constitutionally the only difference is that different parts of the Constitution are now emphasized; but the constitutional role of the Court remains in most essentials what it was in 1917.

Another aspect of this story is the changing nature of the federal system—the gravitation of power to higher levels. This will be an important part of the next chapter.

CHAPTER 2

The Federal System

TO say that the study of the American constitution is complicated by the existence of a federal system is to repeat an observation so old that it is both obvious and banal. Yet most treatments of the subject devote a chapter or two to the relations between the states and the national government and let it go at that. This is hardly to do justice to the importance of the states and their local units, which play in many respects a constitutional role equal in importance to, if not exceeding, that of the national government. I find no writer on the constitution since Lord Bryce who has tried to deal with the states as a working part of this constitutional system. And since Bryce was writing in the period covered by this book, there is no better source: consequently I rely on him heavily in the latter portions of the present chapter.

First let us deal with the federal system itself. What were the notions of its nature held by Americans between 1877 and 1917, and how closely did these square with the reality? In what respects did the system change during the period under discussion?

Historians have shifted their interpretations of American history; political scientists are no less subject to revisionism. At the present time a wave of reinterpretation of the federal system is taking place. The old version was that the federal system was a kind of "layer cake," in which the allotted functions of government were divided fairly cleanly between the national government and the governments of the states according to a constitutional scheme developed by the Founding Fathers and interpreted by the Supreme Court. According to this traditional theory the national government has little or nothing to do with the cities and other local units of governance. In the 1880's Bryce could even say the same about the states: ". . . the national government has but little to do with the States as States. Its relations are with their citizens. . . ."[1] Since those days, of course, the received theory assumes that more and more functions of government have risen upstairs to the national government, thus necessitating a great increase in national power but also in the number of formal and informal relationships of the national with the state and even the local governments. This aggrandizement is often considered to be illegitimate or unconstitutional even if necessary; and even when its necessity and desirability are conceded it is still regarded as a great and fundamental change in the constitutional system.

Revisionist theory proceeds on a different historical basis. It assumes that the federal system is not only now but always has been a "marble cake" rather than a "layer cake." The basis for this approach is found by the revisionists both in the Constitution and in historical practice, but primarily in the latter. Consequently the revisionists' case rests at bottom on the adequacy of their historical research. In its most extreme form, the revisionist claim is that "all levels of government in the United States significantly participate in all activities of government."[2] This approach is characterized by a more relaxed view of the trend toward centralization at the national level: revisionists do not think that it is seriously eroding the power of state or city governments.[3]

From the standpoint of the Constitution, the older view has it that the framers intended a clear separation of function, apportioned by the constitutional formula of enumerated powers being given by the Constitution to the national government, while the left-over powers (by far the greatest in number, scope, and significance) remained with the states, where they had resided before the writing of the document. This view largely explains why not only southerners but conservatives in general were opposed to the Fourteenth Amend-

[1] James Bryce, *The American Commonwealth*, 2d ed., rev. (2 vols., London, 1891), I, 312.
[2] Morton Grodzins, *The American System: A New View of Government in the United States*, ed. by Daniel J. Elazar (Chicago, 1966), p. 13.
[3] *Ibid.*, p. 15.

ment, which made revolutionary changes in the nature of the ante-bellum system. Liberals, on the other hand, even if they shared the traditional view of the federal system, felt that the shift in power which the amendment embodied was on the whole a desirable one.

The revisionists assert that the framers had cooperation or sharing in mind: they point to the election process, joint administration of the militia, and the amendment process, and to the great number of shared functions which came into existence during the early constitutional period, when the men who wrote the Constitution were running the governments.[4]

The theory of the federal system in use during the period 1877–1917—or accepted by most writers and politicians—was the older "received" theory. Bryce's analysis of the interrelationships of national and state governments, for instance, sticks almost entirely to the formal categories laid down in the Constitution, and he does not so much as mention any type of direct relation between the national and the local governments. Similarly, despite a brief recognition that "each State has its own system of local areas and authorities, created and worked under its own laws,"[5] he relies on an old-fashioned institutional description of types of local government and shows little awareness of the interdependence of the state and local levels. Even his mention of the necessary relationships between cities and the counties in which they are located shows the same formalism. He also adopted what was a basic component of most American thought: the idea that sovereignty was split between states and nation (he did not discuss the position of the local governments in terms of sovereignty).

The Federal Government [he wrote] clearly was sovereign only for certain purposes, i.e. only in so far as it had received specified powers from the Constitution. These powers did not, and in a strict legal construction, do not now, abrogate the supremacy of the States. . . . But the American nation which had made the Constitution, had done so in respect of its own sovereignty as paramount to any rights of the States.[6]

Thus, at least according to Bryce—and probably most Americans would have agreed, although they might not have been familiar with the ins and outs of the technical distinctions as to where sovereignty

---

[4] These will be discussed in a volume in this series covering an earlier period.
[5] Bryce, *American Commonwealth*, p. 561.
[6] *Ibid.*, p. 409.

lay (most Americans are bored by the legalism of the Austinian insistence that sovereignty must be "found" somewhere)—sovereignty in the American system is split three ways, and it is located in the national government, the state governments, and finally—basically—in the Constitution itself. The fact that the latter aspect of sovereignty could be exercised only by the national government did not seem to bother Bryce any more than it has bothered most Americans.

Judge Thomas M. Cooley, the most influential legal writer in the United States during the latter half of the century, perhaps provided the immediate basis for Bryce's comments. For Cooley, sovereignty resided in the people, who had exercised it by framing the Constitution, but practical sovereignty—the kind that is used every day in the making of laws and in the performance of the myriad tasks of governments—lay in the national and state governments.[7]

While there were writers who disagreed, this was the commonly and popularly accepted theory. Alexander Stephens and Jefferson Davis might thunder from their southern redoubts that the states held all sovereignty, and war veteran John W. Burgess might proclaim from his haven in academia that it is held by the national government, which could even dissolve the states.[8] The American people knew better, as did the Supreme Court, which adopted what was later baptized as the doctrine of "dual federalism." In cases coming to the Court, the judges ordinarily assumed that the enumerated powers of the national government are limited by the existence of the states' reserved powers, and that both sets of powers are fixed, so that they can be changed only by amendment.[9]

In a typically American fashion, then, the niceties of well-rounded theory were ignored in favor of other niceties based on a rather legalistic view of the words of the Constitution. Lawyers were in the saddle anyway where such matters were concerned, and undoubtedly most of them, with Cooley, accepted the Bryce version. It had the merit of being at one and the same time formally satisfying and pragmatically effective, for although it looked very neat and final, in practice it left to the courts of law a world of room for interpretation.

[7] Anwar Syed, *The Political Theory of American Local Government* (New York, 1966), p. 63.

[8] Walter Hartwell Bennett, *American Theories of Federalism* (University, Ala., 1964), pp. 184–185, 191–193.

[9] The term "dual federalism" was first used by Edward S. Corwin, *The Twilight of the Supreme Court* (New Haven, 1934).

In court cases questions always arose concerning exactly what the specified powers of Congress included, with the "necessary and proper" clause providing all the room for interpretation anyone could desire. At the same time in state cases, the courts proved perfectly capable of constructing limitations on the otherwise limitless reservoir of state power which they could apply or not as the case seemed to demand. Thus could theory be ignored even while it was being observed.

Constitutional history is the history of practice, not theory, so let us turn from these cursory observations to actual practice. That practice did not consort with theory to any great degree is perhaps to be expected. The revisionist school has pretty well exploded the older idea that the functions of government, before Wilson's presidency at least, were neatly separated into two or three levels with the courts standing as watchdogs to see that the twain never met. As an English commentator remarks,

The foremost characteristic of American federalism . . . is the interdependence of Federal and State government, not their mutual independence. Nor is this view of American federalism confined to the twentieth century; it can be applied to the earlier phases of American history as well, and indeed it enables us to give a unity to the history of American federalism that escapes more legalistic definitions.[10]

This may be somewhat of an exaggeration: there is more truth to the received theory than the revisionists are willing to grant (and vice versa). There are numerous examples of federal-state cooperation in various forms long before 1917; but the number, variety, and significance of the interactions has increased dramatically, especially during and after the New Deal years. The revisionist argument depends a good deal on another factor which revisionists tend to ignore, the general growth of *all* types of governmental activity. It is only natural that as these functions increased, the amount of "partnership" activities would also do so. What the revisionists need in order to prove their case is a quantitative comparison of the *proportion* and *significance* of shared functions from one period to another.

On the other hand the received theory depends for its validity on the assumption that there is a new federalism, which is often dated

[10] M. J. C. Vile, *The Structure of American Federalism* (London, 1961), p. 3.

as beginning in 1913 with the accession of Woodrow Wilson to the presidency.[11] This is not easily proved, and the number of examples of earlier cooperation the revisionists have already found seems to explode any such assumption.

There is also an older theory, which holds that the Fourteenth Amendment was meant by its framers to work a revolution in the federal system by taking away numerous powers from the state level and vesting them in the national government.[12] There is enough truth in this idea, as we shall see later in this chapter, to make the whole story rather complex.

There was in fact considerable cooperation and interaction between the states and the national government long before 1917. This took varied forms, most of which have, surprisingly, been started upon federal initiative rather than that of the states (as, for instance, the decision made in the Civil War, World War I, World War II, and the postwar era to allow the states a role in the administration of the military system).[13]

The most obvious, easiest, and least effective variety of sharing is *informal cooperation*. By now this exists in a bewildering and uncountable variety of situations. In the period 1877 to 1917 it was not so common, but did exist. One way in which this activity can be conducted is for one of the levels of government voluntarily to legislate cooperatively: that is, to enact laws which complement laws already existing at the other level, so as to make a complete network of law on the subject and thus lead to more effective enforcement. Such a law, to give but one example, was the Harrison Anti-Narcotic Act of 1914.[14] This is a federal law through which the government attempted to increase the effectiveness of existing state narcotics laws, as well as to provide for effective control at the international level. In addition, there has for a long time been much voluntary cooperation between federal and state law enforcement officials, not only in the narcotics field but in the whole field of criminal law.

With the entrance of the national government into regulation of

[11] Jane Perry Clark, *The Rise of a New Federalism* (New York, 1965).

[12] Joseph B. James, *The Framing of the Fourteenth Amendment* (Urbana, Ill., 1956); Jacobus ten Broek, *The Antislavery Origins of the Fourteenth Amendment* (Berkeley, 1951).

[13] Clark, *New Federalism, passim*; Daniel J. Elazar, *American Federalism: A View from the States* (New York, 1966), pp. 67–72.

[14] 38 Stat. 785 (1914); Clark, *New Federalism*, pp. 14–15.

interstate utilities, starting with the railroads in 1887, there was provided a basis for similar federal-state cooperation in this field, since the states had long been regulating utilities—with only partial effectiveness because the industries involved were national in scope in many cases. Such cooperation began almost immediately upon the creation of the Interstate Commerce Commission: in 1889 the states requested that agency to cooperate with them, and since that time informal joint hearings, coordination of fact gathering and of statistical work, and attempts to secure some degree of uniformity in the accounting and reporting of utilities companies have been continuous.[15]

The United States Surgeon General was authorized to call joint meetings with state health officials as early as 1902.[16]

Informal cooperation, because of its voluntary nature, is often not effective even when it exists. The problems were illustrated early in our history, with the difficulties the Continental Congress had in securing military, financial, and supply assistance from the state governments. The enforcement of the fugitive slave laws, as demonstrated in *Prigg* v. *Pennsylvania*,[17] was a somewhat different problem, since the states perceived no common interest in carrying them out. Whenever cooperation is expected without shared interest, it will fail; and as the American Revolution and the Civil War both indicate, interstate rivalries, local self-interest, and jealousy of the power of the national government make concerted action in a federal context difficult even during grave emergencies. Informal cooperation does, however, indicate the awareness of the officials involved that they are dealing with parts of the same problems. Such cooperation began and still exists largely without benefit of theory, although the revisionists have in recent years imposed a theory upon it.

A second type of sharing exists in the form of *agreements* or *contracts*. The federal government may make such arrangements, including legally binding ones, with states, local governmental units, or individuals, and of course state governments may do the same. The most famous of the interstate contracts is the Colorado River agreement; but the Supreme Court upheld federal contracts with states as early as 1900, when it sustained an agreement which made Minne-

[15] Clark, *New Federalism*, pp. 17–20.
[16] *Ibid.*, pp. 20–21.
[17] Prigg v. Pennsylvania, 16 Pet. 539 (1842).

sota's admission to the Union contingent upon a limitation of its right to tax lands granted to railroads.[18] Perhaps informal agreements are the most common; but they are also likely to be the least durable and effective. The United States and California have for many years had an agreement of this sort governing the naturalization process for immigrants.[19] The national government, again, insisted before the passage of the Smith-Lever Act of 1914 that it must agree to the state colleges' selection of directors of extension services and experiment stations, since it was providing part of the money.[20]

There are so many such agreements—and this has been true for such a long period of time—that it would be fruitless to catalogue them. They concern subjects such as irrigation (1884), agricultural research (1887), highways (1916), and vocational education (1917).[21] Nowadays agreements accompany practically every federal grant program, as the national authorities strive to make sure that the grants are handled efficiently and effectively. As to formal compacts, the national government has long been a party to many of them, and of course there are quite a few more between groups of states, some of which (mostly in settlement of boundary questions) date back to the early days of the constitutional system. There is a formal national role even in purely interstate compacts, since the Constitution requires congressional approval of them; but in major questions such as the control of water from the Columbia or Colorado river systems, the stake of the whole nation is so obviously great that officials in Washington take a much more active part than a mere ratification, and sometimes enter the agreement as a formal party. Federal interest in the New York Port Authority, for example, goes back at least to 1910.[22]

Formal federal-state or federal-local agreements depend basically for their effectiveness on national control of the purse strings, and are most common where grants are involved. Using the grant as the lever, national agencies can force the acceptance of agreements covering personnel practices, accounting procedures, construction standards, criteria for the acceptance of research projects, etc. This

[18] Stearns v. Minnesota, 179 U.S. 223 (1900).

[19] Clark, New Federalism, p. 47.

[20] Ibid., pp. 48–49; 38 Stat. 372 (1914).

[21] Ibid., pp. 46–80.

[22] Ibid., p. 76. See Felix Frankfurter and James M. Landis, "The Compact Clause of the Constitution," Yale Law Journal, II (1925), 691.

type of grant, conditional upon agreements about administration, began with the Morrill Land-Grant Act of 1862 and has been a feature of most federal grant programs ever since.[23] From a constitutional standpoint such arrangements are important, because they mean that there is a sense in which the national government takes over (in practice, not in law) some measure of control of programs which are nominally in the hands of the states or their agents. This does not necessarily mean that the federal government can always impose such agreements regardless of the wishes of the states: in fact the still strong feeling of obligation of Congressmen to their states guarantees that state interests will be heard, and they often seem to be dominant. Even in such an area, where national power would seem greatest, cooperation is anything but a one-way street. States have "virtual representation" on congressional committees, and their interests are also served by individual Congressmen.[24]

The *joint* or *cooperative* use of personnel is still another means of sharing within the federal system; perhaps one ought to include under this head the use of state officials to perform federal functions, since both Madison and Hamilton envisaged it as a distinct possibility under their new Constitution and it has existed since it was first used as a means of attempting to prevent the slave trade in those states where that was forbidden.[25] One little-known usage of this type came under the ill-fated federal child labor law of 1916, invalidated by the Court after only a year:

The federal administration of this act hinged so completely on state forces that in no case could it have been less truly said that a great federal network was controlling not only the states but also the daily home lives of all the children throughout the country. The campaign waged against the act was based more on hypothetical fears than on knowledge of administrative practice under the law. . . . So satisfactory was the cooperation developed between federal and state personnel in the administration of the law that the experiment was recalled by a state administrator . . . as an "outstanding effective administrative technique." [26]

This form of sharing, too, can be a two-way proposition: states can use federal personnel.

[23] *Ibid.*, pp. 140–141.
[24] Elazar, *American Federalism*, p. 145; Clark, *New Federalism*, pp. 48–49.
[25] Clark, *New Federalism*, p. 8, citing Federalist Papers 17 and 45.
[26] *Ibid.*, pp. 95–96.

Sharing can take the form of arrangements by which the salary of an employee is paid jointly; by which one inspector does the job for more than one government; or by which an employee is jointly deputized (this practice has been used by the Food and Drug Administration at least since 1917, and by California in forest protection since 1910).[27] In the state agricultural colleges, as is well known, experiment station and extension service personnel—in fact the entire operations—are jointly paid and have been for many years.[28] Then, too, the states depend heavily on local personnel for the carrying out of state policies; this is particularly clear in the use of local sheriffs, district attorneys, and police to enforce state criminal law.

A fourth form of federal-state cooperation flourishes in *interdependent law and administration*. Some types of this go back as far as 1789, for the first national law regulating the use of navigable waterways provided that pilots in federal waters must conform with "existing or future" state laws, and that violations would be punishable by the states.[29] No count has been made of other laws which were in existence by 1917, but it is known that there were many. On the other hand, state laws are sometimes dependent on federal action: obviously so in matters which are or may become covered by treaties. A most famous and significant case of this type, because it involved the whole reach of the national government's treaty power, involved the fairly insignificant matter of the treatment of migratory water fowl. The states did not prove uniformly responsive to the pressures of organized conservationists, but they were successful in persuading Congress, in 1913, to regulate the shooting of birds. Birds were not thought of as items of commerce, however, and lower federal courts held that only the states had the sovereign right to deal with the matter for the benefit of their people.[30] Meeting this constitutional rebuff, the government negotiated a treaty with Canada which pledged both countries to adopt such measures. This was upheld by the Supreme Court as a valid exercise of the treaty power; as Justice Holmes remarked, in a rather casual manner, in the famous

---

[27] *Ibid.*, p. 105.

[28] Under the various land-grant college acts.

[29] Clark, *New Federalism*, p. 109.

[30] U.S. v. McCullagh, 221 Fed. 288 (D. Kan. 1915); U.S. v. Shauver, 214 Fed. 154 (E. D. Ark. 1914).

case of *Missouri* v. *Holland,* "acts of Congress are the supreme law of the land only when made in pursuance of the Constitution, while treaties are declared to be so when made under the authority of the United States." [31] Thus, the treaty clause can justify a regulatory power not otherwise constitutionally held by the national government; but for present purposes the important point is that since the treaty superseded existing state laws, all such laws had to be redrawn to satisfy the standards laid down in the treaty.

Similarly, after the passage of the national pure food and drug laws, many states either adapted their own regulations to those of the federal government or else repealed their laws entirely, specifically adopting the national standards for use by state officials. State inspectors were also given the power to aid in the enforcement of the federal laws, so that the whole process of food and drug enforcement has become a cooperative one.[32]

There are also numerous instances, going back at least as far as the fugitive slave laws, in which the national authorities aid in the enforcement of state law. By 1917 there were quite a few examples of this: the Mann Act of 1910 lent federal aid when prostitutes were transported across state lines; [33] the Dyer Act of 1910 prohibited the transportation of stolen automobiles into another state; [34] the Wilson Act of 1890, reinforced by the Webb-Kenyon Act of 1913, attempted to use Congress' commerce power to aid in the enforcement of state liquor laws; [35] and the regulation of interstate sales of oleomargarine was undertaken in 1902 in order to aid the state regulations of those states in which the butter lobby was strong.[36]

In fields in which state and federal governments have concurrent powers—usually this means the national commerce power and the police powers of the states—the state governments may continue regulating even after national laws are adopted, provided they do not positively conflict with the federal regulations. In addition, of course, there may be a high degree of cooperation in enforcement. Both levels of government may punish violations. "A man who catches black bass shorter than the length allowed by Vermont law is liable

[31] Missouri *v.* Holland, 252 U.S. 416 (1920).
[32] Clark, *New Federalism,* pp. 113–114.
[33] 36 Stat. 825 (1910).
[34] 41 Stat. 324 (1910).
[35] 26 Stat. 313 (1890); 37 Stat. 699 (1913).
[36] 32 Stat. 193 (1902).

to pay a Vermont fine, and if he sends his fish across to a friend in New York state, he violates the federal law and is liable to a federal penalty as well." [37]

Some federal laws, however, do not allow federal punishment after a state conviction. In more recent times such legal situations might run afoul of the Supreme Court because of the double jeopardy rule—but this did not occur until long after 1917.

Finally there is *financial aid* flowing from one level of government to another. Since in our day this is largely a one-way flow we have lost sight of the possibility that states could aid the national government (as indeed they did under the Articles of Confederation, when the central officials had no taxing power). Grants go far back into American history and take many different forms. There is the land grant, in which states are allowed to use the proceeds from federal land use or from the sale of federal lands. Grants have had great significance in our history, and "whatever was at the focus of state attention became the recipient of national grants," at first usually land grants but later more typically grants of money.[38]

The theory behind grant programs of course is that federal aid will lure the states into becoming partners in some area of activity in which the federal government is interested. But in practice it is often the states which have the interest and which succeed in luring the national government into aiding them.[39] Consequently, it is improper to view the use of grants purely as a deliberate device for federal intervention. Since originally the states were expected to aid the national government in many fields, it would not have seemed improper for the central officials to help pay for this aid.

The beginnings of these practices involve periods of our history long before the one under review. Suffice it to say here that both the land grant and the cash grant were regular and well-known parts of American political practice and expectations by 1877. An additional device, started in 1862, became habitual during the period after 1877: the practice of trying to make sure that federally derived money would be properly spent. The Morrill Act went only so far as to earmark specifically the proceeds of the land grants, to require annual

[37] Clark, *New Federalism*, p. 133.

[38] Grodzins, *American System*, p. 31; Clark, *New Federalism*, pp. 137–185. See in general V. O. Key, Jr., *The Administration of Federal Grants to States* (Chicago, 1937).

[39] Grodzins, *American System*, p. 31; Elazar, *American Federalism*, p. 63.

reports from the spending agencies, and to require provision of military training.[40] Minimal controls soon became regular features of grant acts, and slowly more elaborate regulations were attached. The Weeks Act of 1911 (for forest fire prevention) required each state to submit its plans to federal officials in order to qualify for the grant,[41] as did the Smith-Lever Act of 1914 (for agricultural extension work).[42] By 1917 the foundations had thus been laid for the extensive and complex web of federal rules which control practically every federally aided program today.

Grant programs involved all of the types of cooperation already discussed. State personnel might be hired according to federal regulations, personnel could be shared, there were both state and federal laws involved, the grant programs required agreements or contracts, and in general there was as complete a sharing of function as could be achieved without actual merger of the agencies. The techniques involved become more and more elaborate and sophisticated as we approach the present day, but the approach is as old as federal attempts to control the interstate slave trade. It is equally true that the states maintain grant programs for their local governments, in which much the same considerations apply: education and highways are obvious examples.

Because the sharing of functions in the federal system is more a response to felt need than to theory, it makes little sense to inveigh against federal usurpation of state functions. If the states could perform the functions adequately there would have been little incentive for the national government to enter the picture at all. The moral, here as elsewhere, surely is that as the economy became national so did the problems which had to be handled. In many cases these were modern developments of old problems; but many other times they involved matters with which the states themselves had never dealt. In some instances the federal government could constitutionally have assumed complete control, but it often decided instead to allow the states to play a role: the grant program for interstate highway construction is an obvious case in point. We have here the best possible exemplification of the "web of government."

Clearly the national government bulked much larger in the total

---

[40] Clark, *New Federalism*, pp. 140–141.
[41] *Ibid.*, pp. 142–143.
[42] *Ibid.*

picture of American government in 1917 than it had in 1877, just as it was to bulk larger in 1937 than in 1917. While all governments had become more active in response to the changing problems of the day, the national level gained more dramatically because it had done less to begin with—and perhaps also because for some reason it had always been the primary center of citizen attention. By 1917 not only was the citizen *watching* events in Washington: he was going off hat in hand to that city asking for solutions to problems which had evaded solution elsewhere. If one had to look to Wall Street as the financial capital and to such places as Wilmington, Delaware, as the corporate capital of the country it was natural to suppose that only the political capital was in a position to deal with the titans of finance and industry.

This pilgrimage to Washington did not occur without misgivings on the part of many Americans, and many roadblocks were thrown up in attempts to prevent it. The very businessmen who, in a sense, created the problems were at the same time engaged in strenuous attempts to prevent their solution. Doubtless the captains of industry did not see the same problems as did their employees, or the embattled farmers, or the declining professional middle class which had dominated American life for so long. What is identified as a "problem" is largely a matter of the point of view. To Rockefeller and Carnegie monopoly was not a problem, but an opportunity, and it was natural for them to attempt to prevent governmental regulations which would interfere with their businesses. Some of these attempts had constitutional implications.

The industrial leaders and the finance capitalists found—it is an old story—that their interests generally lay in the absence of governmental regulatory activity, since the regulations would regulate *them*. Naturally they would try any political method open to them, as would any other group, to secure their interests. The balance of political forces in individual states often favored the agrarian interests; and even in states where it did not, such as Massachusetts, surviving principles of *noblesse oblige* retained by the old professional classes often produced the same results. So dependence upon lobbying in the state capitals was found to produce uncertain results, and the battle against state regulation was often lost. Consequently the lawyers who, as one wag has said, always retained the courage of their retainers' fees, were put to finding a constitutional means by which they could approach the courts, with the hope that judges would see their point of view and strike down the offensive statutes. This battle went on in both state and federal courts. At the state level the story is not well known, but insofar as it is known at all, it appears that the battle was as uncertain as in the legislatures, since the state courts were closely tied to political opinion: judges were usually elected to limited terms of office and thus tended to reproduce on the bench the political feelings of the day.

Approach to the federal courts posed a different problem, since there was often no obvious constitutional provision which prevented states from regulating business enterprise. But slowly the lawyers were able to convince federal judges that the due process clause of the new Fourteenth Amendment not only could but should be used to effect this purpose. The movement proceeded from the dissenters' opinions in the Slaughterhouse cases in 1873 and did not reach fruition until the 1890's; it will be fully discussed later—but there is one aspect of it which bears directly on the nature of the federal system. This is the development by the Supreme Court of the set of principles that has later been christened "dual federalism."

The same business interests which were opposing regulation by the states found themselves, surprisingly enough, fighting the same battle against the national government. For Nelson Aldrich and his conservative cohorts occasionally lost control of congressional processes, and domineering Presidents sometimes wanted legislation which industrial barons had advised them against. When the titans of business lost in the Congress and the White House the recourse was the same: to try to recoup their losses by resort to the courts. In a sense this was easier than with state legislation, for the national government was (all the textbooks said it) a government of enumerated powers, and all that was necessary was to prove that the particular piece of legislation involved a power that was not enumerated. Most often this directly involved theories of the federal system, since those powers not given to Washington were presumably left to the states: therefore the argument was that such-and-such a law could be passed only by the states (which in most cases were not about to do so). Obviously the commerce clause lent itself readily to such argument; it could be applied as a two-edged sword, preventing state regulation in one instance by use of the doctrine that the power belonged exclusively to Congress, and federal regulation in another, using states' rights.

Thus dual federalism led to the construction of a "twilight zone," in which states could not legislate because that was a violation of a natural law principle found by the courts in the due process clause of the Fourteenth Amendment, while the national government could not legislate on the same subject because there was no such power given in the constitutional enumeration.[43]

There was also the problem of practicality, which sometimes added to the defensive bulwarks of corporate interests: not only could these often prevent federal legislation because of constitutional limitations, they could also sometimes prevent state legislation because of difficulties in enforcement. For instance, in the Sugar Trust case of 1896 the Supreme Court held that since manufacturing was a local phenomenon, not part of interstate commerce, monopoly in manufacturing could not be touched under the Sherman Anti-Trust Act.[44] But it was as clear as anything could be that no state could effectively prevent such monopoly either, because the scale of the problem could not be coped with within state boundaries.

Having said all this, it needs also to be said that even the Supreme Court was never completely dependable: judges may have received retainers' fees from corporate interests back in the days before they ascended Mount Olympus, but once on the bench they were unreachable except by persuasive legal briefs. There is no period of American history in which judicial decisions have been all of a piece, and this is as true of the Court's so-called laissez-faire stage as of any other. And while, as Mr. Dooley pointed out, "a statute which reads like a stone wall to a layman can become in the hands of a lawyer a triumphal arch," it is also true that the lawyer has to be able to convince a majority of the Supreme Court that an arch is there rather than a wall: a feat of legerdemain which did not always prove successful.

In explaining the Supreme Court's tergiversations there are many

[43] Corwin, *Twilight of Supreme Court.* See also Benjamin R. Twiss, *Lawyers and the Constitution* (Princeton, 1942), pp. 167–168 and *passim*; Walton H. Hamilton, "The Path of Due Process of Law," in Conyers Read (ed.), *The Constitution Reconsidered* (New York, 1938), pp. 167–190. A somewhat revisionist view is presented in C. Peter Magrath, *Morrison R. Waite: The Triumph of Character* (New York, 1963), esp. pp. 183–196.

[44] U.S. *v.* E. C. Knight Co., 156 U.S. 1 (1895).

possibilities to be considered. There is an imponderable factor in the judicial philosophies of the judges: that is, their personal perceptions of what it means to be a judge and what kind of a role they are called upon to play. In this respect there is a vast difference between a Stephen J. Field, who feels that his role calls upon him to save America from alien ideologies, especially economic ones,[45] and an Oliver Wendell Holmes, Jr., who views such problems with Olympian detachment because he feels that the judges' role is to allow full play to the "reasonable" decisions of representative legislatures.[46] Other judges occupied positions between these two extremes; but until the 1930's perhaps the balance lay with Field.

Then, too, the legal philosophy that flourished in the closing years of the century was a factor. The reigning philosophy in American schools was that of the English legal thinker John Austin; particularly was this so in his emphasis on law as a closed system in which, from already existing principles, answers to new questions could be derived by deductive logic without so much as a glance at the conditions in the real world surrounding the case at bar.[47] The construction by Justice Rufus W. Peckham and his colleagues of the doctrine of liberty of contract to stop the states from regulating wages and other working conditions was a logical deduction from the existing common law. This was first accepted by the Court in *Allgeyer* v. *Louisiana* in 1897; [48] but its most notorious use came in the Lochner case, a 1905 decision which held that the liberty of workers to contract with their employers was unconstitutionally interfered with by a New York law which prescribed the hours of work for bakers. That it was hardly a free bargaining situation between employers and individual workers, and that (as Justice Harlan pointed out) health and other hazards might exist which could make regulation a matter of great public interest, were external considerations which, if noticed at all, were given short shrift.[49] There were

---

[45] See Carl Brent Swisher, *Stephen J. Field, Craftsman of the Law* (Washington, 1930); Robert G. McCloskey, *American Conservatism in an Age of Enterprise* (Cambridge, 1951).

[46] The material on Holmes is practically endless, but he is perhaps his own best spokesman; on this subject see especially his dissenting opinion in Lochner v. New York, 198 U.S. 45 (1905).

[47] John Austin, *The Province of Jurisprudence Determined* (London, 1862).

[48] Allgeyer v. Louisiana, 165 U.S. 578 (1897).

[49] Lochner v. New York, 198 U.S. 45 (1905).

dissenters to such decisions, and they sometimes won the day, but even when they did it often looked like a grudging concession to unlovely reality.

Another, less grudging, concession to reality was the development of a new school of legal thought which has become known as "sociological jurisprudence." Seeded by Holmes in his famous lectures on the common law, published in 1880, it was fostered by lawyer Louis D. Brandeis in cases before the courts in which he had to try to convince judges that the states had the power to use economic regulations in aid of groups other than corporate enterprise.[50] It was expounded in the law schools by Roscoe Pound and his followers [51] and spread to the lay audience through journals of opinion such as that established in 1913 by Herbert Croly and Walter Lippmann: the *New Republic*. Sociological jurisprudence is a high-sounding phrase for a very simple concept—that the law should respond to the underlying needs and desires of society and that it could and should be used deliberately to shape that society. Brandeis developed the use of economic and social facts in court because he knew that the only way that he could win cases was by convincing judges that there was an overriding social need justifying state regulation: thus in *Muller* v. *Oregon* (1908) his brief argued that states could regulate women's working hours not merely because the Constitution permitted it but because it was socially necessary and desirable.[52] Pound and academic writers have made an abstruse principle out of this which is of interest largely to their colleagues but which was important also because it provided respectable intellectual backing for the new approach—backing which could be used by Lippmann and others in approaching the broader elite of public opinion.

The social background of the judges was also a contributing factor to the pattern of their decisions. Most Supreme Court judges were not only (of course) white and Anglo-Saxon, but upper middle class.[53] Their sympathies and habits of thought lay with their own

[50] Muller *v.* Oregon, 208 U.S. 412 (1908), brief by Brandeis.

[51] Roscoe Pound, "The Scope and Purpose of Sociological Jurisprudence," *Harvard Law Review*, XXV (1911), 591. See, in general, Henry S. Commager, *The American Mind* (New Haven, 1950), ch. 18.

[52] A good brief description appears in Leo Pfeffer, *This Honorable Court* (Boston, 1965), pp. 243–244.

[53] John R. Schmidhauser, "The Justices of the Supreme Court: A Collective Portrait," *Midwest Journal of Political Science*, 3 (1959), 1.

strata of society. In addition many of them had been corporation lawyers—more specifically railroad lawyers—during their years in practice. It was not surprising that they were often unable to divest themselves of the legal principles which they had espoused at the bar merely because they now approached the bar from the opposite side. Some rose above their backgrounds: Harlan (sometimes) and Brandeis because of their humanitarian feeling for their fellow man; [54] Holmes perhaps because he had never been dependent on the practice of the law and because his study of history had accustomed him to the idea of change; [55] Hughes because as a practical politician he saw the necessity of temporizing when public opinion seemed to require it.[56]

Nor is it clear that public opinion was on the side of the reformers. Mr. Dooley's comment that the "Soopreem Coort follows th' iliction returns," in context, merely pointed out that the elections favored the status quo. While not entirely unambiguous, election results at least in presidential years were not usually such as to give comfort to reformers or encouragement to progressivism on the part of Supreme Court judges. It is ironic that President Taft's appointments (1909–1913) came at the very time when public opinion was in reality shifting, so that the Taft conservatives on the bench saw themselves as soldiers at Armageddon fighting the progressive hosts exposed by the 1912 election. While Charles Evans Hughes could be considered liberal, the other Taft appointees—Edward D. White promoted to Chief Justice, Horace H. Lurton, Willis Van Devanter, Joseph R. Lamar, and Mahlon Pitney—were pronounced conservatives. Taft himself was a man with a streak of humor: he expected his appointees to outlast the doubtless temporary aberration exposed by the election, and charged them, probably with a chuckle shaking his

[54] There is no good biography of Harlan; for an over-all view of his opinions as expressed on the Court see Loren P. Beth, "Justice Harlan and the Uses of Dissent," *American Political Science Review*, XLIX (1955), 1085–1104; for Brandeis, an excellent treatment is Alpheus T. Mason, *Brandeis, a Free Man's Life* (New York, 1946).

[55] See especially the magnificent but unfortunately unfinished biography by Mark deWolfe Howe, *Justice Oliver Wendell Holmes* (2 vols., Cambridge, 1957, 1963). A more popular treatment is Catherine Drinker Bowen, *Yankee from Olympus* (Boston, 1944).

[56] Good, but a little unreliable because he depended too much on Hughes' own version of his ideas, is Merlo J. Pusey, *Charles Evans Hughes* (2 vols., New York, 1961).

hugh frame, "Damn you, if any of you die I'll disown you!" [57] But there was an undercurrent of seriousness in the remark, and it was true that most of the time since 1877 voters had shown no disposition to choose the more radical of the alternatives facing them—not that the alternatives were usually very great.

The uncertain slide of the Supreme Court into laissez-faire had begun with the Court's decision in the Slaughterhouse cases in 1873. Here the Court had staved off by a 5–4 vote the claim of former Supreme Court Justice John A. Campbell (a Confederate leader from Alabama) that the due process clause of the newly adopted Fourteenth Amendment should be turned to the protection of private business from the depredations of government. The majority had other game in view—the preservation of as much as possible of the ante-bellum Constitution, more particularly the old federal system. Campbell's interpretation would have made the amendment a bill of rights against the states, enforceable by the national government, which is in effect what it has now become anyway; but in 1873 the Court would have none of it. Four dissenters were not so sure that the federal system should not be changed, but they seemed to be more concerned with the protection of business property than with individual human liberties. It is significant that in the first case seriously to introduce the idea that due process of law could be applied to the substance of laws rather than merely to legal procedures, four judges could be found in support. Justice Field was in the forefront.[58]

From the standpoint of the development of the federal system, the rise of substantive due process meant two things: one, that a national agency—the Supreme Court—was to decide (in many instances) what the states could and could not do; it thus meant a diminution of state autonomy. Second, to the extent that the Court used substantive due process to frustrate state attempts to regulate business, there would be more pressure exerted by nonbusiness interests for the national government to act, thus accelerating the march to Washington and the accretion of power in the hands of federal officials. The upholders

[57] Quoted in C. Herman Pritchett, *The Roosevelt Court* (New York, 1948), p. 17.

[58] Slaughter-House Cases, 16 Wall. 36 (1873); see for a fuller account Loren P. Beth, "The Slaughter-House Cases—Revisited," *Louisiana Law Review*, Vol. XXIII (1963), 487–505.

of substantive due process were thus unwitting nationalists in the battle over the nature of the federal system.

The commerce clause was more directly at issue in many cases than the Fourteenth Amendment, for here both state and federal governments were directly involved, and cause-and-effect relationships are more easily identified. When, for instance, the Supreme Court held that a state may not regulate the rates charged by railroads on interstate shipments (as it did in the Wabash case in 1886) [59] this constituted almost an invitation to the federal government to do so: an invitation which was immediately accepted by the creation of the ICC.[60] And this kind of situation was not infrequent: there were numerous such instances between 1877 and 1886, although the federal government was not always so eager to take up the burden which the Court had found unconstitutional when carried by a state.[61]

The constitutional doctrine governing such cases was the "Cooley rule," deriving from *Cooley* v. *Board of Wardens* (1851), in which the Court had decided that states could regulate *interstate* commerce, provided Congress had not done so and the particular matter was one not requiring (in the Court's judgment) a national, uniform set of regulations.[62] Thus, when the Court upheld the power of Illinois to regulate grain elevator rates in 1877, it was either saying "this is not interstate commerce and therefore can be regulated by states," or "this *is* interstate commerce, but Congress has not seen fit to regulate it and we do not feel that in this instance it requires uniform national treatment." [63] Consequently, in every such case, no matter which way it was decided, the Court was making a rough pragmatic judgment in economics (this is—or is not—interstate commerce) or a practical political division of powers between states and the national government, or both. The Court had thus effectively maximized its own power as a governing agency in the American polity; but at the same time there was a good deal of practical wisdom in the feeling that some things were better regulated by the states and others by the

[59] Wabash, St. Louis & Pacific Ry. Co. v. Illinois, 118 U.S. 557 (1886).

[60] Interstate Commerce Act, 24 Stat. 379 (1887).

[61] The most relevant of such cases were Foster v. Masters, etc., of New Orleans, 94 U.S. 246 (1877); RR Co. v. Husen, 95 U.S. 465 (1878); Hall v. de Cuir, 95 U.S. 485 (1878); Pickard v. Pullman Southern Car Co., 117 U.S. 34 (1886); Moran v. New Orleans, 112 U.S. 69 (1884).

[62] Cooley v. Board of Wardens, 12 How. 299 (1851).

[63] Munn v. Illinois, 97 U.S. 113 (1877); actually, the Court did not decide which of these alternatives it was using.

national authorities. The power could also, if the judges wished, be used to minimize the amount of regulation by either government and thus to express the economic predilections of the Court majority. In most instances, when the Court struck down either a state or a national regulation it was exposing its preconceptions rather than its economic or political wisdom.

On the other hand, there was no ineluctable reason why the Court needed to accept federal commercial regulation either, for the same doctrine which in some cases prevented the states from acting could also be used to block the federal power in other cases. The judges seemed especially distrustful of legislation favoring labor: they struck down, in 1908, a federal statute imposing upon railroads liability for injuries to employees—because it applied to all employees regardless of whether or not they were physically engaged in interstate commerce.[64] The Court did not go into the knotty question of how it is possible to disentangle the interstate from the intrastate aspects of railroad employment; nor did it seriously consider the possibility that the act might be approved insofar as it did apply to those engaged in interstate activity. It was therefore fairly obvious that the purpose of the majority was to rid the railroads entirely of such burdensome regulation. The attempt, of course, failed, since the government proceeded to re-enact the law so that it applied only to those to whom the Court had said it could; and the states increasingly adopted their own laws covering intrastate workers. The effect was to make a cumbersome set of regulations in which the claimant often could go shopping around for the most favorable jurisdiction in which to try his case, thus perhaps actually hurting the railroads more than the original law would have done.

In the antitrust field, we have already seen that the Court began in 1895 (in the Sugar Trust case) by drawing a strict distinction between "manufacturing" and "commerce": the former was a matter for states to regulate while the latter could be subsumed under the Sherman Act. Since it was mainly manufacturers whom Congress had sought to curb, the act would seem to have been effectively emasculated. But not so. The Court's tough pragmatism, which always reasserts itself when least expected, prevented it from using this distinction with maximum effect. Under the leadership of Holmes, it soon began to whittle away at the definition of "manufacturing." In

[64] First Employers' Liability Cases, 207 U.S. 463 (1908).

1905 it found that stockyards owned by meat packers (meat packing was considered to be manufacturing) were, while not commerce themselves, a "throat" through which commerce must pass.[65] Throats could apparently be regulated by the national government. Then, too, the Court found that in practice many companies which were primarily manufacturing concerns also maintained their own supply facilities, owned transportation companies, and had their own sales forces and distribution facilities.[66] So inextricable were the interstate from the local aspects of such industries that the Court gave up the attempted distinction when they were involved, as it did in the Standard Oil and American Tobacco cases.[67]

There are several morals to be drawn from all this. One is that the Supreme Court, while talking in terms of a layer cake theory of federalism, was in many cases actually baking a marble cake. For by maintaining a rigid distinction between state and national functions, it was often in effect forcing both levels to deal with the same problems in similar ways. For instance, both the national and the state governments had to enter the field of employees' liability for railroad employees; both had to enter the field of rate regulation; both had to engage in antitrust activities and in pure food and drug regulation. The effect was not a functional division of power but the same functions exercised on either side of a supposedly rigid line. This at the same time encouraged government officials to engage in cooperative approaches to their functions.

Then too, the history of the latter half of the nineteenth century demonstrates that the Constitution does not stand in the way of changes in the location of governmental functions. Given the will and imagination, politicians and judges can find ways, within the Constitution, of dealing with national problems nationally and local problems locally. Historically, there seem to be, if not fewer and fewer local problems, certainly more and more national ones; but as we have seen, even national problems have often been dealt with through the means of over-all national control with at the same time

[65] Swift & Co. v. U.S., 196 U.S. 375 (1905).

[66] To some extent illustrated in Addyston Pipe & Steel Co. v. U.S., 175 U.S. 229 (1899).

[67] Standard Oil Co. v. U.S., 221 U.S. 1 (1911); U.S. v. American Tobacco Co., 221 U.S. 106 (1911).

a good deal of devolution and delegation to state or even to local (such as law enforcement) officials.

If, as it is sometimes optimistically said, the genius of America and its major contribution to philosophy is pragmatism, there could be few better illustrations than the adaptation of the eighteenth-century federal system to the problems posed by nationalization of business, industry, and commerce. Whether this adaptation was in the long run to prove enough could not have been told by 1917, perhaps not even by 1970.

CHAPTER 3

State and Local Government

A MERICAN state government derives its significance from the fact that, aside from the limited powers given the national government (mostly in Article II, Section 8, of the Constitution), it is the states which legally exercise the routine, daily operations which most intimately touch the lives of citizens and most completely regulate their social and business affairs. With allowance made for the mixing of functions already described, it is the states (or their local subdivisions) which organize and maintain the local units of government, regulate the suffrage and conduct elections, provide the basis for the organization of political parties, levy and collect a high proportion of our taxes, exercise the police power to preserve the peace and protect public health, welfare, and morals, erect and maintain systems of education and the supply of public services, have in their hands the enforcement of almost all criminal law and control the areas of private law which are responsible for the regulation of many of the most essential of social relationships—the law of marriage and the family, the regulation of private property, the incorporation of businesses and a large share of their regulation, and the law regulating most business relationships.

The framers of the Constitution no doubt expected that such would be the case, and despite the passage of time and the accretion of powers in the national government it still is; certainly it was so in the period before 1917. Much of the power is shared in varying measure with the national government, and even more is delegated to the county, municipal, and other local units which make up the patchwork quilt of the American political map, but the states are still in some ways the basic units of American government.

That being so, it is surprising how little need be said about the constitutional structure of the state government. Although there was in the beginning a good deal of variety, by 1877 state governments without exception reproduced the federal government in miniature. Usually this resemblance has been the result of states copying federal rather than vice versa. One need hardly quibble about the origins of the tripartite separation of powers or the bicameral legislature: the fact is that by 1877 all states had them and there was not, until after 1917 at least, any tendency to experiment with other arrangements, at least in any formal sense. The states, particularly the newer ones, went through Jacksonian democracy with perhaps excessive enthusiasm, taking wholeheartedly to the ideas of frequent elections, weak and fragmented executive branches, legislatures which were restricted by numerous provisions existing in the state constitutions, and courts to which the judges were elected on party ballots. Some of these features of state government were not entirely eliminated even by the last quarter of the twentieth century. The difficulty of amending the federal Constitution accounts for the fact that the national government underwent few of these democratic innovations.

Jacksonian and American thought in general has always placed greater faith in human nature out of, rather than in, power. As Bryce pointed out in 1890, state constitutions were "witness to a singular distrust by the people of its own agents and officers," [1] and both the Populist and the Progressive movements reinforced these feelings, with the possible exception that, as in Washington, there was a tendency to look to a popular executive as a check upon and a leader for the presumptively corrupt or unresponsive legislature. This trend never went to the extent of the creation of a single executive—state governors were always accompanied by many other elective officials who also performed executive tasks and headed important executive departments; some states also had appointive officials whose terms did not coincide with those of the governor. When Theodore Roosevelt assumed office in Albany in 1898, the board of railroad commissioners was almost independent; its members' terms extended beyond

[1] James Bryce, *The American Commonwealth*, 2d ed., rev. (2 vols., London, 1891), I, 442.

the governor's, and Roosevelt had no need to concern himself with its work.[2] Thus, in their zeal to keep political power from corrupting the regulation of railroads, the people of New York had removed it from any control whatever; Roosevelt, being the man he was, would probably have loved to "concern" himself.

State executive power did not, in any case, amount to a great deal. Until after 1900 few governors assumed the role of policy leader; no state had an executive budget; the term of office was short—often only two years, and in some cases one; and many executive tasks were performed by officers not subject to the control of the governor. On Governor William E. Russell's assumption of office in Massachusetts in 1890, "His governorship promised to be one long ceremony. The prize he had won was a half-empty honor, annually competed for, imposing few responsibilities and fewer powers, and a wearing burden of social obligations."[3]

The same kind of public distrust of the elected official showed itself in the tendency, progressive throughout the nineteenth century and only partially reversed since, to burden the state constitutions with restrictive details. It almost seemed as if the more democratic the political structure was, the less power the people were willing to entrust to it. Thus the chief distinctions between federal and state governments were that the state constitutions were longer and more detailed. While the United States Constitution contains about 6,000 words, Missouri's 1875 document (not exceptional as to length) required 26,000 to outline the frame of government for that state. These constitutions typically specified with great exactitude even such things as the per diem to be paid legislators during the session. The state executive was even weaker than the federal both by way of possessing little affirmative power and by way of being divided among many elective officials.

From the beginning, indeed, there had been a tendency for state and national units to borrow ideas from each other.[4] Thus as the power and prestige of the President gradually increased after 1896, the states in their turn gradually entrusted more power to their gov-

---

[2] G. Wallace Chessman, *Governor Theodore Roosevelt: The Albany Apprenticeship, 1898–1900* (Cambridge, 1965), p. 254.

[3] Geoffrey Blodgett, *The Gentle Reformers: Massachusetts Democrats in the Cleveland Era* (Cambridge, 1966), p. 102.

[4] Daniel J. Elazar, *American Federalism: A View from the States* (New York, 1966).

ernors. This movement was not uniform in all states and was never carried as far as in the federal government; it was, however, stimulated by the Progressive movement, which in its state phase depended heavily on gubernatorial leadership. Before 1900 many states were subject to boss rule, which had the effect of minimizing the role of the governor since the boss himself seldom cared to hold that office: he was more likely to be a Senator.

Governors came and went, but the party remained. The boss, therefore, exercised leadership which was continuous, and it was hard for the procession of transient governors to build up power against him. Governors could not be re-elected sufficient times to remain head of the party; and if one boss were overthrown (Conkling, for instance), another soon arose. Elihu Root attributed boss rule directly to the division of powers among the constitutional elective officers, the "six-headed executive." He could, just as truly, have attributed it to the shortness of the governor's tenure.[5]

One of the jobs of the new wave of progressive leaders like Wisconsin's La Follette was to get rid of bossism: which usually meant becoming the boss themselves and building up personal rather than party machines. Hiram Johnson in California, Charles Evans Hughes in New York, Woodrow Wilson in New Jersey, and other governors both earlier and later played primary roles in restoring the prestige of the governorship. Perhaps even before TR's presidency these governors realized that the new demands upon government could be met only by legislation, and that legislation could be secured only by building a type of party leadership which was concerned with policy as well as with patronage, so that political power would be a means rather than merely an end.[6] By the middle of the twentieth century almost all states had—at least sporadically—strong policy leadership from their governors.

The progressives did not realize that strong administrative leadership was also essential if their programs were to be carried out efficiently and responsibly: thus they did little about the hydra-headed character of the administrations of their states. By a series of well-intentioned and on the whole praiseworthy civil service reforms they tended to make it impossible for governors to perform as effectively in their administrative roles as they came to do in their legislative

[5] Leslie Lipson, *The American Governor from Figurehead to Leader* (Chicago, 1939), p. 49.
[6] *Ibid.*, pp. 47–63.

capacities. Thus, strangely, the effect was to weaken the separation of powers, by making the governors stronger legislatively and weaker administratively.[7]

Another aspect of administrative weakness was shown in the series of experiments in methods of administering publicly run utilities, or public regulation of private utilities. One method which was developed, and which we have seen was later used extensively also at the federal level, was the creation of the autonomous board or commission, which might be either appointive or elective but in either case was unresponsive to gubernatorial control and usually was only formally subject to control from the legislatures. In fact, it may be that one reason for the power of American courts in general has been that they have had to be used as political checks on the activities of commissions, since the "political" branches of the governments were structurally incapable of such use. The development of such agencies was very early: we know that Virginia had a state Board of Public Works to manage "the internal improvement activities of the state" as early as 1816,[8] and it is well known that state regulatory commissions (probably first used for regulation of canal companies) [9] were common at least a decade and often much longer before the creation of the Interstate Commerce Commission in 1887.[10] Thus the development of the "fourth branch" of government came much earlier in the states than in the federal government, even though the same lip service was given to the strict version of the tripartite separation of powers. As early as 1890 it could be said of Massachusetts (which was possibly a little extreme in this respect) that

the great bulk of state business was conducted by independent boards and commissions, over whom the governor had little control beyond his periodic appointments to fill carefully staggered vacancies. The marked increase in the policing function of the state since the Civil War had sprouted a swarm of new commissions. By 1890 there were twenty-six such bodies, twenty-two of which had been created since 1865.[11]

[7] *Ibid.*, pp. 61–62.

[8] Daniel J. Elazar, *The American Partnership: Intergovernmental Cooperation in the Nineteenth-Century United States* (Chicago, 1962), pp. 36–53.

[9] *Ibid.*, pp. 58–61.

[10] Robert E. Cushman, *The Independent Regulatory Commissions* (New York, 1941), pp. 19–36.

[11] Blodgett, *Gentle Reformers*, p. 103.

Often, too, states actually performed an entrepreneurial role in "internal improvements" during the early canal- and road-building era—a role from which they had by 1877 largely retired, and which the federal government was later to enter, as were the local governments. It thus is obvious that the United States never really had laissez-faire in any strict sense; particularly in building communications systems in a huge territory, and in local utilities, there is a long and continuous tradition of governmental construction and operation of "business" enterprises. When practical problems were encountered, neither state nor federal constitutions were likely to serve as effective bars to such governmental activities. As far as the state governments themselves were concerned, however, after 1877 they were more likely to use regulation than ownership as a means of mitigating the worst of the problems of burgeoning industry and commerce. When Wisconsin, for instance, decided that it must enact employers' liability laws to protect workers against industrial accidents, it did so in conjunction with a system by which the employing companies took out private insurance to cover their liabilities. This was done in conscious preference to a system of government insurance. At the same time an independent state commission was necessary to investigate claims, arbitrate, and when necessary make awards. So while preserving private enterprise the state nevertheless had to set up a fairly large bureaucracy to run the system.[12]

In 1891 Bryce could still aver that the administrative services of the states were of little importance; he characterized them in telling words:

Of the subordinate civil service of a State there is little to be said. It is not large, for the sphere of administrative action which remains to the State between the Federal government on the one side, and the county, city, and township governments on the other, is not wide. It is ill-paid, for the State legislatures, especially in the West, are parsimonious. It is seldom well-manned, for able men have no inducement to enter it; and the so-called "Spoils System" . . . makes places the reward for political work. . . .[13]

By 1917 Bryce would have had to change his assessment in several respects, for the state services had by then grown markedly in response to the new demands for governmental services. They had,

---

[12] For descriptions of the Wisconsin experience see Carl A. Auerbach *et al.*, *The Legal Process* (San Francisco, 1961), pp. 534 ff., 585 ff., 725 ff.

[13] Bryce, *American Commonwealth*, I, 478–479.

however, grown without plan or theory. The executive branch was essentially headless even though governors had by then gained considerable political power. Qualitatively there had been little improvement. There was nevertheless a good deal of pressure for reform based on a growing realization that large, headless, patronage-based bureaucracies were not likely to be efficient, responsible, or responsive, and in 1917 Illinois passed the first great executive reform act,[14] while two years earlier New York had a proposed constitutional revision which would have eliminated several (not all) of the elected executives, broadened the governor's appointive powers, consolidated more than 150 separate agencies into a small number of manageable departments, strengthened the classified service, created an executive budget and decreased the legislature's freedom to change it, and increased the governor's legislative role. This was not, however, approved by the voters, for political reasons probably not largely connected to these particular proposals.[15] The tortuous political processes necessary to secure such reforms were such that major efforts had to be mounted and they were generally rewarded with only limited success: in Illinois the use of a legislative act meant that constitutional changes could not be made, so that despite the reduction of the number of separate agencies and the introduction of an executive budget, those agencies which were sheltered by the constitution, such as the elected executives and boards (Secretary of State and Board of the State University provide examples) went unreformed. Attempts at reform were sporadic in various states throughout the period after 1890; but most of these came to fruition only after 1917.[16]

If the state executive structure was ramshackle and weak, the situation was not very different in the legislative branch. The legislative power, quite strong in the early state governments, had been seriously weakened by the time of the Civil War,[17] and widespread corruption in politics following the war and the reaction in the South against Reconstruction governments brought further limitations. The people across the nation had little confidence in their

[14] Lipson, *American Governor*, pp. 82–85.
[15] *Ibid.*, pp. 90–94.
[16] *Ibid.*, pp. 81–126.
[17] Arthur N. Holcombe, *State Government in the United States* (New York, 1916), pp. 106–139.

legislators, and this was widely reflected in the new constitutions and amendments adopted by 1917. The party boss system made for boss control of many legislatures, and the bosses themselves were often directly or indirectly representatives of large corporations: the Southern Pacific Railroad in California; Anaconda Copper in Montana; the Pennsylvania Railroad in Pennsylvania. The public was not kept entirely unaware of this phenomenon of politics; journalists, politicians themselves, and even novelists called it to the attention of anyone who read. The American Winston Churchill, for instance, in *Coniston* and *Mr. Crewe's Career,* portrayed the ownership of a New England state government first by a rural boss and then by railroads. While he exaggerated, and was not overly sophisticated in his view of the causes and correctives for bossism, Churchill was writing of a situation that was anything but fictional. Frank Norris did the same for California in his famous portrait of the Southern Pacific Railroad, *The Octopus.*

More often, however, it was the corporate viewpoint that controlled rather than the interests of any single company. The combination of boss rule and political corruption was endemic. The boss operated by means of the carrot and the stick—favors and patronage provided the one, withdrawal of legislative power the other. Legislatures usually contained excessive numbers of overlapping committees, which had the effect of making the procedures more easily controlled by the leadership. The bosses were not usually greatly interested in legislative questions, and legislatures were left largely free: this meant that in fact they were often as leaderless as Congress, and their irresponsibility made them even less acceptable. The Southern Pacific, for instance, was more interested in preventing than in securing legislation, and the bicameral system with its numerous committees and overlapping jurisdictions was ideally suited to such tactics.[18] Partly because they were too large, the legislatures were prey to an overweening localism which bosses, for their own reasons, did nothing to stem, and a legislator was often judged by how much he produced for his own small constituency.[19] The result often was planless extravagance in addition to corruption, and considering the little that state governments did before the twentieth century, they were expensive to maintain.

[18] George E. Mowry, *The California Progressives* (Berkeley, 1951), p. 64.
[19] Bryce, *American Commonwealth,* I, 520–521.

Many states, despite journalistic talk to the contrary, had no one who could be called a "boss." These were hardly better off than the others. For if the bossed legislatures were often leaderless, the unbossed were almost always so. They were clique-ridden collections of petty local politicians, and it is surprising that they accomplished anything at all. Bryce praised the Massachusetts General Court, which in the eighties and nineties did actually succeed in enacting a progressive legislative program. He felt that the "venerable traditions surrounding an ancient commonwealth do something to sustain the dignity of the body and induce good men to enter it." [20] But if this was one of the best legislatures what was the worst? Localism was so strong that state representatives were often rotated between the towns comprising a Massachusetts legislative district, so that reelection was impossible and the office attracted men of no distinction. A more jaundiced commentator than Bryce concluded that Massachusetts had a "body of 240 representatives and 40 senators, annually elected and poorly paid, low on experience and technical skill, parochial and timid in view." [21]

The response of the people of the states, right through the Progressive Era, was to restrict the powers of the legislatures. The major restrictions were (1) exclusion of a subject from the competence of the legislature (debt limit provisions are an example); (2) definitions of legislative procedures (such as prescriptions of the method of voting on statutes); (3) restrictions on legislative operations (such as prescription of the length and frequency of sessions).[22] If legislative sessions were, as one writer remarked, "an unmitigated disaster," the obvious remedy was to render them as powerless and infrequent as possible. So the Progressives enacted the various forms of direct legislation by the people—referendum, initiative—which could only further diminish the powers and responsibility of the legislatures, lower them still further in the public esteem, and discourage the more responsible citizens from serving in them.

Thus by 1917 the status of the state legislatures was if anything even lower than it had been in 1877; the muckrakers raked over this matter among others, but could not halt further deterioration. If

[20] *Ibid.*, 515.

[21] Blodgett, *Gentle Reformers*, p. 106.

[22] Bryce, *American Commonwealth*, I, 526–528; Holcombe, *State Government*, pp. 106–139, points out additional limitations imposed later.

there was any improvement at all it came because the Progressives were honest men and the Progressive Era was a period of declining public tolerance of dishonesty. It is likely that by 1917 the average legislator was more honest—less likely to engage in grand or petty corruption, less firmly tied to particular pressure groups. But it is also likely that the Progressives used their power too enthusiastically, in the manner of a wrecking crew which in tearing down an unsound building succeeds in wrecking the neighboring structure as well. The moral the Progressives drew from bossism and corruption was that parties and party feeling were bad; and lacking any well-thought-out substitute for party government they ended up by weakening or destroying it without putting anything in its place. When strong governors were in office weak parties might work out well, particularly if the governor was astute and charismatic enough—like Hiram Johnson and "Fighting Bob" La Follette—to build his own personal "party." [23] Progressive states drew both immediate benefits—honest government and progressive legislation—and long-run sources of trouble from their experience with progressivism. Without strong gubernatorial leadership the legislatures after the progressive period were perhaps incapable of major evil, but they were also incapable of major good and perfectly capable of minor evil—localism, pork barrel, and governance by shadowy and shifting coalitions (having little to do with party or policy) which could be easily influenced by well-organized lobbies.

Thus by 1917 many states were as dependent upon executive leadership for effective government as was the national government; but they were less likely to get it, since few state constitutions permitted governors anything like the powers of the President. In democratic societies we seem to have found, thus far, only two avenues to effective governance: party government, in which a strong party organization which knows what it wants can dominate both the executive and the legislative branches (this is the British pattern); and the strong executive, in which the executive possesses both institutional power and personal charisma as in American national politics. The American states have too often failed to provide either avenue; the national government has increasingly relied on the executive. Whether this is the right choice we do not know, but it

[23] Mowry, *California Progressives*; Allen Fraser Lovejoy, *La Follette and the Establishment of the Direct Primary in Wisconsin, 1890–1904* (New Haven, 1941).

is likely that party government is more difficult in our presidential form of government than in the cabinet system, and this may explain the drift into executive aggrandizement. What is certain is that by 1917 the state executives, like the federal, had gained in power at the expense of the legislatures, if not so spectacularly.

Comparatively little need be said—little is known—of the state judiciaries. With some striking exceptions they were neither as prestigious nor as incorruptible as the federal. On the other hand, they were quite certainly not less powerful. For in addition to the same type of participation in political change through constitutional reform which is possessed by the federal courts when using judicial review, the state courts also possessed the extremely broad policy-making powers of the English common law courts. This gave them not only the power to influence policy by the interpretation of statutes, but the power also to make policy initially in all the common law areas to which statute law did not penetrate.[24]

In each jurisdiction the judges were engaged in adapting the principles of the common law to the facts of American life. So far as Americans were concerned, much of the law was unwritten. Courts as well as people were engaged in pioneer work. Both in the development of the unwritten law, and in the interpretation of that which was written, each state judiciary was equally free to apply the utilitarian test in the light of local conditions. Law was copiously made, or as people often preferred to say, discovered, by the judges themselves.[25]

State judges were not always sufficiently aware of the desirability of seeming—and being—nonpolitical. This was a result, no doubt, of the fact that the system in most states tended to emphasize that they were political. They were in most cases elected, on party tickets, and in many cases as the result of patronage. Thus they both were and acted as politicians. They may not often have been as open about this as was Justice Henshaw of the California Supreme Court, who was in 1916 described as "the ablest, the narrowest, and the bitterest representative of the old Southern Pacific machine still surviving in the public life of California," [26] or as active as Roujet D. Marshall,

[24] J. Willard Hurst, *Law and the Conditions of Freedom in the Nineteenth Century* (Madison, 1956).

[25] Holcombe, *State Government*, p. 249.

[26] Mowry, *California Progressives*, p. 249.

of the Wisconsin Supreme Court, who played a major role in the
passage of that state's workmen's compensation law of 1911.[27] Nevertheless they did—because they had to—represent the interests responsible for their ability to reach the bench.

Here again the Progressive answer to the problem was "more
democracy," by which was always meant more popular direct participation and more election. The new states of the West all copied the
already widespread practice of electing their judges to limited terms
of office, and the practice even spread into some of the eastern states.
Bryce, in 1891, found only eight of the older states which still used
gubernatorial appointment for their judges: except for Mississippi
and Louisiana, these were all among the original thirteen. This, he
believed, threw "this grave and delicate function into the rude hands
of the masses, that is to say, of the wirepullers."[28] In addition, the recall of judges by popular referendum was proposed in many places
by progressive forces which hated the judges' subservience to "the
interests." Progressives sincerely believed that "the interests" were
always bad and that they themselves represented "the public," which
was inevitably opposed to "the interests." This oversimplification of
the nature of politics led them to the belief that no office could be
democratic unless its occupant was elected, to a preferably brief term,
and (hopefully) subject to recall even before that term was over. As
applied to judges such an idea could only end by making them even
more subservient to different interests. Subservient, yet powerful, the
American state courts represented perhaps the highest point judicial
power has yet reached in Western civilization.

Organizationally, the state judiciaries were based upon the federal
model (though it may be that historically the process was reversed)
of three levels—a supreme court with exclusively appellate power,
a set of appellate courts usually divided into districts geographically,
and a trial level. Throughout the latter half of the nineteenth, and
on into the twentieth, century the trial level, however, underwent a
great deal of growth and diversification. Originally there were a great
many trial-level courts because of the large territories and difficult
communications characteristic of the early states. Later, the growth
of population centers, of business and industry, led to the multipli-
cation of trial-level tribunals with specialized jurisdictions (probate,

[27] Auerbach, *Legal Process*, pp. 593 ff.
[28] Bryce, I, 484.

juvenile, police, domestic relations, land, etc.), and to courts of general jurisdiction for municipalities (beginning in Chicago and Cleveland).[29] Judgeships were ordinarily good jobs, well paid by the standards of the time and carrying a certain amount of social prestige; they were thus ideal for political patronage use where politically valuable lawyers were involved.

The corruption endemic in politics in the eighties also touched the courts: they were powerful enough politically to attract corruption in a corrupt era, and not politically independent enough to resist it, especially in those areas where state or municipal party machines controlled the electoral process. Thus the state courts inevitably shared in the low esteem attached to all politics by public opinion during the turn-of-the-century years, and were a natural target of the reformers.

Nevertheless, the state courts seem to have grown more, rather than less, powerful during these years. Certainly they used the power of judicial review to strike down state legislation more and more frequently: during the six-year period 1903–1908 "nearly four hundred state laws were declared unconstitutional by state courts." [30] This seems to have been due to the great increase in the amount of legislation; to the great distrust which people had for their legislatures and their consequently increasing tendency to turn to courts for redress; to the increasing detail of state constitutions, which provided numerous incentives for legislative evasion and thus numerous opportunities for judicial veto; and to the success with which business lawyers found both state and federal constitutional grounds for striking down regulatory legislation.

This last factor may require some elucidation. For one thing, once a constitutional doctrine based upon the federal Constitution was developed or accepted by the U.S. Supreme Court, it was fully as available to the state judges as to their federal colleagues. As a result, state judiciaries, particularly in those states where business interests controlled access to the bench, adopted the substantive use of due process with alacrity; the "rule of reason" adopted by the federal judiciary in 1911 for use in antitrust cases was imported by state courts in those states which had their own antitrust laws; in fact, the very idea of a rule of reason was a common-law conception

---

[29] Holcombe, *State Government*, p. 350.
[30] *Ibid.*, p. 356.

which had been used in state courts at least as early as 1885 in cases involving labor legislation: in that year the New York court threw out a statute regulating labor conditions in the manufacture of tobacco products.[31] While the court conceded that ordinarily the legislature had complete discretion in so-called police regulations, it also maintained that this discretion could not be arbitrarily used when the resulting law constituted a limitation on the use of private property. Laws must have a reasonable relation to their ends, said the court, and "under the mere guise of police regulations, personal rights and private property cannot be arbitrarily invaded. . . ." When they are, "it is for the courts to scrutinize the act" so as to enforce "the supreme law." [32]

As in the federal instance, not all state judges or all state courts approved of decisions of this nature, but there was a strong tendency for the state courts to be even more business oriented than the federal, and to have discovered the legal doctrines needed to defend business long before the federal courts did so. The New York courts seem to have led in this respect: they invalidated a prohibition law in 1855 [33] and a law prohibiting the sale of oleomargarine in 1885.[34] Some of the first workmen's compensation laws,[35] laws regulating the weighing of coal,[36] and laws attempting to prohibit firing because of union membership [37]—to name but a few well-known instances— were similarly treated by some state courts.

The dates of such cases make it obvious that such uses of the rule of reason were not based upon any interpretation of the *federal* Constitution. State courts would, in general, have had to wait for the adoption of the Fourteenth Amendment and the acceptance by the Supreme Court of substantive due process before they could so use that document. But they always had the similar power to interpret their own state constitutions, and beyond that the power to

---

[31] *In re* Jacobs, 98 N.Y. 98 (1885).

[32] *Ibid.*

[33] Wynehamer *v.* People, 13 N.Y. 378 (1856).

[34] People *v.* Marx, 99 N.Y. 277 (1885).

[35] Ives *v.* South Buffalo Ry. Co., 201 N.Y. 431 (1911).

[36] Among others, see Millet *v.* People, 7 N.E. 631 (Ill., 1886); *In re* House Bill No. 203, 39 Pac. 431 (Colo., 1895).

[37] See, for instance, Gillespie *v.* People, 58 N.E. 781 (Ill., 1900); State *v.* Julow, 31 S.W. 781 (Mo., 1895). The literally dozens of other cases on widely varied subjects are cited in Rodney L. Mott, *Due Process of Law* (Indianapolis, 1926), pp. 338, 342.

interpret for their jurisdictions the meaning of common-law rules. Thus they could, as in Massachusetts, use the common law governing "master-servant" relations to refuse to allow financial awards to railroad workers injured on the job; [38] or as in New York, use the state constitution for striking down an early attempt to enact workmen's compensation laws that presumably violated common law.[39] In addition they frequently used the judge-made maxim that "statutes in derogation of the common law are to be construed strictly" to minimize the effects of laws which were upheld.[40]

It may be said, of course, that judicial decisions then as now were dependent upon the willingness of other governmental agencies to enforce them or at least to accede to them. Such willingness came down at last to the respect still held for law by the general public. Public respect constituted an underlying "given" upon which judges could, during this period, always rely. As a result, there was little tendency for government officials to ignore the courts. They could at times be evaded—by constitutional amendment or by the redrawing of statutes—but they could seldom be ignored.

Judges came from the ranks of lawyers who were largely imbued with the closed-system theories of John Austin which we have noted earlier, and by the nature of legal practice they were inclined to take the side of business, to hold an exaggerated notion that holding corporate property was just like owning a farm or a tailor shop. In any case there was little about the American experience which was likely to inculcate feelings of restraint or humility in its judges: they were as willing to use the power they possessed as anyone else. And as with the federal judges, it is difficult to say with certainty that they were not on the whole acting in the public interest and with the public's approval. Certainly there is no evidence that they were not, in the main, public-spirited men who, given power, exercised it as they thought best for the common weal. With certain exceptions, they could present perfectly sincere explanations of how their decisions advanced the public good. It does not do to attribute to them bad motives, even though latter-day liberal historians may feel that the drift of their decisions was wrong and that it delayed the development of public regulation and welfare concepts which

[38] Farwell *v.* Boston & Worcester R.R. Corp., 4 Metc. 49 (Mass., 1842).
[39] Ives *v.* South Buffalo Ry. Co., 201 N.Y. 271 (1911).
[40] Auerbach, *Legal Process*, pp. 492–518.

were both inevitable and desirable. If, in the American constitutions, courts are designed to be checks on the "popular" branches of the governments, they performed this function, if not admirably, nevertheless effectively.

One should not ignore, in any discussion of American constitutional developments, the extent to which judicial functions have been entrusted, gradually, to administrative tribunals. We have already alluded to this development in the federal creation of the Interstate Commerce Commission and other so-called "regulatory" agencies. There were also, at the federal level, the military courts of justice which had always existed side by side with the civil courts and which assumed great importance during the Civil War. In some ways, however, the states pioneered the development of administrative adjudication as they pioneered in the regulatory field generally. Regulatory agencies were commonly given some of their own enforcement powers, and the use of such powers made judging—of at least a preliminary nature—necessary. We do not know how much of such adjudication existed in the states by 1917: we do know that it was extensive. We know little about its quality; it was not likely to rise above the level of the particular state government in which it was found. Agency decisions often had the force of law, although they were usually subject to court review. The administrative agencies thus became in a sense "trial level" courts for cases within their ambit, with appeal possible to the same appellate courts which handled other cases. The Wisconsin Industrial Commission, created in the 1890's, was a good example. Among other things, it had to investigate claims based upon the injury or death of workmen; but as a result of the investigation it also made awards, just as a court would do. These awards were subject to court review, but since in most cases neither party would appeal, the Commission was effectively the "judiciary" which decided workmen's compensation cases.[41]

That this kind of procedure constituted a significant alteration in the traditional theory of the tripartite separation of powers seems to have gone at the time largely unnoticed. Americans were apparently blinded by nomenclature: an administrative agency was just that, no matter what its actual powers. But the powers were there, and state government was to that extent fundamentally changed by 1917.

[41] *Ibid.*, pp. 725–851.

Most of the developments noted in this chapter were accompanied by and resulted from the great burgeoning of functions of the states which was their response to the new conditions of urban-industrial society. This change was fully as drastic for the states—particularly the older ones—as it was for the national government. For early in the nineteenth century they had, like the national, been governments of an essentially caretaker nature. Vested with enormous latent power, they used relatively little of it. A great deal of the actual burden of what governing did exist was, by a process of devolution, actually put in the hands of the local units of government. Every state constructed a set of such units which covered the entire territory of the state; and these units were then vested with broad police, legislative, and administrative powers. While it cannot be said that this situation entirely changed after 1877, it is yet noticeable that as the states began to realize that new functions would be needed to cope with the new problems, they also began to feel that in the administration of these functions devolution was not always the answer. As a perhaps minor part of this picture, federal grants and other federal programs were usually made available to states, not to their local units, so that state agencies had to be created in order to satisfy federal conditions. In other words, part of the general growth of American governments in the period 1877–1917 took place at the state level, and to some extent state growth meant centralization either of functions which were new or of functions which had earlier been entrusted to local government, or (perhaps more commonly) centralization of supervision but leaving a good deal of administration and discretion at the local level. The states, then, extended the already existing "marble cake" by including in it more and more functions.

For instance, Ohio's new constitutional amendments, adopted under progressive leadership in 1912, included one which affirmed the central legislative power to control the school system of the state, the assumption of state financial responsibility for the building of more good roads, a state conservation measure which placed this new function in state hands, and the vesting in the legislature of the power to fix working hours and wages. All of these placed increased power in the state even though they did not necessarily take away from the localities.[42] Similar centralizing tendencies existed in al-

[42] Hoyt Landon Warner, *Progressivism in Ohio, 1897–1917* (Columbus, 1964), pp. 312–353.

most every state, particularly after 1890, but the process varied greatly from state to state. The socio-political conditions existing in one state were very different from those in another, and as a result some states—particularly those in the South and West—had long traditions of "centralism," so centralizing trends were foreshadowed by these states even though they were also predominantly rural and agrarian. On the other hand the older states of the Northeast tended to retain, despite their early urbanization, strong elements of localism, which was traditionally based on the town and township. Centralization in these states proceeded reluctantly and in most cases did not reach the same extent as in the rest of the country, at least not by 1917.[43] Again, Ohio provides a good example, and it was reluctant to undertake any degree of centralized control or financing in the fields of education, taxation, charities and corrections, and public health: as of 1903 local autonomy was still very strong in these fields.[44] Various states in the Northeast were still in the 1960's providing less state support for public schools or for public higher education than were most other states; not only Ohio but New Jersey and Massachusetts (indeed all of New England) provide examples.

Nevertheless the trend to centralization—particularly of new functions—was evident everywhere, and in fact the rate of change was perhaps faster in the "localistic" states of the Northeast, since they had less "centralism" to begin with: and centralism was the dominant tone of the new age. Anyone attending a New England town meeting will be aware of the many ways in which town action is dictated, limited, or financially aided by state laws, often dating from the early years of this century or the latter years of the nineteenth.

Another way of indicating the differing ways and degrees in which various states responded to the need for more government is to look at the history of progressivism. Wisconsin and California were two of the leaders in this movement, and the centralizing tendencies of progressivism there were obvious: everything that they did, beyond reform measures, involved the restructuring of old functions or the creation of new, from the revitalization of public utilities regulation to the setting up of employers' liability systems. Nevertheless, the emphasis on the dramatic leadership of such men as "Fighting Bob"

[43] Elazar, *American Federalism*, pp. 180–193.

[44] Samuel P. Orth, *The Centralization of Administration in Ohio* (New York, 1903), pp. 11–12, 23–24, 126–127, 163–174.

La Follette and Hiram Johnson has obscured the fact that most of
what they accomplished in their own states was also accomplished in
most of the other states, often somewhat later than in Wisconsin—
but sometimes earlier. This was notably true in Massachusetts: even
"before 1900, with a few exceptions, Massachusetts had enjoyed in
practice if not in form all the democratic innovations which progressives emphasized after 1900. It had, in addition, the most effective
corporation laws in the nation, and it led the country in labor legislation." [45] What it lacked were some of the political reforms which
were so much a part of progressivism, such as the direct primary,
woman suffrage, and popular election of Senators. The same could
be said to a lesser extent of New York. In these states progressivism
was achieved without the progressives, by "the gentle reformers,"
who were Democrats and their Mugwump allies—the people who
were too honest to be able to support Blaine in 1884 and thus became,
for a season, Cleveland Democrats. Their leaders were for the most
part wealthy businessmen and lawyers, indistinguishable materially
from their regular Republican brethren and motivated by a tradition
of public service and fair play.[46] Their programs, too, led to centralization; and like the progressives their sympathies were limited to
those problems they could understand directly.

For instance, neither they nor the progressives understood or were
much interested in unionization of the workers. Direct improvement
of material conditions was something they could understand, so
they sponsored hours legislation, child labor regulation, sweatshop
laws; but they did not support collective bargaining or other arrangements which might enable workers to achieve these things
without legislation. They tended to be, if not actually xenophobic,
at least ethnocentric: they distrusted foreigners and especially wished
to keep them out of political leadership. In Massachusetts, for instance, a complex of factors led to state assumption of various functions of Boston. The state led the country in metropolitan planning,
and this was due in perhaps equal measure to fear of the Boston
Irish in politics, to a sincere hope that the standards of urban life
for working people could be improved, and to the obvious political
fact that planning for a metropolis could not be left in the hands of

[45] Richard M. Abrams, *Conservatism in a Progressive Era: Massachusetts
Politics, 1900–1912*, pp. 2–3.
[46] Blodgett, *Gentle Reformers*, ch. 1.

innumerable local units. It was perhaps ethnic fear which primarily led to the state's takeover of the Boston police in 1885.[47]

Finally, the great tide of municipal reform was utterly dependent on state legislation for its achievement. Everywhere the municipal reformers had to turn to the state for permission to introduce the structural change which swept the nation after 1900. Reformers could, by themselves, introduce honesty and integrity—for as long as they could stay in office. But they could not produce new forms of municipal government. The interplay between the urban reformers and the state governments thus provides one of the most striking illustrations of the "marble cake" theory of American politics.

The constitutional status of American local governmental units has always been an anomalous one. Despite much talk about "the grass roots" constituting the wellsprings of American democracy, local government has typically been weak, suffering from public and official neglect, overlapping of jurisdiction, bossism, or oligarchical rule, and lacking a defined constitutional position.

The conventional wisdom of the matter is fairly simple: local governments (of whatever category) are creatures of the states. State governments can create, abolish, or alter them at will. The states can add to or subtract from the powers, duties, and functions of their local units. They can prescribe the offices and structure of the local governments. This view was forcefully stated as the so-called Dillon rule:

The true view is this: Municipal corporations owe their origin to, and derive their powers and rights wholly from, the legislature. It breathes into them the breath of life, without which they cannot exist. As it creates, so it may destroy. If it may destroy, it may abridge and control. Unless there is some constitutional limitation on the right, the legislature might by a single act, if we can suppose it capable of so great a folly and so great a wrong, sweep from its existence all of the municipal corporations in the State, and the corporations could not prevent it. . . . They are, so to phrase it, the mere tenants at will of the legislature.[48]

By 1900 this was in a formal sense the prevailing view. Nevertheless it hardly does justice to the complexities of the American politi-

[47] *Ibid.*

[48] Syed, *Local Government,* p. 68; cited from Dillon's opinion in City of Clinton *v.* Cedar Rapids & Missouri River R.R. Co., 24 Iowa 455 (1868).

cal structure. Nothing in our political life is that simple. In fact, the state constitutions which govern legislative action have for many years placed severe restrictions on what can be done with local units. California's 1879 constitution, for instance, prevented the state from abolishing the office of county school superintendent, an elected officer; it was forced to "provide for" county school boards which were constitutionally given the powers to examine teachers and grant teaching certificates; counties were recognized and by implication could not be abolished (though they could be divided); the county seat could not be changed by legislation; some county offices were prescribed; some features of the structure of government in large cities were prescribed, and they were given a fairly large degree of home rule; local units were given broad legislative powers—and so on, almost indefinitely.[49] California was not exceptional. The result was that while the judges and the theoreticians mouthed the Dillon rule, political practice observed the "Cooley rule," which emphasized the limitations on state power:

> Some of these limitations are expressly defined; others spring from the usages, customs, and maxims of our people; they are a part of its history, a part of the system of local self-government, in view of the continuance and perpetuity of which all our constitutions are framed, and of the right to which the people can never be deprived except through express renunciation on their part.[50]

As Judge Cooley's statement stressed, the limits to state power were only partly due to constitutional provisions; his theory assumed that local government, by virtue of its ancient origins and its closeness to the people, had attained a prescriptive right to exist and to exercise these powers with which it had traditionally been endowed.

It should be added that while the legislative power was in practice thus limited—a limitation which was reinforced by the inherent nature of the area-based localism of state legislators—the people of the state were not. Acting through constituent assemblies (constitutional conventions) they might do as they pleased so long as they did not (a rare instance) contravene some wandering provision of the national Constitution. Connecticut could thus, in the 1960's, totally abolish its counties.

[49] Reprinted as an appendix in Bryce, *American Commonwealth*, I, 683–724.
[50] Quoted in Syed, *Local Government*, p. 62.

Whether or not it comported with the received theory, in the latter part of the nineteenth century every state had a patchwork quilt— or better, a crazy quilt—of local governments. These consisted, broadly, of three types. In New England the basic unit was the "town." The towns in theory covered the entire area of each state, although there was by 1900 a trend toward consolidating towns in the larger urban areas and converting the larger unit thus created into a city. The towns were supposed to perform all the day-to-day chores of government except the judicial ones. Police and fire protection, road building and maintenance, public schools, the care of the aged and the poor, and a general legislative power were all in their hands. But to complicate the picture, counties had been superimposed, which had minimal functions but served conveniently as boundaries for judicial and some electoral units. And of course there were the cities. Special districts such as (in the Boston area) the metropolitan police district and the metropolitan park district further added to the confusion.[51]

In New York, Pennsylvania, and the Middle West the counties were a good deal more important, assuming most of the functions of the New England town except for the control of schools and the legislative function. Schools were the province of units into which the counties were divided, called townships, or in some cases of municipal governments which were in but often not of the counties: cities typically had their own police, schools, and other appurtenances, and also had a broader legislative power than the counties. Here too special districts had begun to make an appearance by 1917.[52]

In the South and West the governmental structure was considerably simpler, since there were no townships. The counties were the general-purpose local units except in urban areas; again, except in Louisiana, municipalities existed within counties and were in some respects dependent on them, in other respects duplicatory. Special-purpose districts again complicated the picture.[53]

These "systems" grew Topsy-like, largely unplanned; the interrelationships between the various units were the result of *ad hoc* de-

---

[51] The best source on special districts is John C. Bollens, *Special District Governments in the United States* (Berkeley, 1957).

[52] *Ibid.*

[53] *Ibid.*

cisions made to meet specific problems rather than according to any rational scheme of development. The ability—and willingness—to create new special-purpose units provided some flexibility and gave an impression that problems were being satisfactorily dealt with; but at the same time these new units were superimposed helter-skelter on the traditional general-purpose governments and added greatly to the difficulties of coordination and cooperation. Then, too, the whole system resulted in a diffusion of public attention and interest and a decline in popular participation. It left many dark nooks and crannies in which bosses and corruption could flourish unnoticed; but paradoxically the end result (since one of the motives for special districts was to remove certain areas from the control of local party leaders) was to weaken the party system by handing decisions on important matters to agencies beyond local party influence.

The total amount of power held by local governments—which lay in law enforcement, administration of important functions such as utilities, and legislation (which was often disguised by calling it "the ordinance-making power" or, for administrative agencies, simply the power to make decisions as to what they would do, as a school board might decide to have a daily prayer ceremony)—this total was truly impressive. At any time before 1917 it undoubtedly bulked larger than the power exercised by either the national or the state governments. It was, however, so thoroughly diffused among the units that the public often lost sight of its importance; particularly lost sight of was its political character. The progressive reforms were based on the theory that local government consisted largely of routine administration which had little relevance to "politics" (by which was meant partisan politics and policy making). Consequently the progressives saw the problem as one mainly of organization, and they tended to believe that the finding of a simple organizational formula would solve all the myriad ills of local government.[54] Actually some ills were dealt with—alleviated if not solved—but this may have been more owing to the progressive atmosphere, to the growth of a public conscience which refused to put up with the more blatant evils of corruption, bossism, franchise dealing, and spoilsism, than to the structural reforms themselves. It was thus a mistaken simplistic view of politics, based on a mechanistic approach and an unbounded

[54] For an example of this tendency see the valedictory of the great reform leader, Richard S. Childs, *Civic Victories* (New York, 1952).

faith in the goodness of the average man, that accounted for such a view as that of the municipal reform leader Richard S. Childs: "The difficulties of democracy . . . are mechanistic, not moral, and respond to mechanistic corrections. . . . It is the mechanism that makes the difference." [55]

Not only were progressives organizationally minded, however: at the same time, in one of those sets of contradictions which is simultaneously both inexplicable and most human, they were individualist, elitist, and democratic. They combined an almost naïve faith in the goodness of the ordinary (native, Protestant, rural?) American with the feeling that reform could be achieved only through leadership by the "better elements" in society, which in turn could act effectively only when a strong individual appeared who could weld them into an effective political movement. Thus was the role of a municipal leader like "Golden Rule" Jones or Tom Johnson justified; they were sometimes seen as latter-day Don Quixotes who would, however, be more successful than Cervantes' hero.

Perhaps unfortunately, there is in fact no reason to suppose that the award of a franchise to construct and run a trolley system, the decision which streets to pave this year, which school needs a new building first, where to build the new bridge, whether or where to preserve open spaces as parks, and (as in Boston in the 1890's) whether or where to build public baths and swimming pools are less "political" and "moral" questions than whether to raise the tariff another notch or pass a workmen's compensation law. The progressive reformer was thus engaged in the fruitless enterprise of trying to remove politics from politics, and he found somewhat to his dismay that when you throw politics out the front door it is likely to come sneaking back in somewhere else.

The period 1877 to 1917—especially the latter half of it—was pre-eminently a "reform" era, and this reform largely concentrated on local government. The reformers were, of course, moved primarily by the prevailing corruption of local government in the post-Civil War years and by the association of "the bosses" with this corruption. Less proximately, they were unconsciously responding to those great changes in American society which constitute a basic theme of this

[55] Childs, quoted in John Porter East, *Council-Manager Government: The Political Thought of Its Founder, Richard S. Childs* (Chapel Hill, 1965), p. 56.

work. Local government reform, in practice, turned out to be largely *municipal* reform: and it did so not so much because there was more or worse corruption there than in the other units of local government but because it was more obvious, more open—and more written about. The reformers themselves were either city men who were shocked by what they saw in their own experience or rural people who saw the city as the Biblical Sodom which provided a perfect target for their political lances. The first type is well illustrated by Richard S. Childs (1882–19—). Brought up in a wealthy family in unreformed New York City, he spent a lifetime in reform politics, spurred on by its obvious deficiencies as an urban polity. He became the father of the council manager and short ballot movements and at one time or another headed "just about every civic organization of note" in the city, in addition to being the major leader of the National Municipal League. Like many of the reformers, Childs made political reform an avocation: he never held an elective office. He was a pressure politician instead, working through good government (to the cynic, "goo-goo") organizations. But his long-run influence on urban reform was greater than that of most politicians.[56]

Jane Addams (1860–1935) was also an urban "patrician reformer." Founder of Hull House, the first private settlement house, she spent a fruitful lifetime helping Chicago's poor. Not only was her help at the immediate level, but like Childs she sponsored and led numerous reform campaigns which were aimed at improving Chicago as a place to live, especially for the immigrants and the poor.

Men like Hazen S. Pingree (1840–1901), Tom L. Johnson (1854–1911), and Samuel M. "Golden Rule" Jones (1846–1904), on the other hand, were of rural origins. Each of them grew up in poverty-stricken surroundings, went to urban factories at a tender age, and rose in true Horatio Alger style to fame and fortune. They went into active elective politics because of their distress at the conditions in their adopted cities (Jones was particularly interested, contrary to most of the reformers, in measures that would directly benefit workers). Pingree became a (largely unsuccessful) mayor of Detroit and governor of Michigan; Johnson and Jones were astonishingly creative and successful mayors of Cleveland and Toledo,[57] who succeeded in eliminating most of the commoner forms of corruption in their city

---

[56] For a summary on Childs, see *ibid.*, pp. 3–14.
[57] *Dictionary of American Biography*, X, 122–124; XXI, 453–454.

governments, rid their cities of the venal private transportation franchises and sponsored various other reforms or advances.

The reform movement hit the cities and—because of the close legal relationship—the states, while largely skipping over the other local units. Counties and townships are (in today's political scientese) "areas of low visibility," and apparently always have been. Reforms at other levels have usually had little effect in these areas; the politicians active in them have great negative powers of resistance, but perhaps more important, the reformers do not see them as being great problem areas, perhaps because they do not regard such units as important enough to worry about.

In any case, a description of county, township, and even to some extent of New England town, government as of 1877 would not differ tremendously from one written in 1917 or even in 1967. The major change lay in a slow attrition of function. For while cities became increasingly important and powerful, counties and townships went in the opposite direction. The New England town, which has always performed the same functions as a municipality, has not suffered to the same extent, and even in the rural areas it retains a good deal of vitality. Even areas of some urbanization and industrialization such as the Brockton of 1890, as Bryce found (somewhat to his surprise), still used town government, although Boston, Cambridge, and other larger communities had for some years been converted into cities, complete with corporate charters, as was the pattern in the middle Atlantic and Midwestern states.[58] Town government, in rural areas, was even in 1900 almost as simple in operation and concept as it had been in the seventeenth century. In theory at least it revolved around the town meeting, an annual assemblage to which all voters were eligible for membership. This meeting passed on the annual budget, item by item, performed minor chores of legislation, and served as a principal social event as well. The town would also have a chief clerk and a board of selectmen who ran the day-to-day affairs of the community, various local officers such as the constable, and a school committee. Bryce was something of an Anglophile and tended to overpraise the town government; but there was doubtless much to praise in it. "Where it is of native American stock," he wrote, "and the number of voting citizens is not too great for thorough and calm discussion, no better school of politics can be imagined, nor any method of

[58] Bryce, *American Commonwealth*, I, 565.

managing local affairs more certain to prevent jobbery and waste, to stimulate vigilance and breed contentment." [59] In fact, it seems that town politics were not quite that idyllic, and in any case the larger towns would lose to a great extent the face-to-face character which Bryce so admired. The clerk tended to be permanent even in the smaller towns, and the job was sometimes passed on from father to son, so that through him and the selectmen the solid citizens were usually in complete control of town affairs.

Long before 1917 the larger towns had added finance committees which could attain a degree of expertise in the planning of rational budgets; and the town meeting was too large to function properly, so "representative" town meetings were developed, at which several hundred members, elected by the townspeople, carried on the old functions. But even this altered form of government was too amateur to serve as an efficient administrative unit for good law enforcement or for the increasingly complex community services required in a larger community, such as sewage disposal, utilities, street maintenance, and so on. Either these were poorly done or (in some cases) they were administered by the state, or perhaps by a special-purpose district.

Counties and townships were more affected by this trend, since they were less important to their people to begin with. Especially in the case of the township, it never gained the hold over citizen affection that the New England town attained. This was partly because it was rather an anomalous creation to begin with: most of the significant functions of local government were entrusted to the counties or cities, and while the township served conveniently as an administrative unit for some functions, these usually could as well be performed by some larger unit.[60]

Then, too, the hold of these units in the public imagination was probably affected by the fact that they held little legislative power; and while some of their functions (such as the sheriff's duties of law enforcement and court administration) were of a good deal of importance, they were in general not *seen* to be so important. Sheriffs and various other county officials, too, were elected and thus were not responsible to the executive-administrative-legislative unit of the

[59] *Ibid.*, 566.
[60] Clyde F. Snider, *Local Government in Rural America* (New York, 1957), pp. 44, 229–233.

county, which usually consisted of a board or commission of perhaps three elected functionaries. As in state government, this dispersion of responsibility had the effect of dulling public interest and reducing accountability and visibility. Townships often served as school districts, but this was more a matter of marking convenient boundaries than anything else, for the school boards were separately elected and not responsible to the township "government." Township meetings, where they were held at all, were neither as well attended nor as important to the functioning of the local community as in New England. The more thickly settled portions of the township were probably hived off as municipal corporations, which ran their own affairs, in some cases including their schools, and which not infrequently sprawled across township lines.[61]

Townships west of the Appalachians (and to some extent counties as well) were not natural growths from the life of the community, as they were in New England. They were, instead, lines drawn on a map, often in advance of any settlement and unconnected with settlement patterns. If they still survived—as they did outside the urban areas—it was more because of inertia and the fact that they were incapable of doing great harm (or good) than because they were either very useful or regarded with great affection.

As regards the quality of rural local government, politicians tend to be much the same wherever found. Because of the small population and restricted area, politics no doubt was typically a good deal more personal than in urban areas or at the state and national level. This meant not only that politicians knew each other, with the "you scratch my back, I'll scratch yours" proclivities common to such situations, but that small cliques tended to control through informal wheeling and dealing. The following description of politics in a southern county seat is probably a fairly good picture of an average rural local government situation anywhere in the country and at any time between 1877 and 1917:

The creed of this banker-merchant-farmer-lawyer-doctor governing class is worthy of study. It explains more about Southern politics than any analysis of structure can possibly do, though it is the decentralization of power into these semirural units which makes its existence possible. . . . The member of the governing group will be a leading church member, probably an officer. He will observe the religious forms and pass the collection plate on Sunday. During the rest of the week his religion may be stored away unless he sings in the choir or belongs to the quartette which sings at funerals. . . . He may even pray about the brotherhood of man, but in his day-to-day activities he may like others overlook his conscience in the interest of business.[62]

The local leader is conservative, "accepting current political and social behavior without questioning its major premises." He tends to be anti-intellectual and wants his schools old-fashioned and inexpensive: he "offers lip-service to the democratic credo of liberty, equality, and majority rule, but to his way of thinking liberty has nothing to do with labor leaders or college professors, and equality does not include people with black skins." The governing elite

is not incapable of a *beau geste* in a community chest drive or at a charity bazaar, but it is careful to keep its assessments low and thereby contributes to low standards of schools and other public services. The leaders control the election processes and thereby keep political and economic power alike in their own hands. In this fashion they keep assessments down, tax rates fixed, and the schools in proper hands.[63]

With such an ironic and perhaps exaggerated glance at the leadership of the rural and small-town governing units, we may turn to conditions in the larger, urban units. These came by 1917 to contain just about half of the American people. The government of cities was a major preoccupation of the progressive reformer and the muckraker, and there was much to occupy their attention. Because the stakes were higher, corruption was more prevalent and at the same time involved more people and larger sums of money or property. The stakes were higher not only because potential "profits" were great, but because the cities had more political power. Cities were to a much greater degree than other local units truly general governments, and therefore their actions could affect the lives and properties of their people to a much greater extent than could the activities of county or township. For the people who lived there, indeed, it may be said that as late as 1917 the city government was the most impor-

---

[62] Jasper Berry Shannon, *Toward a New Politics in the South* (Knoxville, 1949), pp. 38–53.

[63] *Ibid.*, pp. 44–50. Another writer claims that "rural local governments are probably more frequently boss-controlled than any other American governments." Morton Grodzins, "Centralization and Decentralization in the American Federal System," in Robert A. Goldwin (ed.), *A Nation of States* (Chicago, 1961), p. 13.

tant single unit. It affected them in more ways, more intimately, and more often than any of the numerous governments to which they were subject. Thus it was in the American constitutional scheme of things a most important element.

City government may conveniently to our purposes be divided into two major periods. The prereform period lasted from well before 1877 into the 1890's (and some cities never did undergo "reform"), while the reform period extended on past 1917. The timing was closely associated with the first great growth of American cities. City dwellers totaled barely 5 million in 1860; by 1890 there were well over 18 million. These cities were closely packed; they were the homes of most of the rush of the "new" immigrants, difficult to assimilate, from Italy, the Balkans, and Russia. And the rapidity of the growth brought tremendous problems along with it:

Water supply systems, sewers, and facilities for the removal and disposal of garbage and rubbish had to be provided. Property had to be protected against fire and theft. Especially acute was the problem of public health, which required constant attention. The provision of public utilities such as light, gas, and transportation became a necessity. . . . The paving, lighting, and cleaning of streets, planning of boulevard systems, and building of bridges became important aspects of city administration. There were school systems and public libraries to be planned and administered; playgrounds, parks, and other educational and recreational facilities to be provided.

The surge of expansion found cities woefully unprepared. . . . Thus the problem usually became one of expediency rather than of efficiency. As a result, there were vastly increased expenditures. Enormous public works programs were undertaken. Valuable public franchises were given away for political reasons. Unprecedented borrowing led to huge public debts. Excessive waste was inevitable for lack of time to plan.[64]

While most of the reformers tended to stress the essentially administrative aspect of these problems, they had their political side as well. Not only were "politics" (pejorative) involved in the "giving away" of franchises, but politics (in the usual sense of the term) were also inevitably involved in decision making: Should we have a park system? If so, who should it be for, and following that, where and what kind of parks? As recent experience has indicated once more,

[64] Frank Mann Stewart, *A Half Century of Municipal Reform: The History of the National Municipal League* (Berkeley, 1950), pp. 2–3.

ignoring the political side of such problems tended to lead to their solution by "experts" who represented primarily—if not the middle class directly—at least middle-class attitudes and values about what should be done for other classes. Thus, looking at the "urban problem" as an administrative one created problems of its own, even though it may at the same time have solved others.

Up to 1890, as Bryce remarks, the political structure which existed to try to meet these problems was to a marked extent a reproduction of state government. There was normally a divided executive: a mayor was the formal head, but he often had comparatively as little power as a governor over the executive branch, since there would be a set of other executive boards or officers, some of whom would not be under the mayor's appointive power. The school systems, especially, were sequestered from "politics" by being run separately; they were not controlled by either the mayor or the council; ordinarily the schools were run by an elective board (how this kept them out of politics has been a problem to some generations of political scientists).[65]

The legislative branch consisted of a city council, often (we have forgotten this) in the larger cities bicameral. This was in general, as in the states, the dominant branch of the city government. The judiciary was kept largely in state hands, although some of the minor courts might be municipally organized, especially in the larger cities.

All of this (except the schools) was organized under a sort of municipal constitution called a "charter," which was granted by the state either by general law to many cities within its jurisdiction or by special law to individual cities. The details of these charters varied widely, and I have made no attempt to account here for their variety.

By 1890 it was plain to intelligent observers that the problems of the cities were outrunning the capacity of their governments to solve them. In the process of trying, the city administrations—run under the spoils system—proved to be woefully inefficient; the temptations of graft led to the corruption associated in the American mind with the boss system; and the inordinate profits to be made from the buying and selling (and occasionally operating) of the franchises for provision of municipal services led many "respectable" businessmen to buy and sell politicians along with the franchises. It seemed at the time that Bryce was correct in his famous judgment that city government

[65] Bryce, *American Commonwealth*, I, 567, 571, 574–575.

was "the one conspicuous failure" of the United States.[66] Bryce's view, because contemporary, was exaggerated, and he attributed the failure to that ubiquitous American whipping boy, the political party, which in hindsight appears to have been at most a mere accessory. Bryce was neither the first nor the last in his ability to delineate symptoms while being unable to diagnose accurately. For the symptoms were certainly plain for all to see, and there was no doubt that something had to be done.

The reform movement thus had its most striking successes with cities. By this I do not mean that it solved the cities' problems, although it certainly alleviated some of them. By 1917 cities normally had paved streets, street lighting, dependable water supplies, and the other appurtenances that we take for granted. It also seems to be true that the reformers were most successful in two ways: one, in the reconstruction of the *structure* of municipal government; and two, in the small and medium-sized cities. In the largest cities, reform almost uniformly meant the substitution of the strong for the weak mayor—that is, the concentration of greater executive power in the mayor's office. It meant also the change from bicameral to unicameral councils, and the beginnings of municipal merit systems for city employees. Without denigrating these changes as unimportant, they are yet something less than constitutionally fundamental. The reformers also succeeded in getting rid of most of the existing bosses; their places were taken in many cases by others sometimes more benign, but only sometimes. Consequently, by 1917 our largest cities were significantly more honestly and efficiently run. Whether they were, apart from the general American rise in living standards, better places to live in was perhaps still somewhat of a question, the answer to which depended partly on who you were.

More fundamental were the changes in the smaller communities. In many of these the whole municipal structure was changed. Two entirely new constitutional frameworks were developed: the commission plan and the council-manager plan. Both involved a considerable simplification of city government; both also were aimed at efficient, honest, "business type" government rather than at wise or democratic decision making.

The commission form eliminated both the mayor and the city council. Substituted for both was an elective commission, usually of

66 *Ibid.*, 608.

five members, who held all the executive and legislative powers of the city. Each commissioner had charge of a group of municipal functions. They were typically elected at large, and thus all five tended to represent the same population segment. The commission plan provided a simple, intelligible structure quite different from the confusing maze presented by nineteenth-century mayoral government. It enjoyed a great vogue, especially in the Middle West, between 1905 and 1920.

Nevertheless, over the years the plan lost favor. It seems to have been inadequate in some specific respects; for instance, it did not provide concentrated executive control, it was inadequately representative, it did not guarantee that administrative efficiency would result, and competition among the commissioners often resulted in a pronounced lack of leadership. Even before 1920 some cities which had adopted the plan dropped it again, and it had become obvious that it was not the "wave of the future" for urban America.[67]

The second plan—most commonly called "council-manager" government—proceeded directly on the analogy to private business. This required two large assumptions, both of which the reformers made without even realizing in most cases that they were doing so. First, they assumed that the business corporation was actually organized ideally for its purpose. Although the rate of business failure in this country has always been high, which does not seem to prove the assumption true, I will grant it for present purposes. The second assumption is politically more dangerous as well as being more doubtful: they assumed that the government of a city was analogous to the running of a corporation. The manager plan has been most successful in small cities, and this seems to have been because small cities are often more homogeneous, single-purpose units than large ones and therefore are in practice more similar to corporations. The polyglot nature of the metropolis, on the other hand, leads to a multiplicity of group interests which makes it more similar to larger political units such as states or nations than to businesses.

Manager government is simple in design. It is based upon a small elective council (proponents have always insisted that this council be both small and elected at large, which produces some of the same difficulties to which the commission plan fell prey). This council is

[67] The defects of the commission plan are summarized in Duane Lockard, *The Politics of State and Local Government* (New York, 1963), p. 113.

the legislative organ of the city, but in concept it is more like the board of directors of a corporation. But unlike the commission form, it performs no administrative functions except that of general oversight. Instead, it is responsible for selecting a "manager," who becomes responsible to it for the conduct of the administration. The manager serves an indefinite term, at the pleasure of the council; he holds the appointive power, and typically there are few or no elective officials; he also serves as an adviser to the council, theoretically on technical matters.

Manager government has some obvious advantages, and when these only are considered, the success of the plan is easily explained. Particularly in smaller cities, the advantage of securing a "business manager" is great: he is trained in management techniques and has some knowledge of a broad range of technical questions. He is capable of expert fiscal management and of making up a budget; he is in a sense an administrative efficiency expert, and cities which have the manager system are typically well managed. These explain why 300 cities—most of them small—had adopted the plan as early as 1917.

As noted earlier, the reformers who sponsored manager government in cities across the nation had a strong tendency to think that politics—especially party politics—had no place in city government: "There is no Democratic or Republican way to pave a street," they would say. At that level they were right, and they seldom considered the matter at any deeper level. There is no doubt that American cities were better governed, on the whole, and (despite their problems) are better governed today than they were at any earlier time in our history. But this is true of American cities almost regardless of whether they have managers, commissions, or mayoral governments. The fact that it *is* true of most cities seems to point to the fact that it was the progressive spirit rather than its specific institutional reforms which made the difference. It should be remembered, of course, that even in mayor-governed cities there was a degree of institutional reform in response to the demands of the progressives.

It is also true that in those cities where the manager system has been tried and then discarded, the experience seems to have been that it did not allow enough scope for politics: in other words, significant groups in the life of the city felt that their needs and desires were being ignored. And when managers got into trouble and were discharged by the council, it was most often because they had got embroiled in questions of policy, had tried to assume policy leadership (there is nowhere else it is likely to come from), and had become identified politically with one view. The point here is not precisely that only fools will contest forms of government: it is rather that all government is ineradicably political and that if any government is to work successfully over a long period of time some place for political leadership must be found in it. There may be no Democratic way to pave a street, but there may well be a Democratic solution to the question of which street should be paved, or, indeed, whether the city's money should be spent on something else first. In the days of affirmative government which arrived with rather startling speed after the Civil War cities no less than the state and national governments found that political leadership was the key to meeting their needs. Good, honest leaders like Pingree were of course to be preferred over the Tweeds of this world, but it may be that in the long run it is more important to have leaders who are responsive to public needs. And as the middle classes have progressively (a fitting term) deserted the center city for the suburbs, it has become more obvious that it is the lower classes to which the leaders must respond: and that typically these classes do not consider honesty or efficiency the *sine qua non* of government—their immediate needs are too great.[68]

Progressivism sponsored the middle-class ideals of honesty, efficiency, integrity, and technical expertise, secure in the belief that these would result in policies satisfactory to the middle classes. In cities where these groups are still dominant—which means most cities with populations under 100,000—manager government performs very well and is still spreading. In lower-class suburbs it was never adopted at all, and in rather few of our large center cities. All government must in the final analysis be judged on the basis of whether it meets the needs of its citizens. If it can do so efficiently, well and

[68] The literature on council-manager government is enormous; the treatment presented here is an attempt to summarize the latest "revisionist" views, which tend strongly to take a less favorable view of the system, especially for large cities. See Edward C. Banfield and James Q. Wilson, *City Politics* (Cambridge, 1963), pp. 168 ff.; David A. Booth, *Council-Manager Government in Small Cities* (Washington, 1968), p. 125; Harold Stone, Don K. Price, Kathryn H. Stone, *City Manager Government in the United States: A Review after Twenty-Five Years* (Chicago, 1940), pp. 221–223.

good; but no amount of efficiency will substitute for acceptable policy judgment.

The Progressive movement, despite its obviously high purposes, ended by tending to enfeeble the governments it touched by destroying the possibility of sound party government. Leadership came more and more to depend on individual charisma; when the charisma was lacking, government was ineffective. Charisma is, however, a dangerous quality in a democracy. People come to depend on it, to the detriment of the representative institutions which are the basis of all democratic government. We may have ended up by fostering "Caesaro-papism"—government based on the strong executive—in our efforts to escape the evils of "party." [69]

But it is now time to give attention not to the formal aspects of constitutional structure, but to the informal. Dicey as early as the nineteenth century realized that the actual working of a representative system depended primarily on the functioning of effective mechanisms by which public opinion could be brought to bear on the formal policy-making institutions. Let us turn to this aspect of our constitution.

[69] Henry Fairlie, "Thoughts on the Presidency," *The Public Interest*, 9 (1967), 28–48.

CHAPTER 4

The Public and Its Government

IN any political system those men who wield the legal powers of government represent larger groups in the society. In a democracy, theoretically at least, they represent everyone. In studying our constitutional history we are forced to face two basic questions: To what extent was theory made real (that is, did the power holders in practice represent everyone, and if not, who was left out)? What were the mechanisms which brought (or failed to bring) popular or group desires to the attention of the formal institutions?

No group of substantial size which holds the vote and uses it so as intelligently to advance its interests can be ignored in the world of democratic politics. No minority is likely to get all it wants; but without the franchise, discriminatingly used, it may get practically nothing. This is because under our system groups must have proximate power if they are to gain attention; this power may be economic or military, but if a group's major asset is numbers it can only maximize its effectiveness through the ballot box.[1] Meaningful choice among candidates and policies, and the existence of group interests sufficiently distinguishable from those of the general populace so that the group is not merely a microcosm of the electorate as a whole, are also necessary. The latter consideration is of great importance when considering the history of the suffrage during the period 1877 to 1917, since two of the major disfranchised groups as of 1877 occupied quite

---

[1] Harold F. Gosnell, *Democracy, the Threshold of Freedom* (New York, 1948).

different positions in this regard. The Negroes, because of their slave background and the continuing presence of race prejudice, certainly had a clearly definable group interest, quite different from that of the electorate. It would be rational voting, then, for them to stick together and vote as a bloc. Women, on the other hand, have no such clear bloc interest, except in the rare kind of political issue which turns on sex. For this reason, one would not expect to find women bloc voting; rather, their vote would probably be cast in roughly the same way as that of men. Perhaps this is why the political system accommodated itself to women voting sooner than it did to Negroes. Yet before women's suffrage politicians were not sure enough how females would vote to be happy with the prospect. Victorian morality tended to assume that women were morally superior to men (and for this reason it was sometimes argued that they could not work effectively in the "practical" world of politics); the effect of this assumption was the fear (among male politicians) that women, voting, would immediately "throw the rascals out." In other words, it was assumed that their higher morality constituted a kind of bloc interest which would hold women together at the polls. Like other groups seeking political status, the women themselves fell prey to the same delusion, so that the claims they made as to the beneficent effects of granting them the vote took on at times an almost apocalyptic tone.

Self-conscious groups having the power to vote have, at least potentially, the power also to influence the choice of the formal power holders and the policies adopted by them, while groups not holding the vote largely lack this power. This is what makes the question "who can and does vote?" a constitutional one.

The limitations of American democracy in 1877 are well known. Three groups either could not or did not vote: Negroes, women, and the poor.

Formally the Negro right to vote was guaranteed by the Fifteenth Amendment. It was a right which was exercised by large numbers during the Reconstruction period. However, one of the major effects of the "Compromise of 1877" by which Rutherford B. Hayes ascended to the presidency was the tacit agreement that the Republican party, and the federal government as a whole, would turn a blind eye to the efforts (if they were not too obvious) of the Bourbon leaders of the South to keep Negroes away from the polls.[2] This practical disfranchisement, accomplished at first largely by coercion and violence, became increasingly institutionalized as the period wore on and clever lawyers found ways around the amendment. By the mid-1890's these efforts had succeeded in largely eliminating the Negro voter in the South, and thenceforth the influence of that unhappy race on Southern politics and policy was negligible except when a politician threatened with defeat at the polls would use race as a scare question so as, hopefully, to unify the white voters behind him.

Negro weakness was so pronounced, indeed, that even northern writers customarily wrote essays on "Southern Opinion" in which the only opinion discussed was that of whites. Negroes disappeared completely from public life, and even the great "Teddy"—after the outcry caused by one attempt—found it politic not to invite Negro leaders to the White House.[3]

Negro disfranchisement, when not the result of apathy, force, or intimidation, was putatively "legal" and "constitutional." Even the Supreme Court accepted its less crass forms without question. The Mississippi Constitution of 1890 has sometimes been regarded as a "model" in such matters. It provided for a two-dollar poll tax as a requirement for voting and required that the receipt for this tax be shown at the polling place upon request. In 1892 a constitutional understanding test was added, as well as a "good character" requirement. The important aspect of all these provisions was that their enforcement was largely left to the discretion of the election officials, who are local functionaries; and in the conditions of the time this meant that they would be strictly enforced when Negroes tried to vote and loosely enforced (or not at all) for white voters.[4] (There were at times exceptions to the latter, which we shall discuss when we come to the handicaps of poverty when one wished to vote.) As one speaker at a Virginia constitutional convention said, speaking of the "understanding" test: "I expect the examination with which the black man will be confronted to be inspired by the same spirit

[2] The compromise is best treated in C. Vann Woodward, *Reunion and Reaction* (Boston, 1951).

[3] George E. Mowry, *The Era of Theodore Roosevelt* (New York, 1958), p. 165.

[4] C. Vann Woodward, *Origins of the New South, 1877–1913* (Baton Rouge, 1951), pp. 321–336.

that inspires every man upon this floor and in this convention. *I do not expect an impartial administration of this clause.*" [5]

The Supreme Court upheld the Mississippi literacy test in 1898, using the common doctrine that it could not look behind the face of the statute, and since it was not on its face calculated to prevent Negroes *as such* from voting it did not violate the Fifteenth Amendment.[6] A few years later the same court upheld the Alabama constitutional understanding test: the Court this time felt that it was legally inconsistent for a Negro to try to register under an act which he felt was void.[7] It is true that in the Guinn case in 1914 the Court overturned an Oklahoma "grandfather clause," which allowed anyone to register whose ancestors would have qualified to vote before 1866 but refused registration to others unless they registered by a stated, very short deadline. The grandfather clause does not, however, seem to have been of prime importance in keeping Negroes from voting.[8]

The development of the primary election system gave southern states another opportunity to deprive Negroes of political influence. Under southern conditions, the one-party system was safe only so long as the voters were predominantly white. If the Democrats could keep Negroes out of the primaries in addition to the general elections, they could ensure that Democrats would win in November, and that those Democrats would be whites who were not tied to the Negro vote in any way. The constitutional argument was that primaries were not elections within the meaning of the Fifteenth Amendment, and that therefore the southern states could legislate openly to prevent Negroes from voting in them. Usually this was done by laws limiting the membership in the Democratic party to whites. Since only registered Democrats could vote in the Democratic primary, this effectively kept the franchise safe for the white man. These laws did not come before the Supreme Court until the 1920's.[9]

The result of this array of legal and extralegal measures was the

---

[5] Kirk Harold Porter, *A History of the Suffrage in the United States* (Chicago, 1918), p. 218.

[6] Williams *v.* Mississippi, 170 U.S. 213 (1898).

[7] Giles *v.* Harris, 189 U.S. 474 (1903).

[8] Guinn *v.* U.S., 238 U.S. 347 (1914). Assessments of its importance may be found in Porter, *History of Suffrage*, p. 224; and Woodward, *New South*, p. 343.

[9] Gosnell, *Democracy*, pp. 96–97.

practical disfranchisement of the Negro. Thus was about one-tenth of the American population rendered politically powerless—a situation which remained in effect long after the First World War.

The struggle of women for the vote, which came to fruition at the very end of our period, was marked by mass demonstrations, sometimes accompanied by scuffles, mass arrests, and even hunger strikes. It resembled in its moral fervor the civil rights movement and the antiwar demonstrations of a later era. But given the changing status of women in society—the new freedom, the addition of women to the industrial labor force, the rise of the "career woman"—the result was a foregone conclusion, legal discriminations were slowly dropped, especially in the West, and some of the new states began giving the franchise (Colorado began the procession, for school elections only, in 1876) at least in limited forms.[10] A suffrage amendment drafted by Susan B. Anthony was introduced into Congress in 1878—which was only finally to pass in 1920.[11] By 1900 most states permitted women to vote for certain purposes, most often for school board members—the male American tended to turn the schools over to women anyway. Wyoming, however, had practiced full equal suffrage as a federal territory as early as 1869, and continued this in its first state constitution adopted in 1890. Colorado, Utah, and Idaho followed by the turn of the century.[12] Paradoxically the movement slowed a little in the early stages of the Progressive era, but gained renewed vigor as a result of the First World War, when women were in great demand as factory workers. By 1920, when the Nineteenth Amendment extended the vote to women everywhere, women had the vote in 15 states, most of them in the West.

The effect of woman suffrage was to double, at one stroke, the number of potential voters. It did not, however, do so in practice, since many women did not seem eager to assume the burdens of full citizenship, especially those among immigrant groups, and as a result the proportion of eligible voters who actually went to the polls fell even lower in the 1920's than before. In general, however, the political opinions of women tended to follow those of "their men," and the change in the suffrage has not, therefore, been as important constitutionally as the rise of the Negro voter at a later date or as the

[10] Porter, *History of Suffrage*, p. 243.
[11] *Ibid.*, pp. 228–254.
[12] *Ibid.*, p. 244.

New Deal's successful effort to mobilize the political force of the poor. The suffragettes provide a colorful chapter in American history; the political millennium supposed to be marked by their success still seems, however, to elude us.

The third large disfranchised group—the poor—presents quite a different case from the other two. The main reason for this is that the poor were not, during this period, *legally* disfranchised at all. "Social disfranchisement" took the place of legal. It resulted from a whole string of causes—ignorance owing to lack of education or recent immigration and consequent unfamiliarity with American politics and language, and the lack of a secret ballot, which tended to intimidate the frightened or halfhearted. Then, too, there was a form of disfranchisement which resulted all too often even when the poor actually did vote, for their votes were often stolen and quite as often bought, especially by the urban machine bosses (and sometimes, reputedly, by employers).[13] In the long run the bosses introduced successive generations of immigrants to American politics; but in the short run their votes were simply used.

One might say, with some exaggeration, that the immigrant generation itself did not vote; the second generation voted as the bosses told it to; while the third generation tended strongly to absorb the machine and provide the bosses. By the 1890's the Irish were in the third generation. John F. Fitzgerald ("Honey Fitz") was boss of Boston's North End, "where a small remnant of Irish families with firm business and political stakes clung to power against the tide of voteless Italians and Jews. . . . It was an Irish rotten borough." [14] Analogous situations existed in the other great cities, especially in the East.

In American conditions, the immigrant's descendants could gain effective political power partly because there were so many of them and partly because they did not stay poor. Like "Honey Fitz" (John Kennedy's grandfather), many sons or grandsons of immigrants were solidly established in business, politics, or the labor movement. The advantages were with the Irish: they arrived earlier, they had no pronounced language barrier to overcome, and they came in such great numbers and congregated in such a way that politicians could hardly ignore them.

[13] See Ray Ginger, *Altgeld's America* (New York, 1958), pp. 92–100.
[14] Geoffrey Blodgett, *The Gentle Reformers: Massachusetts Democracy in the Cleveland Era* (Cambridge, 1966), p. 169.

Even so, it could not be said that by 1917 America's poor were a working part of the constitutional system. Most of them did not vote and were not encouraged to do so.[15] Perhaps this was especially true in those rural sections (for instance in the South, where they were almost all native stock) which contained large numbers of semisubsistence farms, sharecroppers, or commercial farms on which the margin of success or failure was extremely problematic. To a certain extent, especially in the South during the Populist years of the 1890's, the poor white farmers were disfranchised by the same legal measures which we have already described as being aimed at the Negro. There was nothing about a poll tax receipt requirement or a constitutional understanding test that could not be used as well against the poor whites who might vote Populist as against the Negroes. There is, in fact, a good deal of evidence that the southern vote restriction laws were actually adopted to perpetuate Democratic dominance by preventing Populists from voting. The Negro was not ignored—he, too, might vote Populist; and in any case it was more acceptable for Bourbon rhetoricians to worry about "the Black tide" than about fellow white men, at least in public.

The specter of a coalition of the poor haunted the South, and Populism actually did raise such a threat. In Louisiana, for instance, the beginnings of such a coalition came as early as 1888; Negroes were not as yet disfranchised, and in 1896 the Democrats were faced by a combination of "Republicans, disgruntled sugar growers, and the People's party"—the latter openly bidding for the poor farmer vote, both white and Negro. While the Democrats squeaked through this election (probably with the aid of widespread fraud), the moral was to prevent such coalitions in the future; and while this could have been accomplished by preventing Negro voting alone, the mood of the Democrats was such that the disfranchisement of the poor white (Populist) was not looked upon with disfavor. Consequently the 1898 constitution drawn up by Louisiana Democrats, while justi-

[15] Voting in post-Civil War United States apparently reached its peak around 1880 and declined sharply in the 1890's. The decline was, of course, greatest in the South, for reasons explained herein; but significantly, the second greatest decline came in the industrial East, where ignorant immigrants and disenchanted workers did not have the interest necessary to wish to go through the increasing inconveniences attached to voting. See Cortez A. M. Ewing, *Presidential Elections* (Norman: University of Oklahoma Press, 1940), charts on pp. 199 and 200 and accompanying text. And see, for corroborating data, Walter Dean Burnham, "The Changing Shape of the American Political Universe," *American Political Science Review*, LIX (1965), 7–28, especially noting his data on Pennsylvania.

fied in terms of white supremacy, in effect disfranchised 20,000 to 30,000 whites, almost one-fourth of the white electorate; and "it was the poor, illiterate, but certainly not necessarily ignorant, farmers who had lost the suffrage." [16] "The real question which was settled in the South was *which whites* should be supreme." [17]

Another reason for low voter turnout among the poor was that for most of the period they were politically invisible. While William Jennings Bryan, and (perhaps even more) the Populists, appealed to the poor to some extent, they were largely concerned with the rural native-born white, nor did they offer solutions which were comprehensible to an ignorant sharecropper. The poor had not yet learned to organize in order to achieve their aims—this was a lesson which in the latter years of the nineteenth century was only beginning to be learned by their more prosperous brethren.

The political ideas of the time did not help. National intervention, even aid in times of panic or catastrophe, was almost nonexistent, and there was little feeling that the government in Washington had any responsibility for the poor. If they were to be helped at all (many writers and politicians thought they should not—"social Darwinism" was born during this era) it was to be by the local governments, which had traditionally maintained poor farms and which were now just beginning to provide such urban amenities as parks and public baths. President Cleveland thought the problem of poor relief belonged to private charity; vetoing a bill to provide seed to drought-stricken areas of Texas in 1887 he wrote:

I can find no warrant for such an appropriation in the Constitution, and I do not believe that the power and duty of the General Government ought to be extended to the relief of individual suffering which is in no manner properly related to the public service or benefit. . . . Federal aid in such cases encourages the expectations of paternal care . . . and weakens the sturdiness of our national character. . . .[18]

Theodore Roosevelt and Woodrow Wilson had different views about this, although the results in legislation were slow in coming. Wilson, campaigning in 1912, remarked:

[16] Perry H. Howard, *Political Tendencies in Louisiana, 1812–1952* (Baton Rouge, 1957), p. 103.

[17] *Ibid.*, p. 105; this whole development is masterfully depicted in Woodward, *New South*, pp. 330–345.

[18] Message of Feb. 16, 1887, in James D. Richardson (ed.), *Messages and Papers of the Presidents* (New York, 1900), vol. 8, pp. 557–558.

. . . the individual is caught in a great confused mix-up of all sorts of complicated circumstances, and . . . to let him alone is to leave him helpless as against the obstacles with which he has to contend; and . . . therefore, law in our day must come to the assistance of the individual.[19]

During most of the period, however, government offered little enough to the poor, even in the way of proper policing in slum areas. The poor responded by taking little interest in government.

The electorate, then, was composed largely of white, native-born, middle- and upper-class males, except in cities where large numbers of the poor were regularly shepherded to the polls to support the machine. After 1920 this situation, of course, changed rapidly and is still changing in our day.

What was the well-born male voting for, and how was the vote conducted? To exercise political power, a voter must have a meaningful choice among competitors for offices which possess real political authority. What then of the elective system?

The old frontier tradition of oral voting had disappeared by the 1850's and voting by ballot taken its place. However, in most places during the 1880's the ballots were printed by the parties rather than by the government; they were likely to be of different colors (deliberately), and since they were cast publicly, observers who were interested could see which party was being favored by the voter.[20] "A menacing leer from a fire company bravo secured many a vote." [21] While by this time there were regular ballot boxes, which protected against some of the more obvious forms of vote thievery, the general lack of efficient registration systems led to other abuses such as the floating voter or the nonexistent voter, and election laws were not strict enough to protect against such practices. Elections were thus marked by obvious intimidation and frequently by fraud.[22]

These systems were based on the assumption—still true in the rural areas and small towns—that almost everyone was known to everyone else and that the identity of the voter was therefore well established, making election fraud impossible. Intimidation was, on

[19] Speech in New Haven, Sept. 25, 1912, reprinted in Otis Pease (ed.), *The Progressive Years* (New York, 1962), p. 366.

[20] L. E. Fredman, *The Australian Ballot: The Story of an American Reform* (East Lansing, Mich., 1968), pp. 20–30.

[21] *Ibid.*, pp. 25–26.

[22] *Ibid.*, pp. 22–30.

the other hand, always present though usually shrugged off as being unimportant. In any case, the growth of large cities with their inflow and outflow of large numbers of people, many of them ignorant immigrants in dire need of money, made frontier assumptions untenable. By the eighties it was clear that reform was necessary. The parties were obviously the least likely places from which such reform would come, since they were the beneficiaries of the status quo.

Reform came, instead, from political leaders who were on the fringes of party politics: of these, Henry George, the Single-taxer and perennial candidate, was probably the most important, since he was a prolific writer with ready access to the national press and a vast audience. George publicly advocated the so-called Australian ballot as early as 1883 and fought for it with renewed vigor after a trip to Australia and a few losing campaigns. Such a ballot was first adopted for Louisville, Kentucky, in 1888.[23]

Probably the most influential early reform act was that of Massachusetts, adopted also in 1888. Massachusetts had a tradition of election reform: it had adopted the paper ballot to replace oral voting as early as 1647. (Maine in 1833 prescribed the paper and ink to be used for ballots, and New York adopted a voter registration law in 1859—both of which reforms spread slowly to the other states.)[24] The Australian ballot movement in Massachusetts was sponsored by Richard Dana III, a prominent Mugwump leader.[25] The most important features of the Australian ballot were that it was marked in secret and that there was a single ballot for all offices, printed by the state, so that observers could no longer see how the voter was voting. Various other protective devices, such as numbered ballots, were added later.

The Australian ballot caught on swiftly; ten states had adopted it within a year of Massachusetts. The movement was led by Single-taxers, Mugwumps, and Populists—who had the most to gain from its success; it was opposed by party machine politicians like David B. Hill of New York and Senator Arthur P. Gorman, the Maryland boss, for reasons equally obvious. Farm and labor organizations supported the movement, as did public-spirited citizens and newspapers generally.[26] By 1900 its use was general.

[23] *Ibid.,* pp. 31–34, 65.
[24] *Ibid.,* p. 23.
[25] *Ibid.,* pp. 36–37; on Dana, see Blodgett, *Gentle Reformers,* pp. 26, 113–116.
[26] Fredman, *Australian Ballot,* pp. 42–45.

Other election reforms had to wait for a further spurt of reformist energy, which was to be provided shortly by the Progressive movement. By 1908, "Corrupt Practices Acts"—which were largely directed toward campaign expenditures—had been adopted by twenty states.[27] They were, however, largely unenforceable. There was a determined drive, which nevertheless failed, for compulsory voting.[28] Woodrow Wilson and Richard S. Childs led another movement for a short ballot, the idea of which was to make fewer elective offices more visible and thus reduce the onerous chore of voting; it attempted to reduce the number of executive officers to be elected and thus contributed to the concurrent drive to concentrate executive powers in the hands of the governor, mayor, commission, or manager. Fairly successful at the municipal level, the short ballot movement enjoyed only limited success in the other units of local government and in the states.[29]

Another hallmark of the era was the increasing entrance of government into the regulation of the nominating process. Nominations, at all levels, in the 1880's were accomplished most often by conventions (which could be regarded as representative caucuses), or sometimes by private, party-run primaries. Primaries were, essentially, party "elections" which "elected" candidates to run in the general elections. Both methods were subject to extreme abuse in the hands of party bosses; the private primary, in addition, tended to break down because of the sheer intensity of feelings aroused: a report of an early Democratic primary in San Francisco (admittedly a rowdy town) pointed out that "knives were drawn and freely used, revolvers discharged with a perfect recklessness. . . . The police had they interfered would have stood a chance of being annihilated."[30]

The "direct primary" movement, then, was not the beginning of the direct primary: instead, it was the campaign to universalize the primary and put it under strict state control rather than leaving it entirely to the parties themselves. In the process its functions as party mechanisms were sometimes lost sight of; or, better, they often underwent a transformation. Progressives were determined to destroy the political machine even if they had to build up their own machines

---

[27] Ibid., p. 89.
[28] Ibid., pp. 89–90.
[29] Ibid., pp. 91–92.
[30] Quoted in ibid., p. 20.

with which to accomplish the work of destruction. In any case they tended strongly to believe in "the evils of party." The result was that the state-run primary sometimes (as in Wisconsin's "open" primary) tended to make it more difficult for parties to nominate candidates, rather than easier.

Actually, the first state primary laws were adopted as early as 1866 by California and New York: California's, while comprehensive, was optional with the parties; New York's, while mandatory, was not comprehensive—and in any case neither of them contemplated "anything like complete public control over party primaries."[31] Such laws gradually spread to other states, and their provisions were gradually extended to cover more abuses. Half the states (most of them in the North and West) had some kind of primary law by 1890; these were primarily aimed at the larger cities, where the evil appeared to be greatest.

In the nineties after the Australian ballot was adopted with its official recognition of parties on the ballot, there was a rapid spread of primary regulation: primaries were more often made subject to mandatory state control; primaries were gradually made more like general elections, using the same polling places, equipment, procedures, and officials; voter qualifications were established by law, thus taking the determination of party membership out of the hands of the parties themselves; states began to bear the expense which primaries involved; dates for primaries began to be fixed by the state, with all parties required to have theirs on the same day; in some states the law prescribed the election of party officials at the primary, as well as the selection of candidates; and some laws were adopted regulating conventions and caucuses. Probably the main feature of the direct primary laws, when fully developed, was the mandatory substitution of the primary for the convention as a nominating device, so that the older custom in some states of having a preprimary convention which chose who would go onto the primary ballot became illegal, as did the opposite customs of using a postprimary convention to select nominees already presented through the primary. This development came only after 1900, and some states have not adopted it even today.[32]

[31] Charles E. Merriam, *Primary Elections: A Study of the History and Tendencies of Primary Election Legislation* (Chicago, 1907), p. 12.
[32] *Ibid.*, pp. 123–124.

The best explanation of the sources of the remarkable change in our nominating system is that:

The direct primary method of nomination apparently constituted at bottom an escape from one-partyism. A major heritage of the Civil War in many states was a party system unable to implement the doctrine of popular government by presenting the electorate with genuine alternatives. The impact of the federal system—itself newly molded by the war—on the politics of the states . . . contributed to the unworkability of the party system. With the states of the South irrevocably tied to the Democratic party and with many of the states of the North and West almost equally attached to the Republican party, oligarchical control of party—of which the nominating convention became the symbol and often the reality— amounted to a denial of popular government. Unable to find expression through the channels offered by the party system, the impulses to political conflict in a society with a faith in popular government were bound, as social tensions built up, to break the hold of party oligarchies on the dominant party and to develop an intraparty politics.[33]

"The substitution in considerable degree of intraparty politics for interparty politics"—this is what the direct primary was all about, although it is also doubtless true that some progressives wished to rid the country of parties completely, the difficulty being that they could not think what to put in their place.

This means that in states where one party is dominant, voter interest tends to center in the primary of that party, rather than in the interparty general election, because the primary is where the real choice can be exercised. The primary of the dominant party is more likely to provide alternative policy choices.[34]

Although the primary system arose to save the nation from undoubted evils, like many reforms it brought its own evils in its train. The primary seems to have been a major influence in the disappearance of party organization in some areas, and of the decline of responsible party organization in others. This has been most true in one-party states; in other states in which party competition is close, the parties have been more able to maintain themselves as viable, policy-offering mechanisms. The problem is not how to restore the

[33] V. O. Key, Jr., *American State Politics: An Introduction* (New York, 1965), pp. 88–89.

[34] Julius Turner, "Primary Elections as the Alternative to Party Competition in 'Safe' Districts," *Journal of Politics*, 15 (1953), 197–210; Key, *State Politics*, pp. 104–118; V. O. Key, Jr., *Southern Politics in State and Nation* (New York, 1949).

old discredited convention system, but as Key remarks, how to contrive "circumstances and practices favorable to the development of leadership cliques adequate to the performance of party functions yet subject to popular control." [35] This is a problem that the Progressives hardly even recognized, let alone solved—nor have we today clearly made progress on it.

The direct primary also came to be used in federal elections—for nominating candidates for the House and Senate, for selecting delegates to the national conventions, and for expressing a state's preference as to presidential candidates. As regards presidential elections, however, the primary never made as much progress as in those elections which were confined to a state's boundaries. The reasons were obvious: it was difficult to construct a system which would even *work* nationwide, much less find a way to get each state to adopt it. For these reasons the national nominating convention continued without pronounced change. There is little reason to suppose that these conventions were even as representative then as they are today. Given the suffrage restrictions and the existence of bossism their representative character is, indeed, open to serious question.[36]

On the other hand, until about 1900 the presidency was an office much sought after but not very powerful. When Presidents were not leaders it made less difference who was nominated or how. With the rise of the modern presidency the question became much more important, but neither the Progressives nor their descendants have yet been able to improve on the convention system. And any system that seems conceivable would probably have the effect of further vitiating the party system.

One clear weakness of the convention system was its tendency to subordinate issues to candidates. This was partly a result of the lack of great issues characteristic of American politics in the era after the Civil War. Bryan, in 1896, ran both as a personality and on issues: despite his magnetism he was resoundingly beaten on the issues. But even after the rise of the modern presidency our strong candidates ran more on their personalities than on their policies. This was sometimes despite their own preferences: Wilson, certainly, made a serious attempt in 1912 to present the electors with a set of policy

[35] Key, *State Politics,* p. 131.
[36] See Joseph E. Kallenbach, *The American Chief Executive: The Presidency and the Governorship* (New York, 1966), pp. 142–145.

alternatives. The system was against him, however, and it is likely that Wilson the public figure won the election rather than Wilson the policy maker. It is doubtful that the 1912 Democratic convention even knew what it was getting when it nominated the governor of New Jersey, or cared very much. The delegates were interested in finding a candidate who could lead them out of the wilderness in which they had resided since 1896, and a certain blandness or a lack of definition of the policy positions favored by the candidate was, if anything, an aid to his nomination.[37]

On their part, the Republicans in 1912 would have liked to win with Roosevelt. But here policy considerations did play a part: the party leaders could not stomach "Teddy" in the White House. But even here, it seems likely that party considerations played a larger part than those of policy. Taft men had control of the convention machinery, and party leaders were more concerned with preserving their positions of leadership than they were in advancing or preventing particular policy alternatives.[38]

Clearly the American party system was better at presenting alternative candidates than it was at presenting alternative policies, and often even the candidates differed more in physique and personality than in principle.

Was a two-party system which de-emphasized issues virtue or vice? Controversy raged on this point then as it does now, and each campaign was likely to see its quota of third-party or independent candidates who were trying to buck the system by presenting alternatives. "Greenbackers," Populists, Progressives made their successive appearances on the American scene. They enjoyed limited electoral success except at the state level; but their policies were often adopted by one or another of the major parties, and many of these eventually found their way into law (it is true not as quickly as might have been desirable).[39] The major parties remained stubbornly nonideological—they were not "issue oriented." So long as the American society enjoyed a broad consensus of political and social values—as it did

[37] See Arthur S. Link, *Wilson: The Road to the White House* (Princeton, 1947), pp. 431–465.

[38] Arthur S. Link, *Woodrow Wilson and the Progressive Era, 1910–1917* (New York, 1954), pp. 13–15.

[39] Robert N. Chambers, "Party Development and the American Mainstream," in Chambers and Walter Dean Burnham, *The American Party Systems* (New York, 1967), p. 32.

throughout the period from 1877 to 1917—with only minorities existing outside this consensus, the system worked fairly well. It muted policy differences enough so that losers were willing to abide by the election results; at the same time it accomplished enough to keep the voters from being too dissatisfied with the results. In this imperfect world one can hardly ask for much more. Indeed, the worth of a constitutional system can be judged only in retrospect, and in that light the system up to 1917—with all its rather glaring defects—seems now to have been a striking success. Certainly there were many, at any time during the period, who did not think so, but even if the country did not adopt their prescriptions it seemed to thrive. Historically, any political system which survives without much use of violence has a great deal to be said for it, even though no one would claim that mere survival is enough. Beyond this, however, the system adapted itself to startling changes without violent resistance from those favoring the status quo. If this book has a theme, it is that the American Constitution in 1917 was very different from that of 1877; not the least of these changes came in electoral methods and politics. They were adopted with, perhaps, a maximum of verbal fuss but a minimum of intransigent resistance. A system with such adaptability has much to be said for it.

Two other electoral reforms remain to be mentioned: first, the development of the direct popular election of United States Senators, finally sanctified by the Seventeenth Amendment in 1913,[40] and second, the initiative and referendum, a favorite Progressive prescription for undercutting the power of the party machines and the bosses. The initiative submitted legislative proposals to the electorate (either state or local) as the result of a petition to put them on the ballot, or by reference from the legislature itself. Many states already permitted this for constitutional amendments, but not until the turn of the century was it applied to ordinary legislation.[41] The most commonly used form of it has been the school bond referendum, although the Progressives wanted to apply it on a statewide basis to all subjects of legislation. The movement for the initiative (through which the public may by petition get new proposals onto a referendum ballot) accompanied the referendum in most instances, although it was not

---

[40] See Chapter 2.
[41] Arthur N. Holcombe, *State Government in the United States* (New York, 1916), pp. 95–99, 132–135.

always adopted even in states which accepted the referendum idea.[42] Beginning with Oregon in 1902—another example of individual influence, since it was largely the result of a long campaign by William S. U'Ren, a blacksmith-turned-editor—the twin proposals had been adopted by twelve states ten years later, all of them west of the Mississippi. U'Ren perhaps deserves a larger place in the gallery of fascinating Progressive "characters" than he has so far been accorded. As leader of the direct legislation league he guided the movement for more than a decade; and at the height of his influence it was claimed that: "In Oregon the state government is divided into four departments—the executive, judicial, legislative and Mr. U'Ren. . . . To date, the indications are that Mr. U'Ren outweighs any one, and perhaps all three, of the other departments." [43]

The Oregon movement was sponsored by the direct legislation league and supported by an array of other groups, mainly the farm granges, trade unions, and the Populist party. But the drive attained such great momentum that the major parties endorsed it before its adoption. While it was to spread beyond the West in later years, direct legislation has always been more at home there.

Direct legislation was a further expression of the Progressive temper. It was widely felt that although the legislatures were untrustworthy, the people as a whole were not. As California's Governor Hiram Johnson said, "No man is better able to govern than all others; no man is better in government than any other man." [44] As part of a movement designed to destroy corrupt political machines and bosses, direct legislation was an admirable device; but like so many other Progressive reforms, it at the same time made life more difficult for clean politicians trying to govern through party government, and it opened the way (certainly in California) to a good deal of sheer demagogery.

The electoral reforms of the era from 1890 to 1917, like most human affairs, present a mixed picture. Actuated by the highest of motives, they yet had the total effect of making party government more difficult, of reducing the power of legislatures while at the same time expanding that of executives who, however, had to rely

[42] *Ibid.*, pp. 135–136.

[43] Portland *Oregonian*, July 17, 1906. For more on U'Ren see his article, "Initiative and Referendum in Oregon," *Arena*, 29 (1903), 270–275; and Lincoln Steffens in *The American Magazine*, 65 (1908), 527–540.

[44] George E. Mowry, *The California Progressives* (Berkeley, 1951), p. 149.

on popular appeal more than on party support. Political organizations could no longer be reliably held together; even California's powerful Progressive machine was split six ways from Sunday almost immediately after its fateful decision to leave the Republican party.[45] The electoral system encouraged such splits, and candidates more and more campaigned as individuals rather than as representatives of a party. To understand these developments, we must turn now to an analysis of the political party organizations of the period.

Historians until recently have portrayed the party battles of the late nineteenth and early twentieth centuries as uncomplicated battles of the bad guys against the good; the good were those politicians and parties, like the Progressives, who were supposedly fighting for the little man against the robber barons of industry. The little man included all farmers and all working men (but especially those who belonged to unions), while the barons included all businessmen, regardless of their particular interests. This is, in general, the picture drawn by such writers as Parrington and Josephson.[46]

This picture is overdrawn, but reinterpretation was hampered for some time by a lack of specific data. Historians and political scientists have only in the last decade begun to rummage among the voting statistics of the period; and what they have found presents anything but an uncomplicated picture. It appears, for instance, that very large numbers of urban workers voted for McKinley in 1896, and that the farm vote was far from united at any time.[47] The interpretation of the data presents great difficulties, and several different theories have been advanced. What appears certain, however, is that historians dominated by the progressive ethos tended unconsciously to slant their information, oversimplifying and thinking in terms of black and white rather than the grays more characteristic of human affairs. Parties, it now appears, were not all bad, even in the 1880's; and the Progressives, regardless of the purity of their motives, appear to have been Don Quixotes rather than Sir Galahads. They were often tilting at the wrong objectives.

[45] *Ibid.*, pp. 195–220.

[46] V. L. Parrington, *Main Currents in American Thought* (3 vols., New York, 1938). Matthew Josephson, *The Politicos, 1865–1896* (New York, 1938).

[47] See especially Samuel P. Hays, "Political Parties and the Community-Society Continuum," in Chambers and Burnham, *Party Systems,* p. 159.

The Progressives (at least in their leadership) were not farmers or workers but middle-class and professional businessmen.[48] This basic fact has not been controverted, although the theory that professionals such as lawyers and clergymen, and smaller independent businessmen as well, were revolting against the decline in their social status and political power resulting from the Industrial Revolution seems now to be only partially valid.[49] The mere fact that many members of the middle class were Progressives, however, requires a rethinking of older theories about the nature of the movement.

More recently it has been questioned whether the pre-1890 party system was as bad—as unrepresentative—as the liberal historians had thought. There has been an overconcentration on national politics to the practical exclusion of studies of state and local political movements. In fact the local parties were more highly representative than we have thought. But the parties were organized around local rather than national issues, so that their true character was misconceived by those looking primarily at the national level. Party alignments actually developed around a broad division between "evangelical Protestantism," which stood for prohibition, nativism, and antislavery, and an opposition composed of the Democrats—largely Catholics, German Lutherans, and non-evangelical Protestants. The "evangelicals" were heavily rural, while the Democrats were heavily urban.[50]

The 1896 election resulted in a complete realignment of this old grouping, since Bryan appealed to the very groups which had previously been strongly Republican, while he tended to drive urban workers out of the party because of the evangelical tone of his appeal.[51]

At the local level, a study of Pittsburgh before the 1890's has found that the party system paralleled very closely the actual social structure of the city, or more accurately, that wards tended to be microcosmic one-party districts. City councilmen were elected by wards, and

[48] Richard Hofstadter, *The Age of Reform* (New York, 1955).
[49] Andrew M. Scott, "The Progressive Era in Perspective," *Journal of Politics*, 21 (1959), 685–701; J. Joseph Huthmacher, "Urban Liberalism and the Age of Reform," *Mississippi Valley Historical Review*, XLIX (1962), 231–241.
[50] Hays in Chambers and Burnham, *Party Systems*, p. 158.
[51] *Ibid.*, p. 159.

Working class wards most frequently elected workingmen, labor leaders, or men who provided the focal point of community contacts, such as saloonkeepers or grocers. Middle class wards elected small businessmen such as grocers, druggists, undertakers, community real estate dealers, bankers, and contractors. Upper class wards elected central city bankers, lawyers, doctors, manufacturers.[52]

The rise of common-interest pressure groups (that is, groups representing broadly based interests regardless of geographical location) in the late nineteenth century—groups which transcended the local community in their efforts to secure favorable treatment—forced parties to deal with decision making at a higher level, a development which helped to destroy the vitality of local parties. Widespread alienation and loss of involvement resulted especially at the local level, as indicated by a drastic drop in voter turnout.[53] The Progressives thus attacked the party system not from the bottom but from the top. In cities this often (not always) meant a shift to at-large election of councilmen and to nonpartisan elections, which prevented the type of direct community representation which had existed earlier.

The reformer's model was the business corporation, not the political party. The political party was too open to a variety of compromising and debilitating influences. It had to respond to the multitude of impulses arising from the community electorate; it had to compromise in making legislative decisions to secure majority support; it had to reward friends and defeat enemies on a party basis. . . . [I]ncreasingly through the years those involved in cosmopolitan life sought to divorce decisions from the electorate, in order to enhance the efficiency and system which they felt would implement their goals.[54]

The attempt and the result were "the insulation of industrial elites from the threat of effective, popularly based 'counterrevolution.' " [55]

These developments came about concurrently with a widespread decline in party competition throughout the country. Part of this had already happened in the South as a result of the Civil War and Reconstruction; but in the 1890's it also occurred in many areas

[52] *Ibid.*, pp. 164–165.
[53] *Ibid.*, pp. 173–176.
[54] *Ibid.*, p. 177.
[55] Walter Dean Burnham, "Party Systems and the Political Process," in Chambers and Burnham, *Party Systems*, p. 284.

which had through the seventies and eighties been closely balanced. Three subsystems resulted: the solidly Democratic South, the Republican Northeast, and a quasi-colonial West "from which protesting political movements were repeatedly launched against the dominant components of the system." [56] The primary election came about at least partly in an attempt to restore within one party the competition which had previously existed between the two. The decline in party attachments and of political enthusiasm which accompanied these movements was marked. While we think of Progressivism as appealing to the masses and tapping a great ground swell of popular fervor, voting statistics show the opposite: the hard-fought (even if seemingly issueless) campaigns of 1876, 1888, and 1892 brought out almost 80 per cent of the voters—a figure fully comparable to European elections; in the period 1900 to 1916 this figure dropped to less than 65 per cent, and it has never since reached the earlier figure. While the decline was sharpest (for reasons we have surveyed earlier) in the South, it took place all over the country.[57]

It seems, in other words, that the Progressive attempt to convert American politics into an "issue" politics, while partially successful, achieved its success at the price of alienating a large portion of the electorate. This apparently was because the issues thus posed were "cosmopolitan" in nature rather than "community-oriented"; and since they did not touch many voters directly, these voters lost interest. At the same time structural changes in urban government progressively cut down the power of the bosses either to provide the kinds of services their lower-class supporters were interested in, or to marshal these supporters at election time. This, also, was achieved at a price which we are only now beginning to understand. For it meant that urban government in most places became middle-class government, and the interests, desires, and needs of the lower classes went unperceived and largely ignored. The country is now, perhaps, beginning to reap the fruit of seven decades of "efficient" city government.

Revisionism, in its attempt to compensate for the extremes to which earlier historians have gone, is likely to go to the opposite

---

[56] *Ibid.*, p. 300.

[57] Walter Dean Burnham, "The Changing Shape of the American Political Universe," *American Political Science Review*, LIX (1965), 7–28.

extreme. It is therefore probable that the present revisionists will in their turn need to be revised. Yet there seems to be much that is valid in the foregoing analysis. Progressivism cannot thus be seen as "democratic" in any simplistic, uncomplicated sense; nor can the party machinery of the pre-Progressive era any longer be condemned out of hand.

From the standpoint of a constitutional history, it can easily be seen that (regardless of one's conclusions as to the rights and wrongs of the matter) there were profound changes in the party system between 1877 and 1917; the "benchmark" for the change is the elections of 1894 and 1896, though it might be more valid to regard it as a gradual response to the forces of industrialization and urbanization which extended over the entire period. One can see in the change a response to the nationalization of the economy: a corresponding nationalization of political issues and of party organization and emphasis; yet while losing party strength at the local levels, we did not really succeed in building strong national parties. Pressure groups have increasingly come to fill the vacuum, and the extent to which modern American government has become merely a broker between interests to the detriment of the public interest has long been noted (if, indeed, there is a public interest which is more than the resultant of countervailing pressures).[58]

Of course, despite these changes, the outward contours of the party system remained the same. Ours was basically—despite the alarums and excursions of frequent third-party movements—a two-party system. The typical unwillingness of our parties, in their attempt to secure the allegiance of enough voters to win elections, to deal with issues gave rise to several rather important third parties. The Greenback party dragged on into the 1880's; the Mugwumps of the eighties were Republicans who became Democrats rather than forming a new party; and the Populists and Progressives have already been mentioned. Third parties have often been successful locally. On the national level they have sometimes been spectacular but hardly successful. Yet since the locus of American parties has been local, it was important to party leaders to be able to maintain a local base from which to make their forays into national politics, and a third party successful in Iowa would mean the cutting off of this local

[58] See especially David B. Truman, *The Governmental Process* (New York, 1951).

base for the "regulars" of that state. For this reason the major parties have to react to third-party movements.

Did third parties succeed by having their issues taken up by one of the great national parties? Not uniformly; or perhaps it merely needs to be said that not all third parties were successful, even in this restricted sense. Nor was it necessarily true that the major party which took up the issues would itself profit by their use. The Democratic platform of 1896 consisted of wholesale borrowings from Populist principles, the only immediate result of which was a stinging electoral defeat from which the Democrats were not to recover for sixteen years. It seems from the history of the period—at least until 1900—that there were only two major issues which the parties were willing to face: the tariff and free silver. Even these resulted in tearing the parties apart when either of them insisted on taking an unambiguous platform stance.[59]

The moral of all this is that until the turn of the century the American people were more concerned with local issues than with national. It was not yet clear that economic developments would make state or local action insufficient to meet popular needs, and people had not yet accustomed themselves to look to Washington for help. The result, for parties, was that they were loose, shifting coalitions of local leaders who used their national positions only as far as their local needs permitted. Men like Conkling were interested in maintaining their machines at home more than they were in policy making in Washington, and their attitudes in the latter were usually dictated by the necessities of the former.

The drift toward Washington was, of course, obvious by "Teddy" Roosevelt's time, and parties under the stimulus of Progressivism did become somewhat more issue oriented. Even so, their genius was to mute issues rather than to confront them, and thus to delay their solution until something like a consensus was reached. If this meant that problems were not handled as soon as they might have been, it also meant that the solutions were acceptable to most people by the time they were achieved. The willingness of both parties to accept the inevitable—but usually not until it seemed actually to be inevitable—probably accounted for their ability to ride out the various third-party movements. It also may account for the lack of revolu-

[59] The various articles in Chambers and Burnham, *Party Systems*, document this point in detail.

15—14—13.—THE GREAT PRESIDENTIAL PUZZLE.

1. Senator Roscoe Conkling, the New York boss, was known as a Republican "king-maker" in the 1880's.

(Wales in *Puck*, March 17, 1880)

2. (*Above*) President Arthur as Hamlet—"I say, away! Go on, I'll follow thee!"

(Gillam in *Puck*, December 28, 1881)

3. Boss Croker as Hamlet (to Ghost Tweed) —"I'll follow thee!"

(F. Opper in *Puck*, April 11, 1894)

HANNALET, PRINCE OF $MARK, IN THE MODERN GRAVEYARD SCENE.

4. Republican boss Mark Hanna as Hamlet

(Davenport in *New York Journal & Advertiser*, July 6, 1899)

The Hamlet-like qualities of American political leaders were oft remarked, if not always admired.

5. President Roosevelt as Hamlet—"Thus the tariff does make cowards of us all."

(Keppler in *Puck*, October 30, 1907)

6. "The Raven." Keppler thought the first Harrison's hat too big for the second Harrison.

(Keppler in *Puck*, August 13, 1890)

7. "Where is he?" By the 1892 election Harrison had disappeared in the hat.

(Keppler in *Puck*, November 16, 1892)

THE PRESIDENTIAL HOLIDAY

8. "The Presidential Holiday: He arrives in 'San Antone' to attend a reunion of the Rough Riders."

(McCutcheon in Chicago *Daily Tribune*, April 6, 1905)

Presidents who were not great leaders were not much admired, but neither were great ones safe from ridicule.

DANGER!

TOUCH ME NOT, I'M A LADY!

9. The dominant male saw militant suffragettes as "holier than thou" at times, but nevertheless acceded to the adoption of the Nineteenth Amendment.

(Mayer in New York *Times*, December 18, 1912)

10. Even leadership from the representative legislature was looked upon with suspicion: Speaker Thomas B. Reed was accused of usurping power.

(Coffin in Washington *Post*, November 14, 1894)

T. B. R.

THE CZAR IS DEAD. LONG LIVE THE CZAR.

"THE UPRIGHT BENCH," WHICH IS ABOVE CRITICISM.

11. " 'The Upright Bench,' which is above criticism." The courts were not immune to corruption.

(Nast in *Harper's Weekly*, September 11, 1875)

12. "Our overworked Supreme Court." Nor was the Supreme Court immune to criticism.

(Keppler in *Puck*, April, 1885. The Bettmann Archive)

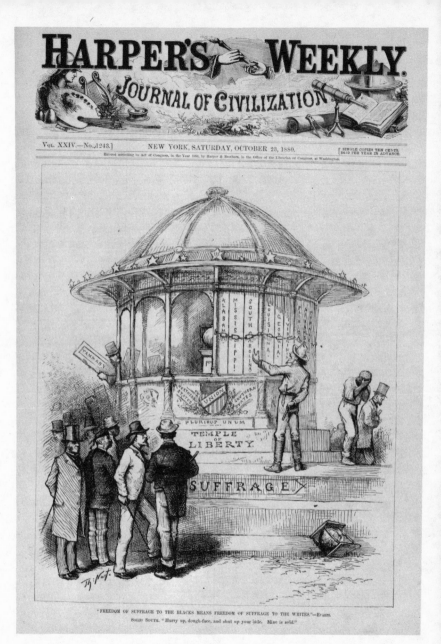

"FREEDOM OF SUFFRAGE TO THE BLACKS MEANS FREEDOM OF SUFFRAGE TO THE WHITES."—Evarts.

SOLID SOUTH. "Hurry up, dough-face, and shut up your side. Mine is solid."

13. Not everyone was in favor of the extension of the suffrage to Negroes.

(Nast in *Harper's Weekly*, October 23, 1880)

WHAT THE POSITION OF A PRESIDENT OF THE UNITED STATES REALLY IS.

14. "What the position of a President of the United States really is." Presidents before 1900 were not widely regarded as strong leaders.

(Nast in *Harper's Weekly*, July 18, 1885)

15. Thomas M. Cooley

16. Louis D. Brandeis

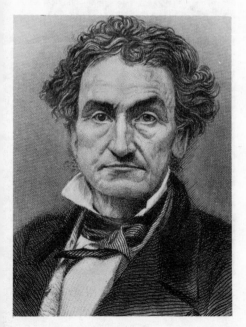

17. Rufus W. Choate

*Three lawyers
who helped shape
the law of
the Constitution*

18. "Fighting Bob" LaFollette of Wisconsin

19. Hiram Johnson of California

Leaders of Progressivism at the State Level

20. Charles Evans Hughes of New York

21. "Golden Rule" Jones of Toledo
(Culver Pictures)

22. Tom L. Johnson of Cleveland
(Culver Pictures)

Leaders of
Urban Political
Reform Movements

23. Joseph W. Folk of St. Louis

24. Charles Doe, New Hampshire Supreme Court

(Harvard University Press)

25. Samuel F. Miller, U.S. Supreme Court

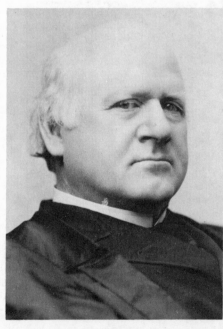

28. Stephen J. Field, California Supreme Court and U.S. Supreme Court

29. John Marshall Harlan, U.S. Supreme Court

26. Roujet D. Marshall, Wisconsin Supreme Court

(State Historical Society of Wisconsin)

27. William Howard Taft, U.S. Circuit Court, 1892-1900

(Cincinnati Historical Society)

SEVEN

GREAT

JUDGES

30. Oliver Wendell Holmes, Jr., Massachusetts Supreme Court and U.S. Supreme Court

31. Richard Croker of New York

32. Abe Ruef of San Francisco
(San Francisco *Examiner*)

33. Edwin H. Vare of Philadelphia
(*The Evening Bulletin*, Philadelphia)

THREE

GREAT

CITY

BOSSES

tions or counterrevolutions, and for the lack of ideologically oriented parties which would have led to a European type of politics in which the parties indeed faced issues, but in which there were as a result so many parties that the adoption of policy was no easier, and in which the parties served as bases for revolutionary coups. Under Roosevelt and Wilson the parties became clusters of interests which were broadly different from each other, but which still contained within themselves so many points of view that most of the American people could find homes within one or the other and accept the election results with some grace. Kipling's witty assessment was both perceptive and exaggerated:

> Now this mass of persons who vote is divided into two parties—Republican and Democrat. They are both agreed in thinking that the other part is running creation (which is America) into red flame. Also the Democrat as a party drinks more than the Republican, and when drunk may be heard to talk about a thing called the Tariff, which he does not understand, but which he conceives to be the bulwark of the country or else the surest power for its destruction. Sometimes he says one thing and sometimes another, in order to contradict the Republican, who is always contradicting himself. And this is a true and lucid account of the forepart of American politics. The behind-part is otherwise.[60]

Suprisingly little is known with any certainty regarding the role and power of pressure groups during the period under review. Few scholars paid much attention to them until recently.[61] There was, of course, a mountain of polemical literature inveighing against "the interests," or "special interests." Such literature was usually a self-serving plea for the public to favor one interest rather than another. Since this literature came typically to identify the "interests" with big business and finance, it tended to obscure the fact that the writer at the same time represented the "interests" of others, such as farmers or laborers. Such groups, in any realistic view, also constituted interest organizations, although they were not always as powerful or as well organized as the business groups.

Pressure groups are of constitutional importance only to the extent that they are powerful enough to influence the making of govern-

[60] Rudyard Kipling, *From Sea to Sea: Letters of Travel* (Garden City, 1915), p. 457.
[61] Arthur F. Bentley, *The Process of Government* (Chicago, 1908).

mental policies. It is, however, almost axiomatic that in any heterogeneous society, with almost any form of government, some groups will exist which will try to press their interests through the most accessible political channels. To some extent, therefore, the interesting question about them is whether they in effect constitute a system of "countervailing" pressures which because of their balance tend to offset each other so that policy does not reflect the desires of any single group, but rather comes as a result of compromise. American government is unique, perhaps, only in the number of points of access which pressure groups have: each level of government and each branch of any single government constitutes such a point of access, as do the party organizations.

There is no convincing reason to suppose that pressure groups have not always existed on the American scene, even though they are sometimes regarded as a twentieth-century phenomenon. James Madison was perfectly familiar with their existence, although he called them "factions" instead of using modern terminology.[62] If there was any change it lay more in the fact that in a largely agrarian society there were fewer pressure groups and that many of those which did exist tended to be difficult to identify because they were so closely identified with the dominant segments of society. Nevertheless, from 1816 to 1836 the Bank of the United States and its stockholders constituted very readily identifiable pressure groups, as did the canal entrepreneurs.

As America grew more complex with the growth of industry and large cities, the number of such groups would be expected to increase markedly, as apparently it did. Also, it would be expected that the business groups would be more powerful, as apparently they were: the literature against them demonstrates their increase both in number and in power. And this growth, in turn, forced the older groups (the farmers, merchants, and professional people) and newer ones in opposition to business interests (such as labor) to organize in self-defense, or at least to increase the efficiency of their already existing organizations. The growth in number, scope, and level of organization of pressure groups was a major fact of the politics of the closing years of the nineteenth century. Some of the accompanying effects have already been mentioned: pressure groups more and more, for instance, tended to exist outside, and independent of, the

[62] James Madison, *Federalist No. 10*.

major parties, and thus to make it even more difficult for the party organizations to maintain an intelligent concern with policy issues, especially at the local level. This seems to have been a factor in the attrition of local interest and participation in politics which was so marked a feature of the new century.

Mr. Dooley commented on some of these tendencies:

What do I think iv it all? Ah, sure I don't know. I belong to th' onforchnit middle class. I wurruk hard, an' I have no money. They come in here undher me hospital roof, an' I furnish thim with cards, checks, an' refrishmints. "Let's play without a limit," says labor. "It's Dooley's money." "Go as far as ye like with Dooley's money," says Capital. "What have ye got?" "I've got a straight to Roosevelt," says Labor, "I've got ye beat," says Capital. "I've got a Supreme Court full of injunctions." Manetime I've pawned me watch to pay f'r th' game, an' I have to go to th' joolry-store on th' corner to buy a pound iv beef or a scuttle iv coal. No wan iver sthrikes in sympathy with me.[63]

Dooley knew that the Supreme Court, too, was a part of "pressure politics." Access to the Court, it is true, was not based on lobbying or an elaborate set of legislative-type hearings; it was instead founded on lawyers' briefs presented in a carefully chosen case—and, to a certain extent, on a knowledge of the economic and political prepossessions of the judges. Mr. Justice Field once came close to sounding like an echo of Mr. Dooley: in the Income Tax case, concurring, he charged that "the present assault upon capital is but the beginning. It will be the stepping-stone to others, larger and more sweeping, till our political contests will become a war of the poor against the rich; a war constantly growing in intensity and bitterness." [64] One-sided as Field's opinion was, it did reveal an awareness of the extent to which the litigants in cases before the Court were the representatives of the great interests. The Court could not decide cases without taking sides, any more than Congress could pass a law without doing so.

Pressure groups were, if anything, more powerful on the state and local level than they were on the national. For one thing, this was where the stakes were most immediate, especially in the years before 1900. Here the municipal franchises were awarded (bought and sold, some might say), and here were concentrated most of the existing regulatory statutes and agencies. Not only that, but the number of

[63] Quoted in Pease, *Progressive Years*, p. 249.
[64] Pollock *v.* Farmers' Loan and Trust Co., 157 U.S. 429, 607 (1895).

effective countervailing groups was fewer: a utilities magnate could control a city, and Southern Pacific or Anaconda could control a state; one writer said that Standard Oil had done "everything to the Pennsylvania legislature except refine it." A George Pullman, indeed, could construct and control his own city.

If one may generalize on a subject so little known, the typical pressure politician before the nineties was the railroad entrepreneur; afterward, the Wall Street financier and the steel or oil magnate. Perhaps the greatest change was that these men came to work through elaborate organizations which, like the American Iron and Steel Institute, printed and distributed large numbers of political tracts in an effort to influence public opinion on the tariff.[65] They might still go off to Washington or to the state capital to lobby personally on occasion; but they had broadened the scope of their interests and their activities. In the 1870's a railroad man would be lobbying primarily in the interest of his own railroad—to obtain a land grant, to forestall state regulation, or to prevent competition from other railroads. By the nineties whole industries had combined to exert pressure for things which the companies had in common.

It is very difficult to estimate the actual influence of particular groups on political decisions. There has been a tendency to assume that the strongest groups always won: but there is no convincing evidence that this was the case. In addition, it is often thought that individual political leadership played almost no part: its only function was to respond to group pressures. This also was unprovable, and seems in retrospect to be wrong. Finally, it seems not to be true that groups always acted only in their own self-interest, and that this interest was in the main economic in nature and rather easily discovered. We are more sophisticated today—it is not all that easy to find the self-interest of the League of Women Voters, nor is it at all certain that economics plays the predominant role we once thought it did.[66]

Nevertheless, interest groups played, then as now, an extremely significant role. Perhaps a major error was an assumption that government agencies do not have group interests of their own, or feelings of their own. Regarding government as an automatic and accurate mechanism, one could see it as responding only to the interests of

[65] S. Walter Poulshock, *The Two Parties and the Tariff in the 1880's* (Syracuse, 1965), p. 177.
[66] Bentley, *Process of Government.*

the groups which at the time were strongest. But our more sophisticated approach is in essence an extension of this theory rather than a denial of it.

If we knew enough, it would be important at this point to go into a sophisticated investigation of just where groups operated in the total system with maximal effect. Did they influence party platforms or the nominating process? Did they attempt to influence the course of legislation? Did they try to control the administration of laws already passed, or the interpretation of such laws by the courts? If they were like present-day groups—I assume that they were—they did all of these and more. But beyond such general statements it is difficult to go. That they formed a channel for the expression of desires, to which governments responded or failed to respond, is certain; and in this sense they played a constitutional role, even though their existence is not acknowledged in any strictly constitutional document. The closest to formal constitutional standing they have come, lies in the string of lobbying regulatory statutes passed by the state legislatures and by Congress. These were for the most part enacted after 1917 and thus fall outside our purview.

It only remains to deal briefly with the question of representation and apportionment. This is complex largely because (as in other areas) of the federal system, the existence of which means that there are multiple sets of representational systems rather than one, and that these systems need not be similar. Despite these facts, American concepts of proper representation have always basically revolved around the principle that equal citizens should have equal votes, so that people—always as organized in geographical districts—were the unit of representation. This was more true in the states west of the Appalachians than in the older states of the East, which long retained the idea that at least one house ought to be organized on a different representational principle, such as property ownership.[67]

As long as the country remained primarily agricultural the strict population principle worked well; although there were frequent squabbles between large and small counties, their basic identity of interest kept these within bounds. The change in the system came when some rural counties began actually to decline in population

[67] American concepts of representation are surveyed in Alfred de Grazia, *Apportionment and Representative Government* (New York, 1963), and Robert G. Dixon, *Democratic Representation: Reapportionment in Law and Politics* (New York, 1968).

while more counties began to contain urban centers.[68] At this time the rural-dominated legislatures began to enact new constitutional provisions which provided for the equality of counties regardless of population, or with only minimal attention to it. This was a common feature of new constitutions adopted in the 1890's and thereafter; by 1910 "the progressive disfranchisement of the urban voter" was well under way, illustrating the maxim that those who have power will normally try to keep it. In 1910 only a few cities—Boston, Milwaukee, New Orleans, Indianapolis—were equally represented by population in their state legislatures; cities like Birmingham, Atlanta, and Baltimore were the worst off.[69]

This situation was often justified by reference to a Jeffersonian distrust of city dwellers; more often it was not justified at all. Some states, like Tennessee, merely stopped reapportionment of legislative districts decennially, so that the situation became progressively worse as the cities grew and rural areas further declined in population.[70] The result was that the legislatures were less and less able to deal with the real problems of the cities and that there was consequent growing disenchantment with the state governments on the part of those who dwelt in urban areas.

At the same time, the urban Progressives were centering their attention on the reform of city governments, and as already seen, this resulted in many places in the substitution of at-large city council elections for the old ward representation. This slowly killed the party machines; it also killed the wellsprings of community interest in local politics and to a marked extent left large urban groups unrepresented in their own city governments.[71]

State legislatures also apportioned congressional districts. It was natural, then, that the House of Representatives also became a malapportioned body which overrepresented the rural areas at the expense of the cities. Since the Senate had been frozen into the "state equality" mold, the situation was often no better there.

---

[68] William J. D. Boyd, *Changing Patterns of Apportionment* (New York, 1965), p. 5; Royce Hanson, *The Political Thicket: Reapportionment and Constitutional Democracy* (Englewood Cliffs, N.J., 1966), p. 14.

[69] Paul T. David and Ralph Eisenberg, *Devaluation of the Urban and Suburban Vote* (Charlottesville, Va., 1961), pp. 9–15.

[70] See the survey of the history of Tennessee redistricting in the opinions in Baker *v.* Carr, 368 U.S. 804 (1962).

[71] Hays in Chambers and Burnham, *Party Systems.*

The underrepresentation of the urban dweller—especially of the working class—in American legislative bodies was thus an endemic feature of American representation by 1917. There seems no doubt that this was a contributing factor in the decline of voting turnout, and as little doubt that it contributed to the continuing decline in the power and prestige of legislative bodies themselves. Perceptive observers noted this quite early. And the decline played into the hands of the movement toward "executive aggrandizement" at all levels of government to which we have previously called attention. Discouraged with their legislatures, people began to regard their mayor, governor, or President as being a more effective representative of their needs, and the executives were not slow to play upon this feeling. Thus could one writer say, in 1925, that

it is assumed quite frankly that the representative assembly is insufficient in itself to reflect the opinion of the nation, which demands that the issues shall be defined by someone in a position to act upon an enlarged view of things. At the same time there has been no movement toward making the President responsible to Congress. This fact is certainly a mute witness of the extraordinary degradation of legislative authority in the United States.[72]

He was talking about the national government, but his words were equally applicable to the states and municipalities. They were less so to those cities which had adopted the manager system, for there the manager was made responsible to the council: but the simultaneous shift to at-large elections meant that in practice he was responsible to an unrepresentative council, so that he could not always take the "enlarged view" that Carpenter saw as the peculiar advantage of the plebiscitary executive.

As we have seen earlier—and the causes are more complex than the failure of representative bodies to reapportion adequately—the bodies which we *call* representative were less and less successful in performing that function, and the executives became more and more regarded as representative in their own right, and as representative, in many cases, of quite different segments of the population than the legislatures. While, as Andrew Jackson felt, our executives have always had something of this quality, the various defects of the legislative systems played into their hands.

[72] William Seal Carpenter, *Democracy and Representation* (Princeton, 1925), p. 70.

CHAPTER 5

The Supreme Court and National Business Regulation

O NE of the distinguishing characteristics of Western constitutional systems, in those countries which have written constitutions, is the formalization of the idea of limited government. This
usually consists of a set of more or less specific statements of
individual or societal rights which are in theory supposed to be protected against encroachment by government. After the American
states, the United States first worked out such a formal "Bill of
Rights"; and it also first developed a means by which the rights
could be enforced (within limits). This means is usually called "judicial review," and it consists of allowing the regular courts to
adjudicate constitutional issues. We have already surveyed at appropriate places the ways in which judicial review, during the period
1877–1917, functioned in relation to the separation of powers and the
federal system, although constitutional compartments are not neat
enough to keep these entirely separate from the concerns of the next
few chapters. But mainly we shall now be concerned with the ways
in which, in this era, American courts did—or did not—enforce
the limitations specified in our bills of rights. Along the way, we
shall have to investigate also the development of constitutional doctrines about these rights, and the reasons why governments might
wish to infringe constitutionally granted rights.

To say that such activities made American courts uniquely agents of government—policy makers—other than merely in the ways in which ordinary civil and criminal courts are is perhaps to belabor the obvious. Nevertheless, there has been and still is enough misunderstanding of this point so that some explication of it seems necessary.

Lawyers will not generally waste their client's time and money pressing cases which cannot be won. For this reason it must be assumed that most constitutional issues arising to the courts involve genuine questions of interpretation: that is, they concern clauses of the Constitution about which there can reasonably be more than one meaning, and the function of the case is to decide which of the possible meanings is the "correct" one. Since there may be several reasonable meanings, the determination of the correct one is essentially an act of political authority rather than of legal discovery. To put this in another way, judges are forced to decide which interpretation is the *most* reasonable: a process fraught not only with the possibility of error but with the probability that individual preconceptions will (at least partially) shape conclusions. Justice Stephen J. Field, for instance, approached cases with a bias in favor of laissez-faire, and thus that side of any case could count him on its side unless the other side succeeded in overcoming the bias. This somewhat oversimplified attitude was shared by many other judges to a lesser extent. But of course one should keep in mind that a judge's preconceptions were not necessarily economic in nature: Justice Holmes had a bias in favor of judicial self-restraint; he believed that courts should not overturn legislative acts unless those acts were obviously unreasonable or arbitrary. Justice John M. Harlan tended to approach federal system cases with a bias in favor of the national government. We have already mentioned the differing views of judges Cooley and Dillon about the constitutional status of municipal governments; these differences did not result from the fact that they lived in states with different constitutions, but from different philosophical presumptions about the "proper" relationship of local government to the states.

Then, too, the process of interpretation described above allows the development of new constitutional theories which when first presented may not be popular (or even seem very reasonable) but which over a period of years may capture a majority of the judges. Thus they are engaged in a "creative" function—the invention of new doctrine to meet the felt necessities of new times and new circumstances.

The development of "substantive due process," which we shall examine in this chapter, is perhaps the best illustration of this in our constitutional history.

Clearly, even judges have a fairly wide degree of discretion, particularly when deciding constitutional cases. Since constitutional litigation involves questions of public interest—often the same questions which have already been considered in the "political" arena—in deciding them courts perform a political as well as a legal function. All courts performing their normal functions of enforcing law and helping to maintain order are of course agencies of government; but to an extent equaled by the courts of no other country our constitutional courts are in addition part of the policy-making machinery.

From 1877 to 1917 the courts were largely (though never exclusively) occupied with defining the proper constitutional role of government in the regulation of the economy. A great deal of judicial creativity went into the development of doctrines which could either justify or limit this role. This will not be surprising to anyone familiar with the profound revolution in the American economy—from agrarianism to industrialism; small local to large national and specialized to integrated industry; simple business organization to the modern corporation; rural to urban patterns of settlement; individual ownership to wage-earning status; handicraft to machine technology; and from simple and slow methods of communication and transportation to rapid and complex ones. These changes began long before 1877, but not until the 1870's did even intelligent Americans fully realize their extent and rapidity.

Periods of great social change bring about correspondingly great stresses on the national fabric. As the changes—or at least their causes—were economic, the strains were also economic, and the public response to them was a demand for government regulation which would in some ways control, not the pace of change, but its damaging consequences. Employees, professional men, farmers, and other groups disadvantaged by change had vested interests in its control; while the great and small entrepreneurs and financiers had just as much interest in maintaining their freedom to earn the profits upon which they believed the whole economic transformation depended. There was thus great incentive for one side or the other to demand protection or regulation from government. When either group failed in its attempts to block legislation, there was a strong tendency—a natural result of the existence of judicial review—to turn to the courts in the hope that judges would reverse the legislative verdict.

It does not do, in this latter day, to take a simplistic view of the judges or the way the courts handled the resulting cases. We are far enough, now, from the events to see them clearly. What emerges is what might be expected of a human institution: a fumbling and vacillating response which in the long run was astonishingly but accidentally successful in allowing both for increasing governmental regulation of the worst aspects of the Industrial Revolution and for the maintenance of the system (sometimes loosely called "free enterprise") which was creating the revolution. We tend to read back into the events of the day a sense of purposefulness which does not really seem to have been there. Judicial response was not all of a piece; and what emerges, finally, is a sort of pragmatism which consorts very well with the *ad hoc* nature of the case system used by American courts. Judges were forced by the nature of the case system to decide discrete issues which arose fortuitously or haphazardly. It is true that many judges almost instinctively supported the free use of private property—a tendency frequently overcome by the arguments for regulation or for the constitutionality of legislative action under our particular constitutions. Certainly there was no plan or conspiracy with big business.

Judicial action was a patchwork of often conflicting decisions reflecting differing views about what could or should be done to solve what were novel and difficult problems in the art of statecraft. The American temperament was to face such problems with no set of ideological principles, and in any case there was no ideology ready to hand other than the vague liberalism which pervades American institutions. Other ideologies were known, of course, but they were alien and extreme, and the American was optimistic enough to think that the problems did not demand such drastic action as their importation.

Attempts to limit the reach of congressional action were centered on the commerce power, and the cases involving this power show as well as any others the ambivalence with which judges approached the problems of the day. Article I, Section 8, of the Constitution gives Congress power "to regulate commerce . . . among the several states." Although they did not have enough foresight to see all of the implications of what they did, the framers seem to have thought this power had been stated clearly, so as to give Congress an unambiguous and plenary power. The mode in which the power was given, however, made it possible for courts, given the motivation, to use the clause as a limitation as well as a grant. Thus, for instance, one could define "regulate" in such a way as to exclude certain kinds of action, and the same approach could be taken to "commerce" or "among" the several states. Since Congress did not do very much commercial regulation, and since most of what it did was along traditional and familiar lines, these implications were not very important early in our history.

It was only after the Civil War that significant segments of American society began to press for effective regulatory measures that could be conceived as hostile rather than friendly to business interests. Earlier governmental action (usually not taken under the commerce clause) had included such notable actions as the creation of the Bank of the United States, protective tariffs, and federal and state grants to canal and railroad companies—measures intended to foster and protect infant industries or to facilitate trade on a nationwide basis. But increasingly after the Civil War farmers and shippers wanted protection against "unfair" railroad rates; laborers against unfair employers; consumers against sharp selling practices, fraudulent claims, mislabeling, or deleterious ingredients; various public groups against the spoliation of our natural resources or the increasing power of "monopoly." Meeting such demands meant limiting the freedom of businessmen to run their businesses as they thought proper—or, put differently, to maximize their profits. In each of these areas there was by 1917 significant federal legislation (added to the already existing state statutes): the Interstate Commerce Act (1887), the Sherman Anti-Trust Act (1890), the Pure Food and Drug Act (1906), the Employers' Liability Act (1906), the Federal Reserve Act (1913), the Federal Trade Commission Act (1914), the various laws extending these, and numerous other somewhat less significant measures. In view of the prevailing conservatism with which historians have accused the courts of approaching such laws, it is interesting to note that none of the above laws was found to be finally or unambiguously unconstitutional. While many of the judges did not like them, and in some cases found ways of limiting their application, the laws stood, and their application could be broadened in later years. A brief look at some of the more important cases will demonstate this fact.

When courts did limit the activity of the national government under the commerce clause they were by implication saying that (unless some other constitutional bar could be found) the same activities *could* be carried on by the states, since the states retained all powers not granted to the national government in the Constitution. On the other hand, under the Cooley rule of 1851 the states themselves were limited to the exercise of powers over interstate commerce which did not (in the Court's opinion) require national regulation and in which Congress had not regulated.[1] Thus in cases involving congressional action the Court asked essentially one question: Did the law or its particular application concern interstate commerce? If not, the national government had no power. In cases coming from states, however, the situation was more complicated. The Court started with the same question; if it decided that the regulation in litigation was not a regulation of interstate commerce, the state regulation (if there were no other constitutional defects) was allowed to stand. But if the regulation was found to be of interstate commerce other questions had to be asked. Were there acts of Congress on the same subject? If so, the Court had to decide whether concurrent state regulation was constitutional—a decision based on the Court's feeling as to whether the national law pre-empted the field, or whether the state law interfered with the operation of national law. An affirmative answer to either question would render the state act inoperative. In the absence of congressional action, the Court would ask whether the subject was one which required uniform national treatment or whether, on the other hand, it might as well be state-regulated despite the fact that it concerned interstate commerce.

Clearly the number and nature of questions involved left broad discretion to the judges. Most of the questions were fundamentally economic, not legal, and this led to the probability that judicial decisions would be based as much on the economic preconceptions of individual judges as on more purely legal considerations. It also meant that decisions would be likely to shift with the shifting nature of the cases coming to the courts as well as with the inevitable shifts

[1] See Cooley *v.* Board of Wardens, 12 How. 299 (1851); and see in general, Felix Frankfurter, *The Commerce Clause under Marshall, Taney and Waite* (Chapel Hill, 1937).

in Court personnel. When a Holmes or a Hughes replaced a Gray or a Brewer, the pattern of Court decisions was likely to change, if only slightly.

The commerce clause, then, could be looked at in several different ways, depending on the case and on the viewpoint of the observer. Sometimes it was used to limit the reach of national power, sometimes of state. At times it was a method by which the courts could "maintain the federal balance," at times one of aggrandizing the national (or the state) government. And if it frequently seemed to be merely a crass and obvious means of preventing business regulation and sanctifying laissez-faire, at other times it appeared to express a conviction that government regulation was a good thing. Considering the mixture of motives characteristic of human beings, it is not surprising that in many cases the judges appeared to combine two or three of these at the same time.

It was John Marshall who, in the leading case of *Gibbons* v. *Ogden,* defined the word commerce to include "every species of commercial intercourse." [2] After 1877 this definition never ceased to trouble the courts. One question was whether new modes of transportation and communication—invented after 1789—were to be included within the scope of the term commerce. This question was posed not because of its intrinsic difficulty but because businessmen engaged in these new occupations were understandably reluctant to accept regulation of their enterprises by the national government rather than the states. The politics of the matter was that state regulation was not likely to be as restrictive as national: states were more amenable to pressure group influences in many cases and, because of their wish to keep businesses, hesitant to regulate more strictly than other states. The courts, however, never felt that they could overturn Marshall's dictum, nor is there any evidence that they would have wished to do so. Quite the reverse, far from removing transportation from the definition of commerce, they had a strong tendency to try to make it *all* of commerce.

The leading case was in some ways very similar to that handled by Marshall: Florida had granted a monopoly, in two counties, to the Pensacola Telegraph Company, and as in Gibbons, the Supreme Court found that a national grant of power (to Western Union) over-

[2] Gibbons *v.* Ogden, 9 Wheat. 1 (1824).

rode the state's grant.[3] Chief Justice Waite, discussing whether the telegraph business was interstate commerce, relied heavily on Marshall and added that the powers of Congress "are not confined to the instrumentalities of commerce . . . known or in use when the Constitution was adopted, but they keep pace with the progress of the country, and adapt themselves to the new developments of time and circumstances." [4] The decision was confined to new modes of transportation, and implied that communication is a form of transportation of messages.

The Pensacola case concerned a state's power over interstate commerce in situations involving concurrent action by Congress, but it did not imply that states could never act if Congress had already done so. The inference must be that the Court found Florida's franchise act in direct conflict with the national law, or that Congress had intended to pre-empt the field. For in cases in which no such conflict or intent was found, the Court upheld the state action. These cases left open the question what kind of state regulation of interstate commerce was allowable in the absence of congressional action, a question answered in principle but not in detail by the 1851 Cooley rule, under which the answer depended on whether the Supreme Court felt that the area under consideration was one which demanded uniform national treatment. Such considerations not only left the Court with a great deal of discretion, but were an open invitation to the entrance of the judges' prepossessions both on the subject of regulatory legislation and of their views of the nature of federalism.

A Louisiana law *prohibiting* segregation on steamboats fell, through the application of the Cooley principle in 1878; [5] but the ambivalence of the Court was demonstrated when, a few years later, it refused to strike down a Mississippi law *requiring* segregation on railroads.[6] Both cases were prosecuted in the courts under the commerce clause. It seems likely that the cases expressed views about national and state power under that clause, rather than views about racial segregation. Apparently in 1878 a majority felt that national

---

[3] Pensacola Telegraph Co. *v.* Western Union Telegraph Co., 96 U.S. 1 (1877).
[4] *Ibid.*, p. 9.
[5] Hall *v.* DeCuir, 95 U.S. 485 (1878).
[6] Louisville, New Orleans & Texas Ry. Co. *v.* Mississippi, 133 U.S. 587 (1890).

regulation was important enough to debar the states from acting, while later the majority shifted so as to permit such action.

But at the same time the Court found that state regulation of railroad rates—at least on the interstate portions of their business—was in violation of the Cooley rule. In the Wabash case, Illinois had attempted to regulate long-distance shipping rates from points in the state to points outside it.[7] The Court opinion thought it clear that "this species of regulation is one which must be, if established at all, of a general and national character, and cannot be safely and wisely remitted to local rules and local regulations."[8] This decision, by abrogating all state regulation of interstate rates, led directly to the passage of the Interstate Commerce Act of 1887, which was then to test whether the Court would accept national regulatory legislation.

Yet two years after Wabash the Court limited the national power over "commerce" drastically by redefining the word. The Kidd case asked the judges to decide whether a state can prohibit the making of liquor for shipment outside the state.[9] In holding that it can, the Court did not resort to the state's police powers as a justification, but to a narrowing of Marshall's version of "commerce." Manufacturing is not commerce:

No distinction is more popular to the common mind, or more clearly expressed in economic and political literature, than that between manufactures and commerce. Manufacture is transformation—the fashioning of raw materials into a change of form use. The functions of commerce are different. The buying and selling and the transportation incidental thereto constitute commerce.[10]

The Court frankly looked at the results which would follow if Congress could regulate manufacturing industries; it found these results not to its liking:

The result would be that Congress would be invested, to the exclusion of the states, with the power to regulate, not only manufacture, but also agriculture, horticulture, stock-raising, domestic fisheries, mining,—in short, every branch of human industry. For is there one of them that does not contemplate, more or less clearly, an interstate or foreign market?[11]

[7] Wabash, St. Louis & Pacific Ry. v. Illinois, 118 U.S. 557 (1886).
[8] Ibid., p. 577.
[9] Kidd v. Pearson, 28 U.S. 1 (1888).
[10] Ibid., p. 20.
[11] Ibid., p. 21.

Since Congress was not attempting at that time to regulate the liquor trade, this restrictive decision had no practical effect, but it made a distinction which was to become very important a few years later in the interpretation of the Sherman Anti-Trust Act. The distinction involved a basic reorientation of the Court's approach to the commerce power: for Marshall had used a "conception of commerce as an organic whole," while Justice Lamar (not without precedent in earlier cases) viewed "the crossing of state lines as the criterion of Congressional power." While such a view is not illogical in itself, it is narrow, and in a world of nationalized industry unrealistic as well—"the artificial and mechanical separation of 'manufacturing' from 'commerce', without regard to their economic continuity or the effects of the former upon the latter." [12] But if a state may prohibit the manufacture of liquor it cannot prevent its importation: two cases contemporary with Kidd dealt with aspects of this, and it appears that since importation does involve the crossing of state lines its regulation can be performed by Congress.[13] As it happened, Congress did not much want this power at the time, and it turned the subject of prohibition back to the states in the Wilson Act of 1890 and the Webb-Kenyon Act of 1913. This kind of delegation of congressional power to the states raises constitutional issues of its own, but the Court upheld the practice in 1891.[14] The Court had also long held that states could regulate the importation of products where quarantine regulations, contagious diseases, and "undesirable" products or persons were involved, and this power was upheld in 1902.[15]

The Supreme Court, as these cases demonstrate, hardly practiced a "foolish consistency" when dealing with the powers of states under the commerce clause. And consistency was no more characteristic of its handling of the commerce power of Congress. If the Court felt that transportation and communication were undoubtedly commerce, it had its doubts about "production," as we have seen. In the Sugar Trust case in 1895 it applied its dictum from Kidd to the coverage of the Sherman Act.[16] This act attempted to prohibit, under the

[12] Bernard Schwartz, *The Powers of Government* (2 vols., New York, 1963), I, 186.

[13] Bowman v. Chicago & North Western RR Co., 125 U.S. 465 (1888); Leisey v. Hardin, 135 U.S. 100 (1890).

[14] *In re* Rahrer, 140 U.S. 545 (1891).

[15] Compagnie Française v. Bd. of Health, 186 U.S. 380 (1902).

[16] U.S. v. E. C. Knight Co., 156 U.S. 1 (1895).

commerce power, all combinations (trusts) "in restraint of [interstate] trade." It could not, according to the doctrines of the day, touch intrastate commerce, or anything that was not definable as commerce. The case was the result of an attempt by the government to break up a combination which threatened to gain control of all the sugar-refining plants in the country, and which would then put it in a position to control the price of refined sugar. Chief Justice Fuller, speaking for the majority, reiterated that manufacturing is not commerce; and in answer to the government's contention that sugar refining had a significant effect on interstate commerce, he drew what came to be an important distinction between "direct" and "indirect" effects. While a monopoly which had a direct effect might come under the congressional power to regulate, one which had only indirect effects would not; and for productive activities "the restraint would be an indirect result, however inevitable and whatever its extent." Granting to Congress power to regulate such industries would mean that "comparatively little of business operations and affairs would be left for state control." The Court, obviously, was more interested in maintaining the federal system within its traditional contours—or in preventing, as far as possible, the successful operation of the Sherman Act—than it was in developing a realistic view of what commerce entailed at the turn of the century.

While the Court did apply this doctrine to other industries, such as liquor production and lumbering,[17] it shortly found it politic to withdraw from some of the extreme implications of the idea. By manipulating the idea that things cross state lines, and also the idea that *direct* effects on interstate commerce can be regulated, the Court was able to recede gradually and gracefully from the Sugar Trust doctrine. For instance, in 1899, in a case concerning a combination of cast-iron pipe manufacturers, the Court upheld the application of the antitrust law, reasoning that this trust had explicitly tried to control prices—a factor probably present also in the Sugar Trust case but not brought forward by the government prosecutors.[18]

The qualification of the Sugar Trust doctrine was carried further in the Swift case in 1905.[19] Here Justice Holmes invented the so-called stream of commerce theory, which resulted from the Court's

[17] Coe v. Errol, 116 U.S. 517 (1886).
[18] Addyston Pipe & Steel Co. v. U.S., 175 U.S. 229 (1899).
[19] Swift & Co. v. U.S., 196 U.S. 375 (1905).

emphasis on transportation across state lines as the basic element in interstate commerce. The defendants in this case were the stockyard firms in Chicago, accused of monopolizing the buying and selling of livestock. The companies argued that their business was a part of production rather than of distribution; but Holmes replied that a stockyard is a "throat" through which commerce must pass and that it is therefore a part of commerce. While this constituted a significant broadening of the Court's view of interstate commerce, it remains difficult for the layman to see why a stockyard should be regarded as a throat through which commerce passes while the meat-packing plant next door is not. The case therefore is an excellent example of the ambivalence in which the Court of this period was caught up. At the most it represents a renewed tendency to look at commerce as "not a technical legal conception but a practical one, drawn from the course of business," as Holmes remarked.[20]

The power of Congress to control commerce is dependent, of course, not only on whether commerce exists, but on whether that commerce is "among the several states." The Court could, here too, manipulate definitions to achieve its own purposes; and here too it must be said that the period under review shows no single dominant purpose, but rather disparate purposes which shifted from Court to Court and from case to case. There was a tendency to require the actual crossing of state lines of something which was (or could be visualized as) a person or physical object.

For instance, in the first Child Labor case the Court invalidated a law in which Congress tried to eliminate the employment of children by preventing the shipment in interstate commerce of items manufactured in plants employing them.[21] The Court apparently felt that Congress was beyond bounds because it was really attempting to regulate factory employment rather than interstate commerce; or to put it a different way, the employed children did not cross state lines and therefore their employers could not be regulated by Congress. And in the first Employers' Liability case a statute was similarly struck down—this time one which required railroads to pay compensation to injured employees—because it applied equally to those employees whose work required them to cross state lines and those not so re-

---

[20] *Ibid.*, p. 398.
[21] Hammer *v.* Dagenhart, 247 U.S. 251 (1918). See Stephen B. Wood, *Constitutional Politics in the Progressive Era: Child Labor and the Law* (Chicago, 1967).

quired.[22] The Court wished to confine the operation of the Act to the workers who physically crossed the boundary, even though it was obvious then as now that there was a sense in which all employees were engaged in interstate commerce.

Nevertheless, these cases should not be taken as expressing any single-hearted desire on the part of the Court to protect business—especially the railroad business. They may instead represent more accurately a hostility to labor regulations, which extends throughout the period and will be dealt with further on. In any event, cases such as the Shreveport case sufficiently illustrate that railroads were regarded as being involved so directly in interstate commerce that Congress did not need to separate precisely the interstate from the intrastate aspects of the business.[23] This case arose because of conflicting federal and state regulations governing shipment from Shreveport (Louisiana), Dallas, and Houston into the area of eastern Texas which was roughly equidistant from the three cities. In upholding the power of the ICC to regulate the rates within Texas in order to protect the interests of Shreveport, Justice Hughes remarked that "whereever the interstate and intrastate transactions of carriers are so related that the government of the one involves the control of the other, it is Congress, and not the State, that is entitled to prescribe the final and dominant rule." [24] This was a means of restating the distinction between direct and indirect effects upon interstate commerce—a distinction which, as we have seen, was always available when the Court wished to smile upon a particular bit of regulation.

The Shreveport case was only one in a long line in which the Supreme Court first opposed and then grudgingly conceded the power of Congress (through the ICC) to regulate railroad rates. While the Court early upheld the existence of the Interstate Commerce Commission as an appropriate exercise of congressional power, it for some years showed a tendency to restrict the powers of the Commission.[25] Congress had, it is true, granted the rate-making power in words that were less than crystal clear, for it merely gave the ICC the power to pass upon the reasonableness of existing rates, and the argument that this necessarily involved the power to prescribe them fell upon deaf judicial ears. Justice Brewer, in one of

[22] First Employers' Liability Cases, 207 U.S. 463 (1908).
[23] Shreveport Rate Case, 234 U.S. 342 (1914).
[24] *Ibid.*, pp. 351–352.
[25] Interstate Commerce Commission *v.* Brimson, 154 U.S. 447 (1894).

the cases, said that "no just rule of construction would tolerate a grant of such power by mere implication."[26]

Such decisions turned out to be mere delaying actions, however, for Congress, in the Hepburn Act of 1906 and the Mann-Elkins Act of 1910, gave to the ICC explicitly the powers which the Court had failed to find in the original act, and the Court, which had long accepted the principle of rate regulation by the states, could find no constitutional reason to refuse to accept the same power when exercised unambiguously by the national government.[27] The Court also upheld the power to regulate other means of transportation even when the transported materials were owned by the carrier.[28]

But the Court was harder to please in those cases which concerned laws in which Congress was trying to regulate industry in order to protect labor. The strict—and in the long run futile—attempt to separate the interstate from the intrastate workers of companies like railroads was as unrealistic as it would have been to try to separate the interstate rates, which the Court did not even attempt. In addition, the Employers' Liability decision made its opposition to labor legislation manifest by striking down the entire law, even though it could have upheld the law as it applied to interstate workers. Some of the judges apparently thought that any regulation of the "employer relationship" was unconstitutional; but the decision was only a 5–4 one, and when Congress re-enacted the law to make it applicable to interstate employees only, the majority upheld the act.[29] Another law, which outlawed "yellow dog" contracts—in which the employer makes employment conditional on the worker's not joining a union—was also invalidated, in a 1908 case in which the Court held that the connection between union membership and interstate commerce was at best indirect, if indeed it existed at all.[30] Railroad safety legislation was, on the other hand, upheld even for equipment not used in interstate commerce, as was a maximum hours law.[31] The

[26] ICC v. Cincinnati, New Orleans & Texas Pacific Ry., 167 U.S. 479 (1897); for other decisions limiting the rate-making and other powers of the ICC, see CNO&TP Ry. v. ICC, 162 U.S. 184 (1896), and ICC v. Alabama Midland Ry. Co., 168 U.S. 144 (1897).

[27] See ICC v. Chicago, Rock Island & Pacific Ry., 218 U.S. 88 (1910); U.S. v. Atchison, Topeka & Santa Fe Ry., 234 U.S. 476 (1914).

[28] The Pipe Line Cases, 234 U.S. 548 (1914).

[29] Second Employers' Liability Cases, 223 U.S. 1 (1912).

[30] Adair v. U.S., 208 U.S. 161 (1908).

[31] Southern Ry. v. U.S., 222 U.S. 20 (1911); Baltimore & Ohio RR v. ICC, 221 U.S. 612 (1911).

Child Labor case, previously mentioned, again showed the Court in its "antilabor" mood, although the other considerations involved in that case make it likely that the law would have been struck down even had it not been a labor regulation.

This observation is given point by a look at the cases which turned on the question of whether Congress could use its plenary power over interstate commerce as a means to prohibit trade: does the word "regulate" include prohibition? Hence, as in so many other areas of action newly undertaken by government during the period, the Court had a difficult time making up its mind. No one wished to deny this power altogether, for it was clear to the judges that trade in some items ought to be prohibited; yet to uphold the power might allow Congress to prohibit anything it wished—a power which property- and business-minded judges could not easily accept. Even so, the Court early upheld full power in Congress to prohibit importation from foreign nations.[32]

In order to try to handle this question for interstate commerce, the Court invented the so-called noxious articles doctrine, which said (in principle) that Congress could prohibit interstate commerce in harmful items but not in harmless ones. Although there is no warrant for such a distinction in the Constitution, Justice Harlan found one anyway: his always strong sense of public morality forbade him from making the power applicable to everything. The leading case involved the interstate shipment of lottery tickets [33]—Harlan called lotteries a "widespread pestilence"—but the doctrine was applied by the end of the period to traffic in diseased livestock, articles violating the Pure Food and Drug Act, intoxicating liquors, and women transported for immoral purposes.[34]

The doctrine was misapplied in some of these cases, for the evil lies more often in the purpose for which articles are transported than in the articles themselves: thus the lottery case and the decision upholding the Mann Act really went beyond the "noxious articles" concept. But the important thing was that the Court had once more arrogated to itself the discretionary power to decide what was good and what

[32] Buttfield v. Stranahan, 192 U.S. 470 (1904).
[33] Champion v. Ames, 188 U.S. 321 (1903).
[34] Reid v. Cole, 187 U.S. 137 (1902); Hipolite Egg Co. v. U.S., 229 U.S. 45 (1911); Clark Distilling Co. v. Western Maryland RR, 242 U.S. 311 (1917); Hoke v. U.S., 227 U.S. 308 (1913).

was bad, for it was the Court which decided whether or not an article (or its use) was "noxious."

The limits of the doctrine were exposed in the Child Labor case.[35] Here the articles transported were in themselves harmless, as was the use to which they would be put. Congress was attempting to get at the way in which they were manufactured: that is, by children. At this the Court balked, pointing out that the evil involved came *before* there was interstate commerce. This was rank sophistry, for in earlier cases the Court had been perfectly willing to allow prohibition when the evil came after commerce had ceased. It was, obviously, the purpose of the legislation to which the Court objected, not the means which it employed.

The commerce clause, although written and first interpreted by Marshall as a plenary national power, was thus by 1917 converted into a major limitation on the powers of Congress; at the same time it functioned as a serious brake on the actions of the states. And it was true also that in many fields which the courts left technically to the states, the growth of the nationalized economy had made it increasingly unrealistic for the states to act: either the political pressures against action were too great or the fear of losing industry in competition with other states made them reluctant to regulate. These effects were probably not wholly visible—particularly to the judges— by 1917. That we see the matter in this light today is the result of a generation of criticism of the legal doctrines used; and most of this criticism came after 1920. In any case, it does not seem likely, in view of the ambivalence evidenced in the decisions themselves, that the judges were following any set theory. American constitutional jurisprudence is not built out of a priori principle, but out of case-to-case *ad hoc* adjudication. Faced with specific cases, courts reacted to "felt necessities" (as Holmes phrased it); and if the necessities were sometimes identified differently than we see them from the vantage point of 1970, it may merely be that we are reacting to a different set of "inarticulate major premises" than the one which impelled the majority of judges during the era of laissez-faire.

Other powers granted to Congress in Article I, Section 8, of the Constitution were, like the commerce clause, sometimes but not always construed as limitations. There was if anything less of a

[35] Hammer *v.* Dagenhart, 247 U.S. 251 (1918).

tendency for free enterprise dogma to enter into decisions, for these clauses were not as easily used by Congress for regulatory purposes; and even when they were, it was quite likely (as we shall see) that the specific regulations would gain the assent of the courts.

The only major instance in which a congressional act was found unconstitutional came in the famous Income Tax cases; while the Court was given numerous other opportunities by businessmen anxious for their profits, it upheld all other major uses of the powers of Congress (sometimes, it must be said, these uses were for the promotion of business, and at other times for the promotion of one business to the detriment of another; so that even a decision upholding a statute could be regarded as a "pro-business" judgment).

The tax cases were perhaps the most important. The provisions of the Constitution regarding taxes are at the same time peculiarly broad and somewhat confining, for while the national government is given the power "to lay and collect taxes . . . to pay the debts and provide for the common defence and general welfare," a clause so sweeping that it has seldom been construed as an interference with any tax measure, it is also provided that there can be no export tax, that "indirect taxes" must be uniform all over the country, and that "direct taxes" shall be apportioned according to the populations of the states. These provisions have seldom proved to be excessively limiting, although they have raised questions of great importance. Do the tax clauses limit the purposes for which tax money may be spent? Can taxes be used as a regulatory device? As a prohibitory device? And what is a "direct" tax? May taxes be levied by the national government on state governmental agencies? During the period from 1877 to 1917 the cases concerning some of these questions were too insignificant, however, to require extensive attention. These I shall deal with before turning to the more important questions.

The Supreme Court had, in 1871, constructed a reverse corollary to the old McCulloch doctrine that states could not tax federal instrumentalities.[36] Thus was born the fertile and complicated field known as "intergovernmental tax immunity" about which Thomas Reed Powell wrote with such magnificent irony.[37] Immediately after *Collector* v. *Day* the Court began to limit the scope of state immunity from national taxation, however, upholding a succession tax on be-

[36] Collector v. Day, 11 Wall. 113 (1871).
[37] Thomas Reed Powell, *Vagaries and Varieties in Constitutional Interpretation* (New York, 1956).

quests to municipalities, taxes on state-controlled liquor businesses, and corporation taxes (against a claim that this limited the power of states to charter corporations).[38] These cases were not of tremendous importance in themselves, although they marked a trend toward a more flexible judicial view of both national and state taxation which has continued to this day, so that the reciprocal immunity is now of very doubtful effectiveness.

Neither were there any important cases concerning the way in which Congress could spend tax revenues: the Court held, as it has consistently throughout our history, that spending for the "general welfare" is a very broad power which it is largely up to Congress to interpret. The only case during this period in which the judges found it necessary to rule on this clause was one in which they upheld the government's power to use tax money in order to buy land for use as national park land—in this case the Gettysburg national military park.[39]

The question of regulation by taxation deserves somewhat more extended treatment. It includes within it the possibility of promotion or, on the other hand, extermination of businesses; in addition, regulatory taxation may in some instances be used so as to achieve purposes which Congress could not reach directly, thus trenching upon the reserved powers of the states. There were no significant cases involving government promotion of business, it being more or less assumed that such activity was constitutional, especially in a period when most of the revenues of the national government came from this source via the protective tariff (which was true until World War I).

Other types of regulation by taxation, however, were the subject of litigation. In several cases of rather minor importance the Court upheld regulations which were attached to tax laws ostensibly to make the taxes easier to collect, but probably in reality to use the tax as a means of making the regulation effective. In cases concerning the packaging of tobacco and oleomargarine, and the sale and transfer of drugs, in which the tax was in effect a fine for not observing the regulations, the tax was nevertheless upheld by the Court.[40]

---

[38] Snyder v. Bettman, 190 U.S. 249 (1903); South Carolina v. U.S., 199 U.S. 437 (1905); Flint v. Stone Tracy Co., 220 U.S. 107 (1911).

[39] U.S. v. Gettysburg Electric Ry., 160 U.S. 668 (1896).

[40] Felsenheld v. U.S., 186 U.S. 526 (1902); In re Kollock, 165 U.S. 526 (1897); U.S. v. Doremus, 249 U.S. 86 (1919).

The most important question of this type was, as one might suppose, whether a tax could be used to exterminate a business. The explicit issue in such cases has not usually been whether the tax power can be used to suppress a commercial endeavor: it has instead been whether the tax was imposed on a business which Congress, under other constitutional provisions, had the power to regulate. Thus, in the first important case—in 1869—the power of Congress to tax state bank notes out of existence was upheld, the ruling being based fundamentally on the fact that Congress had full power to control the national currency anyway, and the tax power was merely a technique in the arsenal of control.[41] This doctrine left it open for the Court, if it wished, to find any tax invalid if it felt that its real purpose was to exterminate a business over which Congress had no constitutional control apart from the tax power. Even so, most taxes were upheld, and there has been most of the time a concurrent doctrine to the effect that the judges will not look behind the face of a tax statute to its purpose. These two doctrines are contradictory, for if the Court cannot look at the purpose it would have no way of finding out whether Congress was attempting to get at a business over which it had no control. In effect, the Court used one or the other of the two doctrines, not both—the former when it wished to find a tax unconstitutional, and the latter when it did not.

Thus, when Congress imposed a prohibitory tax on yellow oleomargarine, the Court (apparently regarding this as a somewhat noxious product) refused to resort to the idea that Congress had no power to regulate this business.[42] If it had done so, it would most likely have had to follow its dictum in the antitrust cases: that production is not commerce and that thus the production of yellow oleo cannot be reached by Congress. But the Court did no such thing. It forestalled the whole question of congressional power by observing that Congress had the power to enact revenue measures; that this was on its face a revenue measure (even though if successful it would have produced no revenue); and that the Court would not go into the motives of Congress in enacting it. The decision had the effect, potentially, of opening a means of regulating businesses which could not—under the then prevailing interpretations of the commerce clause—be otherwise reached by Congress, although it must be ad-

[41] Veazie Bank v. Fenno, 8 Wall. 533 (1869).
[42] McCray v. U.S., 195 U.S. 27 (1904).

mitted that in many circumstances this means of regulation is too clumsy and cumbrous for practical purposes.

In any case, when the Court invalidated Congress' attempt to use the commerce power to eliminate child labor in factories (which we have discussed above), the legislature acted on what it took to be the moral of the oleomargarine case: it attempted to drive out child labor by imposing a 10 per cent tax on the profits of those employing children. But this time the Court, in the famous Child Labor Tax case, *did* look behind the face of the tax and discovered, to its dismay, that the purpose of the measure was to regulate a matter that was within the reserved powers of the states.[43] As in the commerce cases, the Court had discovered alternative doctrines which it could apply as the judges of the day wished. Not until after 1937 was this kind of discretionary power relinquished by the Court.

By all odds the most notorious set of tax cases during the *fin de siècle* era was that turning on the question of whether the national government could impose an income tax. Although these cases are now of historical interest only, since the adoption of the Sixteenth Amendment effectively reversed the decisions, they are yet illustrative of the way in which the economic predispositions of the judges had a strong tendency to get in the way of an objective view of the Constitution; for in these cases there was no doubt that at least some of the majority judges were deeply and emotionally opposed to such a thing as an income tax. On the other side, there was the growing realization that the protective tariff was not an ideal source for the major portion of federal revenue; by World War I it had already become difficult to imagine how national expenditures could be maintained at all without an income tax; the same question had arisen during the Civil War, when the expedient of an income tax had first been used to help cover the extraordinary expenses of that struggle. When the Civil War tax was challenged in court, it was upheld by a unanimous vote on precisely the issue: that an income tax was not a "direct" tax within the meaning of the Constitution.[44]

The income tax law of 1894 was, to be sure, an innovation in peacetime, and it fell largely on those with incomes which in that day were considered large: it was a flat 2 per cent tax on all incomes above $4,000. In judging the extreme reaction of the wealthy classes, one

[43] Bailey *v.* Drexel Furniture Co., 259 U.S. 20 (1922).
[44] Springer *v.* U.S., 102 U.S. 586 (1881).

should consider that only a few Americans had incomes above that level and that they were worried as much by the possibility that the amount of the tax would be increased in future years as they were by the 2 per cent in itself. Even considering these factors the reaction seems more like that of arrogant men who had grown too sure of their power and status, and who were afraid of losing those attributes. Nevertheless a narrow majority of the Court agreed with them, and in reversing the earlier decisions—"a century of error," Chief Justice Fuller called them—held the tax unconstitutional on the grounds that it was a direct tax and thus could not be levied except on a basis directly related to the populations of the states.[45]

The atmosphere in which the case was decided had the effect of raising the temperature of the Court. The judges were asked by counsel to step into the breach to stem "this communistic march." [46] At first argument Justice Jackson was absent because of illness, and on the major portion of the case the result was a 4–4 tie. Ordinarily, in Court practice, this means that the lower court decision which is being appealed becomes the final decision; but in a case which seemed so important, the Supreme Court felt that the nation deserved a judgment from the highest tribunal. As a result, after some efforts to persuade Jackson to retire had failed (he was extremely ill and was to die only two and a half months after the second decision), the Court waited until Jackson returned to Washington and then reheard the portion of the case which concerned the tax on general incomes (which included a tax on income from stock holdings).[47] Jackson, incidentally, voted to uphold the tax, which means that since the tax was struck down by a 5–4 margin, one of the other justices (apparently Shiras) shifted sides. Justice Field, the doughty old warrior for the rights of capital, wrote a concurring opinion which seems best to describe the motivations of the majority:

The present assault on capital is but the beginning. It will be but a stepping stone to others, larger and more sweeping, till our political contests will become a war of the poor against the rich; a war constantly growing in intensity and bitterness. If the Court sanctions the power of discriminating taxation, and nullifies the uniformity mandate of the Con-

[45] Pollock v. Farmers' Loan & Trust Co., 157 U.S. 429 (1895), and 158 U.S. 601 (1895).

[46] Joseph H. Choate in argument before the Court used these words.

[47] The full story is told in Willard L. King, *Melville Weston Fuller, Chief Justice of the United States, 1888–1910* (New York, 1950), pp. 193–221.

stitution, it will mark the hour when the sure decadence of our government will commence.[48]

If this seems an open admission that the Court was more concerned with politics than with constitutionality, so be it. It must be said that the dissenters did nothing to dispel the impression. While Harlan, White, and Jackson all took cracks at the majority, Justice Henry Billings Brown—hardly a liberal himself—entered the most forceful protest, which is worth quoting at length.

. . . The decision involves nothing less than a surrender of the taxing power to the moneyed class. . . . Even the spectre of socialism is conjured up to frighten Congress from laying taxes upon the people in proportion to their ability to pay them. . . . While I have no doubt that Congress will find some means of surmounting the present crisis, my fear is that in some moment of national peril this decision will rise up to frustrate its will and paralyze its arm. I hope it may not prove the first step towards the submergence of the liberties of the people in a sordid despotism of wealth. . . . As I cannot escape the conviction that the decision of the Court in this great case is fraught with immeasurable danger to the future of the country, and that it approaches the proportion of a national calamity, I feel it my duty to enter my protest against it.[49]

"A sordid despotism of wealth," while a happy catch phrase, is quite certainly not what the majority had consciously in mind. Yet it seems beyond doubt that the Court had overreached itself, and that the decision was based more on feelings than on a cool appraisal of the Constitution. Even some conservative opinion was astonished at the Court's action. And perhaps the Court itself felt that it had gone too far, for it shortly upheld taxes only technically distinguishable from income taxes: a tax on sales in business exchanges; an inheritance tax (which the Court said was a tax on the inheritor rather than on the income of the decedent); a tax on the sales of stocks.[50]

And of course, with the support even of President William Howard Taft, the Constitution was amended—one of only three times in our history (the others were the Eleventh and Fourteenth Amendments) that the Court has guessed so far wrong about public opinion that it has been directly overruled by amendment. The Six-

[48] Pollock case, p. 607.
[49] Ibid., p. 695.
[50] Nicol v. Ames, 173 U.S. 509 (1899); Knowlton v. Moore, 178 U.S. 41 (1900); Thomas v. U.S., 192 U.S. 363 (1904); and see also Spreckels Sugar Refining Co. v. McClain, 192 U.S. 397 (1904) and Flint v. Stone Tracy Co., 220 U.S. 107 (1911).

teenth Amendment (1913) came in time to avert the calamity foreseen by Justice Brown, for when World War I broke out a few years
later the government was able to use the income tax to help meet the
drastic increase in its expenditures. No thanks, however, to the
Supreme Court.

One area in which the Supreme Court was consistent was its
hostility to national action favoring the cause of labor. We have already seen that in actions involving the two child labor laws, the first
Employers' Liability Act and the law outlawing "yellow dog" contracts, the Court adopted narrow interpretations of the commerce
and tax powers in order to frustrate congressional intentions. A few
cases in which other parts of the Constitution or laws were concerned will illustrate the same point.

The Pullman strike of 1894 was discussed in an earlier chapter; but
the constitutional litigation resulting from it was also important.
Eugene V. Debs, the strike leader, was convicted of violating the
court injunction which had forbidden the union from acting in such
a way as to interfere with the mail or with the conduct of interstate
commerce. When the case went to the Supreme Court on appeal, the
Court, with Field's nephew Justice Brewer speaking for it, upheld the
national power to protect "interstate commerce and the transportation of the mails." In doing so, he enunciated a doctrine of national
sovereignty which was strangely at odds with the limitations that the
Court, with his enthusiastic cooperation, was in the same year placing
on the scope of the Sherman Act.[51] National sovereignty, it seemed
for the moment, was one thing where labor was concerned, and entirely a different thing for capital.

Moreover, the narrow interpretation of the Sherman Act was not
allowed to interfere with an approach broad enough to bring labor
under its coverage. There is no evidence that Congress meant to include labor unions when it used the phrase "combinations in restraint of trade." And lest there should be doubt about this, the
legislators wrote it more explicitly into the Clayton Act in 1914. But
the Court chose, in the Danbury Hatters' case, to construe the Sherman Act so as to include labor; and even after the passage of the
Clayton Act it persisted in this interpretation.[52]

[51] *In re* Debs, 158 U.S. 564 (1895).
[52] Loewe *v.* Lawlor, 208 U.S. 274 (1908). The Clayton Act was not interpreted
until the 1920's: see Duplex Printing Press Co. *v.* Deering, 254 U.S. 443 (1921).

Two more sets of cases involving the national power remain to be considered, different from those above because, at least to the courts, they were not primarily cases which involved the economic attitudes of the judges. These were the Insular cases and the set which questioned the burgeoning war powers of the government. These have in common the fact that they resulted from the entrance of the United States onto the stage of world power.

The so-called Insular cases resulted from the American victory in the Spanish war and its consequent emergence as an imperial power holding overseas colonies. Constitutional questions soon arose, centering on the basic issue of whether, and to what extent, constitutional provisions were to be applicable to the new territories. As Senator Francis G. Newlands of Nevada remarked,

The difference between the imperialists and the anti-imperialists on this question is that the imperialists wish to expand our territory and contract our Constitution. The anti-imperialists are opposed to any expansion of territory which, as a matter of necessity arising from the ignorance and inferiority of the people occupying it, makes free constitutional government impracticable or undesirable.[53]

In the cases coming before the Supreme Court, the judges had a typically difficult time deciding; but in effect (usually by a 5–4 margin) they took the imperialist side. As to trade, they held that since the colonial territories ceased to be foreign soil when the United States took over, the old tariff system ceased to exist; however, Congress was constitutionally empowered to set up a new tariff system specifically applicable to the newly acquired colonies, despite the prohibition of "import taxes" in the Constitution. The doctrine which ultimately gained a majority in the Court was that developed by Justice Edward D. White, who held that conquered territory did not become a part of the United States constitutionally unless Congress passed legislation incorporating it. Therefore, unincorporated territory was not subject to the import tax provision. Justice White did not seem, however, to know precisely what he meant by "incorporation." In the cases under discussion, which involved Puerto Rico, he felt that it had not been incorporated.[54] But when the Court faced a question of whether Hawaiian criminal procedures had to observe

---

[53] *Congressional Record*, 1996; quoted in Carl Brent Swisher, *American Constitutional Development*, 2d ed. (Boston, 1954), p. 475.

[54] De Lima *v.* Bidwell, 182 U.S. 1; Dooley *v.* U.S., 182 U.S. 222; and Downes *v.* Bidwell, 182 U.S. 244 (all decided in 1901).

constitutional limitations, the Court held that it was not incorporated either, despite the annexation act of 1898—but was incorporated in 1900 when Congress set up a civil government for the islands.[55] Alaska had been incorporated, the Court held (again in a case involving criminal procedures), by a succession of laws setting up government there.[56] But it was also held that neither the Philippines nor Puerto Rico came under the jury trial provisions of the Constitution, since they had not been incorporated.[57]

The unincorporated territories were left in a double limbo. On the one hand, only the Supreme Court, by some process of divination rather than logic, could say whether or when a territory had been incorporated. On the other hand, even for unincorporated territories some—unlisted—constitutional rights existed, which were apparently considered to be more fundamental than jury trial. The results apparently reflected, to some extent, the judges' own feelings about the territory in question: all constitutional rights were to be extended to those in which the people were sufficiently advanced to deserve them, while in more "backward" areas only limited rights were considered possible. Fortunately, the Congress was in the long run wise enough to extend most constitutional rights voluntarily to the residents of the territories.

The entrance of the United States into World War I, the largest war in history up to that time, called for extraordinary expenditures and unprecedented types of governmental controls. The result was a series of economic regulations, some of which would inevitably be challenged by those who were disadvantaged by their operation. The reaction of American judges to these cases was perhaps predictable. Despite their general attachment to laissez-faire and their consequent dislike of governmental regulation of private businesses, the judges upheld all such legislation to come before them. As patriots and nationalists (and perhaps also as followers of public opinion) they realized as well as anyone the necessities behind the various laws enacted, and they were willing to find in the Constitution the power necessary for such action. Broadly speaking, one might say that the courts developed a doctrine of emergency powers which has generally been called "the war power." To an unspecified extent,

[55] Hawaii v. Mankichi, 190 U.S. 197 (1903).
[56] Rassmussen v. U.S., 197 U.S. 516 (1905).
[57] Dorr v. U.S., 195 U.S. 138 (1904); Balzac v. Porto Rico, 258 U.S. 298 (1922).

this war power has the effect of abrogating the usual restrictions on the power of both President and Congress. But there was also the feeling in some of the decisions that other emergencies than war might call forth this power.

The constitutional basis for the war power has not been the subject of a great deal of agreement, although almost all commentators agree on the power's existence. It has sometimes been spoken of as an implied power resulting from the power to declare war; sometimes as an emanation from the clauses of the Constitution regarding war and the military; and sometimes as an inherent power which any national government would have by virtue of its very existence as a sovereign nation, whether it is granted specifically in the Constitution or not. The last interpretation is perhaps of the most interest, since it might include an inherent power to deal with domestic emergencies as well as with international wars. The Supreme Court did not, however, adopt any of these theories as its own until long after the end of World War I, if indeed it has yet done so.

In terms of more recent events, perhaps the most significant constitutional question arising out of World War I was that concerning the power of the national government to institute compulsory military service.[58] While a draft had been used during the Civil War, it had not been challenged in court. The World War I challenge took the form of three claims: that the draft deprived the states of their right to "a well-regulated militia," that the militia power of Congress did not allow compulsory service outside the country, and that draft service constituted "involuntary servitude" under the Thirteenth Amendment. The Court upheld the power of Congress in respect to all three of these claims. The military power of the national government, it said, was superior to that of the states, and Congress had the power, apart from calling the militia, to raise armies. Finally and most important, it pointed out that certain kinds of exceptional services to the state had always been expected of citizens, such as jury service and (in the early states) road maintenance work, and that it was most unlikely that the radical Republicans who wrote the Thirteenth Amendment would have intended to outlaw the draft which had enabled the North to win the Civil War.

There is nowadays a strong body of opinion which believes that

[58] Selective Draft Law Cases, 245 U.S. 366 (1918).

(whether this decision was right or wrong) the Court wrote a weak opinion, and on the whole treated the question as if it were not a very serious one. Such criticism, proceeding from a modern set of circumstances which is greatly different, tends to ignore the situation in which the decision was made and the strong precedents for it. On the other hand, there is also the possibility that the decision approved only a wartime draft, and that therefore there is to this day no constitutional case in which a peacetime compulsory service has been validated. But the idea of national emergency as justifying extraordinary measures is so well established by now—it was first announced just before World War I as a justification for the upholding of the Adamson Act, which compelled the railroads to grant a wage increase [59]—that it is doubtful that hostilities such as those in Korea or Vietnam would be considered as anything less than an emergency justifying a draft.

The Supreme Court upheld also a wartime prohibition law and rent controls in Washington, D.C., but despite the extensive and far-reaching economic control legislation used in the war, little of it was challenged in court.[60] This was perhaps partly because of patriotism, but also because the war was so short and because the precedents for this type of legislation in wartime, set in the American Revolution and in the Civil War, seemed to make the probability of successful challenge very slight.

The only other cases relevant to the war power at this point are those which concern the question of whether these extra powers can be used before hostilities actually begin (and if so, how long before), and after hostilities end (and if so, how long after). It cannot be said that such questions received very satisfactory answers in the World War I cases, or indeed in any succeeding cases. This is probably because no satisfactory answers are possible. The railroad wage cases mentioned above seemed to imply that some legislation could be enacted before hostilities began; and the rent control case did the same for the period after the end of actual fighting. It is also true that when Congress tried to renew the District of Columbia rent controls in 1921, the Court held the law invalid since, as Justice Holmes pointed out, the emergency which justified the original act

[59] Wilson v. New, 243 U.S. 332 (1917).
[60] Hamilton v. Kentucky Distilleries Warehouse Co., 251 U.S. 146 (1919); Block v. Hirsh, 256 U.S. 135 (1921).

was now over.[61] But none of these cases set a time limit, nor did they go very far into the setting up of objective criteria by which the existence or seriousness of a threat of war, or of one just ended, can be judged. The doctrine of emergency powers, even aside from war, developed mostly as a result of the depression of the 1930's, would seem to make the question largely an academic one.

Serious questions of national and state power to abridge civil liberties also arose during the war. These involved attempts by the national government to prevent espionage, but in greater volume consisted of sometimes harsh state laws against seditious speech or other activities. Most such laws were not challenged in court, and such cases as did arise almost always resulted in court acquiescence in governmental action. The cases are more appropriately treated in the succeeding volume of this series, as a part of the developing law of civil liberties. As one might expect, great wars create the opportunity and the necessity for the exercise of governmental powers which might be neither desired nor needed at other times. Once gained, these powers are not only not given up, but they tend to be extended to meet other types of emergencies real or imagined. And we have already seen to what an extent these emergency powers tend to nationalize power as well as contributing to the aggrandizement of the presidency. The moral, for those interested in the maintenance of constitutional limitations, would seem to be that a country should not engage in war; but it must also be admitted that with the world as it is such a cure might be as dangerous to American liberty as the disease itself. The kind of world we might now inhabit had the South been allowed to go its independent way, or Germany won the First World War, or Hitler been permitted to consolidate his European conquests (and to develop the atomic bomb)—these possibilities give one pause. Charles Evans Hughes wrote in 1920 that "we may well wonder . . . whether Constitutional government as hitherto maintained in this Republic could survive another great war, even victoriously waged." [62] In a world of national states, nevertheless, victory may give us a better chance than defeat or nonparticipation.

[61] Chastleton Corp. v. Sinclair, 264 U.S. 543 (1924).
[62] Quoted in Swisher, Const. Devel., p. 1.

CHAPTER 6

The Supreme Court and State
Business Regulation

CONSTITUTIONALISM in a federal system, and certainly the Reconstruction amendments, imply limitations on state as well as national power. One of the basic questions of our constitutional law has been: Just what are these limitations on the activities of the states? Constitutionally, the states have generally been regarded as governments of "reserved powers," which means they possess all powers which are not given exclusively to the national government or specifically denied to them in the Constitution. We have already surveyed the development of constitutional principles in deciding what powers the states hold in relation to the enumerated authority of the national government. The main purpose in this section will be to discuss the powers which were withheld from the states. There are in this field two types of limitations: first, those which are found in the main body of the original Constitution—most of which are in principle if not in application quite specific—such as the provisions prohibiting states from making treaties, coining money, enacting bills of attainder, impairing the obligation of contracts, imposing import or export duties, or conducting wars. The second type— much more important for our purposes—are found in the Reconstruction amendments. These are written in much more general and ambiguous language, and thus have given wide scope for judicial interpretation; the effect has been that they have, historically, proved capable of astonishing growth in often unexpected directions. As might be expected, the most numerous and most important cases tended strongly to revolve around attempts by the states to cope with rising industrialism and the attendant problems, and these will therefore be discussed first.

The reserved powers of the states were essentially and in theory an enormous and illimitable reservoir of governmental authority—illimitable because undefinable. In principle, any power which might be exercised by a government was included, except of course those prohibited by the Constitution. This collection of powers was so broad that it did not even have a name; it was regarded as an attribute of sovereignty, and it was certainly in no sense regarded as a limitation on state action. It was, of course, true that there were many things which the Founding Fathers hoped and expected that the states would not do, sometimes influenced by their natural rights preconceptions; but they made no serious attempt to write these into the Constitution. Some of them were written into the state constitutions, for which, however, the Supreme Court had no responsibility. The Constitution, in other words, was concerned primarily with the limitation of the national government, not of the states.

Natural law beliefs and personal interests combined, of course, to bring to court cases in which litigants wished to impose limits on state action. But before the Civil War the Supreme Court seldom acceded to the wishes of these litigants unless their cases could be decided under one of the specific clauses contained in the original Constitution, such as the contract clause which was used as the basis for decision in the famous Dartmouth College case.[1] The Court proved—especially after Taney's accession to the chair of Chief Justice—quite resistant to claims of natural law limitations, and it held as well that none of the provisions of the Bill of Rights applied to the states.[2]

Even so, the verbiage of some of the opinions in cases which upheld state power contained the seeds of later limitations. Chief Justice Marshall started the process unintentionally when he tried to find a name for the plenary powers held by the states; Marshall was not trying to impose a set of outer bounds to state power, but

[1] Dartmouth College v. Woodward, 4 Wheat. 518 (1819).
[2] Barron v. Baltimore, 7 Pet. 243 (1833).

merely to state what that power was. Unfortunately, definition implies limitation, and consequently the efforts of both the Marshall and the Taney Courts succeeded in implanting the idea that anything beyond the definition—which Marshall denominated "the police power"—was also beyond state power.[3] Even though it happened long before 1877, it may be well to give an example of this process.

If Marshall was content with a name—perhaps feeling the impossibility of doing more than this with a power so vast—the Taney Court felt it had to provide a definition. This came about mostly because litigants persisted in suggesting that there were limits to state power, and the Court hoped to lay this idea to rest by emphasizing through definition the breadth of that power. While Taney restricted himself to the statement that the police powers "are nothing more or less than the powers of government inherent in every sovereignty . . . ," [4] other members of his Court felt it necessary to be more explicit. Justice Barbour, while again stressing the breadth of state power, protested so much that he sounded a little defensive about it:

. . . a State has the same undeniable and unlimited jurisdiction over all persons and things, within its territorial limits, as any foreign nation, where the jurisdiction is not surrendered or restrained by the Constitution of the United States . . . all those powers which relate to merely municipal legislation, or what may, perhaps, more properly be called *internal police* . . . [:] in relation to these, the authority of a State is complete, unqualified, and exclusive.[5]

The fact remains clear that the early Court had no conception of limits to state power which were not contained in the Constitution. It seems clear also, however, that as early as the 1840's the judges were being pressed to develop such a limitation by treating the police power as a set of outer bounds rather than merely as a statement of powers. If successful, this would have required the construction of an essentially natural law approach to the Constitution, since that document never even mentions the police powers.

The adoption of the Fourteenth Amendment, with its vague clauses protecting (against *state* infringement) the "privileges or im-

---

[3] Brown *v.* Maryland, 12 Wheat. 419 (1827).
[4] The License Cases, 5 How. 504 (1847).
[5] City of New York *v.* Miln, 11 Pet. 102, 139 (1837).

munities" of citizens, and the due process of law rights of "persons," provided a new point of attack for business interests which wished to avoid state regulation. They could argue that these new provisions, either by intention or by implication, cut across the police power and in some way limited state action in cases involving economic regulation. This claim was apparently first made by former Supreme Court Justice John A. Campbell in his argument in the Slaughterhouse cases in 1873. Campbell concentrated primarily on the privileges or immunities clause; but the narrow Court majority, with its eye on the preservation of something like the ante-bellum federal system, construed that clause so narrowly that it has never since been useful for anything.[6] The Court gave short shrift to the due process argument—it was treated, indeed, so casually that lawyers were encouraged to present successive cases under it.

The first case in which the Court actually admitted that this clause might in some situations act as a limitation on the police power was the famous Granger case, *Munn* v. *Illinois,* decided in 1877.[7] It is one of the anomalies of American constitutional law, with its written opinions, that the effects of a case are sometimes quite different from those envisaged by the opinion writer. This is almost certainly the case with Chief Justice Morrison R. Waite's opinion in the Munn case. Waite, never known as a great opinion writer whatever his other virtues, phrased the opinion in words which gave away half of what he was apparently trying to save. And the case was so important that it deserves extended consideration.

Munn was one of a set of cases popularly known as the Granger cases. They arose out of the reaction of the farmers of the Middle West to the depressed prices of farm products during the 1870's. There was a tendency for these to be blamed by the rural spokesmen on the railroads and other "middlemen" who were believed—with some justice but in an oversimplified fashion—to be gouging the farmers by charging excessive rates for their services. Newly organized into the first great national farm pressure group, the Patrons of Husbandry (called the Grange), they succeeded in obtaining regulatory laws in quite a few states:

... establishment of maximum rates for railroad freight and passengers and for the storing of grain by direct legislative enactment or by regulatory

6 Slaughterhouse Cases, 16 Wall. 36 (1873).
7 Munn *v.* Illinois, 94 U.S. 113 (1877).

commissions; prohibition of discriminatory rates between places by means of the so-called "shorthaul" clauses; and encouragement of competition by forbidding the consolidation of parallel lines.[8]

If it was natural for the farmers to organize to end their sea of troubles, it was just as natural for the businessmen to attempt to defend themselves against such laws. Failing in some of the state legislatures to prevent the passage of the statutes, and also failing in many places to secure favorable reconsideration, they turned to the courts. Their argument was no longer entirely a new one, for the main lines of it had already been charted for them by John A. Campbell. They argued that their property was being taken from them by the state (profits were a form of property, so that if their profits were reduced they were being deprived of property) without due process of law. This was difficult to argue successfully because of the historical breadth of the police power, which had included regulation by states of such things as bridge, ferry, and road tolls and canal rates. Another difficulty was that it was hard to maintain that the state legislatures had enacted these laws without due process of law (in order to do this they had to invent "substantive due process," a development which we shall consider presently). The Munn case itself challenged the validity of Illinois' regulation of the rates charged by grain elevators in Chicago, which was then the hub of the nation's grain shipping.

In answer to the legal arguments, Chief Justice Waite, while in no doubt that the rate law was constitutional, went unnecessarily out of his way to meet the lawyers' contentions. He could have settled the issue by merely quoting Taney or Barbour on the breadth of the police power, and then pointing out that these rate regulations were merely an exercise of what Taney had termed "the power of sovereignty." What he did instead provides some proofs that the business interest had made some headway: for while upholding the law, he made it plain that "under some circumstances" states might violate the due process clause in some unspecified fashion.[9] This concession, hardly necessary to the decision of the case, was an open encouragement to lawyers to try again in other cases, an invitation which they accepted with an alacrity so great that Justice Samuel F. Miller only a year later was moved to protest:

[8] C. Peter Magrath, *Morrison R. Waite: The Triumph of Character* (New York, 1963), p. 175.

[9] Munn *v.* Illinois, p. 125.

. . . the docket of this court is crowded with cases in which we are asked to hold that State courts and State legislatures have deprived their own citizens of life, liberty, or property without due process of law. There is abundant evidence that there exists some strange misconception of the scope of this provision as found in the Fourteenth Amendment. . . . [It] is looked upon as a means of bringing to the test of the decision of this court the abstract opinions of every unsuccessful litigant in a State court. . . .[10]

Not content with this probably unintentional limitation of state power, Chief Justice Waite went on to develop another one. He argued that in English common law it had always been accepted that businesses "affected with a public interest" could be regulated. Such uses of property cease "to be *juris privati* only." While Waite doubtless meant these observations to illustrate the breadth of the state's power, they had in practice the opposite effect, for they implied that purely private businesses (whatever they might be defined to be) were not subject to regulation. Thus was provided another invitation to future litigation which was not likely to be ignored.

Having thus in two glancing blows destroyed much of the foundation of state power, Chief Justice Waite went on to make some platitudinous remarks to the effect that the state must be presumed to have the power to do those things which it has the power to do, and that "for protection against abuses by legislatures the people must resort to the polls, not to the courts." [11] The laissez-faire decisions of the Supreme Court, it should be noted, are full of such declarations, which the decisions themselves contradict.

Justice Stephen J. Field was even more business oriented than the majority of the Court. He may (or may not) have seen the favorable long-run implications of this decision, but being an impatient man he was not willing to wait for the long run: he objected to the decision itself, which after all did not give the elevator operators what they wanted. But more subtle lawyers were able to take the Waite opinion and turn it to their own purposes, and the flood of "due process" cases had begun. The inherent, plenary power which Marshall had first baptized with a name was gradually to become a power which was "cribb'd and confin'd" and which was to be regarded as the exception rather than the rule. Just ten years later, in fact, even Mr. Justice John M. Harlan (who was a "liberal"

---

[10] Davidson *v.* New Orleans, 96 U.S. 97, 103–104 (1878).
[11] Munn *v.* Illinois, p. 134.

in such matters) was able to define the police power "as embracing no more than the power to promote public health, morals, and safety." [12]

Before American business could maximize the uses of the due process clause one more fundamental step had to be taken. Both in Slaughterhouse and in Munn the litigants had been individuals or partnerships, so that the word "persons" as used in the Fourteenth Amendment posed no legal obstacle to their suits. But such forms of business organization were declining: the world of the future was a corporate world. And there remained some doubt whether the framers of the amendment had corporations in mind when they used "persons" in the due process clause. (Some color to the argument that they did was provided by the fact that the privileges or immunities clause had used the word "citizen.") If the courts were to hold that the clause covered only natural persons, all of Field's efforts and all of Waite's mistakes would do little good to the proprietors of American enterprise.

Corporations had, of course, been considered artificial persons for certain kinds of cases at common law for many years. But since they were artificial, they need not be considered as persons (only persons can ordinarily sue and be sued in legal practice, which is why this question is important) for all purposes. Legislatures could, in passing laws, define whether they meant the word to be restricted to natural persons; but in common law jurisdictions it was much more likely that such decisions would be left to the courts.

It was common law judges who first perceived the desirability of allowing corporations to be parties in cases, and since the common law delights in the use of legal fictions by which to maintain that things which have changed have not changed, instead of merely ruling that corporations could sue and be sued in certain kinds of cases, they muddied the waters by inventing the concept of the artificial person.[13]

The question remained whether in the Reconstruction Congress which framed the Fourteenth Amendment it was intended that "per-

[12] Mugler v. Kansas, 123 U.S. 661 (1887).

[13] The origins and meaning of the doctrine of corporate personality have been best presented in Howard Jay Graham, *Everyman's Constitution: Historical Essays on the Fourteenth Amendment, the "Conspiracy Theory," and American Constitutionalism* (Madison, 1968), pp. 367–437.

sons" include corporations. There is no direct evidence that it was—or that it was not. It is true that one member of the framing "Committee of Fifteen," Roscoe Conkling, made a stirring plea that it was; but this argument (one of the most famous in Supreme Court annals) was made almost twenty years later, when he had the advantage of having gained an extensive legal practice for the great corporations and could use hindsight to see what great value an unambiguous acceptance of the idea by the Court would have. He misquoted the journal of the committee to imply that Congress had deliberately intended to protect corporations. Most of the men who had been on the committee were by now dead, and he was safe enough in attributing motives to them: they were, "in the sunset of life," he implied, endowed with the ability to see into the future so as to realize what the needs of business would be.[14]

The Court, which had regularly been hearing corporate cases under the amendment anyway, did not reply; but a year later Chief Justice Waite gratuitously threw into the argument of a case the specific concession sought by Conkling. "This Court," the Chief Justice said, "does not wish to hear argument on the question [whether the Amendment includes corporations]. . . . We are all of the opinion that it does."[15] The question was therefore decided without benefit of full legal argument, and what had earlier been merely probable was now certain.

While there is no doubt that the due process clause was meant to protect property rights along with those of life and liberty, this protection was of a strictly limited nature until 1877. Justice Story had once described the Fifth Amendment due process clause (which uses the same wording as the later Fourteenth Amendment) thus: "this clause in effect affirms the right of trial according to the process and proceedings of the common law."[16] When the constitution makers framed their documents, they had, of course, many substantive rights which they felt needed protection: these they generally incorporated in the specific clauses of their bills of rights. The due process clauses were part of these, of course, but their meaning seems

[14] Brief to the Supreme Court in San Mateo County v. Southern Pacific Co., 116 U.S. 138 (1885).

[15] Santa Clara County v. Southern Pacific Ry. Co., 118 U.S. 394, 396 (1886).

[16] Quoted in Bernard Schwartz, *The Rights of Property* (New York, 1965), p. 23.

to have been to provide a general statement that courts and law enforcement officials must follow regularly accepted procedures, even though all of these procedures may not have been expressly written into the constitution.

Such an interpretation of the newly adopted Fourteenth Amendment would not, however, have provided any great amount of protection against *legislative* action. The laws passed by the states were presumptively valid unless fraud or some other procedural defect in their enactment could be cited. This, at least, was true until Chief Justice Waite made his damaging observations in the Munn case. One may ask whether the clause would have provided any protection for individual civil liberties either, and the answer seems to be no unless one assumes that the whole bill of rights is, by a sort of shorthand, incorporated into the due process clause of the Fourteenth Amendment. This is what finally happened, although it does not seem to be what the Committee of Fifteen had in mind. As far as we can tell it is most likely that they meant to include individual liberties in the "privileges or immunities" clause, and to use the due process clause merely to achieve the same procedural protection it had been held to provide from national action under the Fifth Amendment.[17] When the Court assassinated the "p & i" clause, due process was left to take up the burden.

There is little evidence that the framers of the Reconstruction amendments thought at all of the protection of business enterprise during their labors. They were concerned primarily to protect the status of the newly freed slaves—which meant protecting their lives, their liberties, and their properties, in the traditional sense. Of course the clause was written so as to apply to all Americans, not only Negroes; but again, it is doubtful that they really had corporations in mind.

At the same time, anyone familiar with American social and political thought knows that there was a strong natural law flavor in the work of the constitution makers, and this seems to have been true as well of the Committee of Fifteen, particularly such of its members as were, like Representative John A. Bingham of Ohio, old

[17] The possible meanings of the Fourteenth Amendment, and the literature concerning it, are summarized in Loren P. Beth, "The Supreme Court and State Civil Liberties," *Western Political Quarterly*, XIV (1961), 825–838.

abolitionists.[18] And these natural law views, it had often been claimed, were a limitation on state power even before the Fourteenth Amendment was adopted; both the abolitionists and many of their predecessors made this argument. Madison, when he wrote the original draft of the Bill of Rights, included in it protection against state action, which his more states'-rights-oriented colleagues in Congress removed. The result was, as we have seen, that there were no limits to state power except those implied by the powers given to the national government or those expressly included in the 1787 document. A state judge said it well when he argued that natural law must be used to achieve these limitations, since the Constitution did not: "Such a construction of the constitution would result in its total destruction, and confer upon the American legislatures all the power that the English parliament ever had." [19]

If there was to be a natural law protection of (corporate) property, it could come only through the Fourteenth Amendment. This is why Campbell's arguments in the Slaughterhouse case were seized upon with such enthusiasm and pressed with such vigor despite the Supreme Court's refusal to accept them in that case. And the Court, despite Miller's rejection of such arguments for the majority in Slaughterhouse, by 1877 was willing to concede that there were likely to be some cases in which the Slaughterhouse dissenters—particularly Field and Bradley—were correct in their contention that due process operated as a surrogate for natural law limitations on state power. It is important to note that when Chief Justice Waite set about writing his strange opinion in the Munn case, he got his most important ideas from that same Justice Bradley.[20] After 1877 the development of this idea was mostly a matter of drawing lines between state acts which were permissible under the clause and those which were not. In time, with such a theory, it was inevitable that a state act would be found unconstitutional, although the idea was so novel that it took some years and significant changes in personnel before the Supreme Court had the courage to do so. The newer judges, many of whom had practiced law as representatives of

---

[18] For elucidation of this point see Jacobus ten Broek, *The Anti-Slavery Origins of the Fourteenth Amendment* (Berkeley, 1951).

[19] Chauvin *v.* Valiton, 20 Pac. 658, 663 (Montana, 1889).

[20] Magrath, *Waite,* pp. 182–184.

railroads and other corporations, and who had observed its development in state courts, no longer found the idea novel, and they came
to the bench ready for its use.

After 1877, then, there ensued two decades during which the
Court adopted a "now you see it now you don't" attitude toward the
substantive use of due process. While never quite finding the laws
unconstitutional, it continually restated that it might, some day, do
so. And as businessmen grew more and more distraught at the regulations imposed upon them by the states the lawyers pressed the
arguments with renewed vigor and the Court edged closer and closer
to the brink. What the business community wanted, of course, was
not merely the limitation of the police power by a natural law interpretation of limitations upon government, but more specifically,
the adoption of a particular natural law theory based upon laissez-
faire and governmental do-nothingism in the field of business regulation. The last they were never fully to achieve; even during the
heyday of substantive due process the courts would not automatically invalidate such regulation—it became the judges' version of
natural law, unpredictable and at times almost quixotic, rather
than the version which the entrepreneurs may have wished.

However, businessmen themselves were seldom united on what
they wanted. The railroad companies might not want their rates
regulated, but many of the companies which shipped by rail
certainly did; and similar conflicts of interest would often be found
in other fields of business. Nor, as we have seen earlier, was the general public unambiguously opposed to "the natural law of laissez-
faire." In those periods when Americans were predominantly prosperous, indeed, they seemed positively to favor it; and if criticism
rose during economic crises there was never a clear majority to be
found for any other system. There is no convincing evidence, in
other words, that the courts were not, here as elsewhere, in touch
with the dominant opinions of the public.

The cases involved in this gradual development fall into two
broad categories: those which directly concerned the limits of the
police power and those which fell into Waite's "public interest"
area—which often concerned rate regulation. The assumption was,
more or less, that price controls were legitimate only in the "public
interest" businesses; whereas other types of regulation might fall
under the general police powers and thus be valid even if they regu-

lated businesses which were not "affected with a public interest." Police power regulation was broader but did not include price controls. Since a public interest business was subject to all the police regulations plus others which were applicable only to it, there was a great tendency on the part of lawyers representing such businesses to argue that they were actually private. Another way in which these cases were often distinguished from one another was that the rate cases were regarded as regulations of property (profits), while other regulations tended to be regarded as deprivations of liberty (for some aspects of which the Court developed a special doctrine called "liberty of contract").

The hesitancies of the Court may be well illustrated in the "police power" area by two cases decided in consecutive years. In one case, a state prohibition law was upheld because the Court, on investigating the background of the law—in effect, substituting its judgment for that of the state—found that the "deleterious social effects of the excessive use of alcoholic liquors were sufficiently notorious for the Court to be able to take notice of them." [21] Justice Harlan, in justifying this procedure, also justified a broad use of substantive due process by the Court; "the courts," he said, "are at liberty—indeed, are under a solemn duty—to look at the substance of things, whenever they enter upon the inquiry whether the legislature has transcended the limits of its authority." [22] This gave everything to the laissez-faire advocates except the decision. However, in the next year, in a case involving a state prohibiting the sale of oleomargarine, the Court seemed to take it all back, holding that it could not go beyond the face of the statute and must accept the legislative judgment that margarine was an impure food, since nothing to the contrary appeared.[23] These two cases had the result of giving the Court alternate lines of decision to be used at its discretion:

For appraising State legislation affecting neither liberty nor property, the Court found the rule of presumed validity quite serviceable; but for invalidating legislation constituting governmental interference in the field of economic relations, and, more particularly, labor-management relations, the Court found the principle of judicial notice more advantageous. This

[21] Edward S. Corwin (ed.), *The Constitution of the United States: Analysis and Interpretation* (Washington, 1966), p. 1086.

[22] Mugler v. Kansas, 123 U.S. 623, 661 (1887).

[23] Powell v. Pennsylvania, 127 U.S. 678 (1888).

advantage was enhanced by the disposition of the Court, in litigation embracing the latter type of legislation, to shift the burden of proof from the litigant charging unconstitutionality to the State seeking enforcement.[24]

In any case, after Mugler the Court had accepted the whole concept of substantive due process where regulations not involving rate control were concerned; the actual use of it only awaited a case in which the judges felt that the boundaries of this essentially natural law principle were transgressed. This was to come in 1897 in the Allgeyer case.

A similar progression may be found in the rate cases. The trick here was to get around Waite's opinion in Munn, since for the corporation lawyers, especially those working for railroads, even control of utilities rates was a violation of natural law. The Court approached this issue with mincing steps. In 1886, for instance, Waite himself led the procession toward Field's position when he said, by way of dictum (that is, it was not essential to the decision—which upheld the rate system involved in the case): "Under pretense of regulating fares and freights, the state cannot require a railroad corporation to carry persons or property without reward; neither can it do that which in law amounts to a taking of private property for public use without just compensation." [25]

Field was able to carry the Court further toward his own position in 1888, when in the course of an opinion upholding the powers of a Georgia railroad commission, he in effect limited the public interest doctrine to public utilities. The criterion was not whether the business had a public interest, abstractly conceived, but rather whether it received special privileges, such as franchises, from the public.[26]

In 1890 the Court went almost all the way. Under new leadership—Melville W. Fuller had replaced Waite as Chief Justice—and with, by now, the Jacksonian Democrats entirely gone from the Court, the judges were willing to accept the burden of deciding for themselves whether or not the actual rates set by the state were "reasonable," and reasonableness became the criterion of whether the due process rights of business had been violated. This signal event occurred, again, in a case which was decided on other grounds. The case came from Minnesota, and the law was found unconstitu-

[24] Corwin, Constitution, p. 1087.
[25] Stone v. Farmers' Loan and Trust Co., 116 U.S. 307, 331 (1886).
[26] Georgia RR & Banking Co. v. Smith, 128 U.S. 174 (1888).

tional on procedural grounds: the Court felt that the state had exceeded its powers by making rate orders exempt from judicial review.[27] The Court was thus able to avoid formally using substantive due process for another few years, but in order to invalidate the law it had to prepare the ground for future use of that concept. As Justice Samuel Blatchford put it,

> The question of the reasonableness of a rate . . . , involving as it does the element of reasonableness both as regards the company and as regards the public, is eminently a question for judicial investigation, requiring due process of law for its determination. If the company is deprived of the power of charging rates for the use of its property, and such deprivation takes place in the absence of an investigation by judicial machinery, it is deprived of the lawful use of its property, and thus, in substance and effect, of the property itself, without due process of law. . . .[28]

The ground was now prepared for judicial supervision of the actual rates set by the states, and again, all that was required was a living, breathing "unreasonable" rate for the Court actually to use the power that it had thus discovered it possessed.

By now the final step in the development of substantive due process was predictable. It came from the police power cases in 1897, and for the rate cases in 1898. The 1897 case was, in itself, of slight importance even though it bulks large in constitutional history as the first use of substantive due process to invalidate a state act, and also as enunciating the doctrine of liberty of contract. Louisiana had enacted a statute which prohibited its citizens from buying ("contracting with" is the legal phrase) marine insurance from out-of-state companies, thus attempting to stimulate local business. Justice Rufus W. Peckham, adopting as his own Field's long line of dissents, wrote the opinion for the Court, holding that the law was unconstitutional as a deprivation of liberty without due process of law. In

[27] Reagan v. Farmers' Loan and Trust Co., 154 U.S. 362 (1894).
[28] Chicago, Milwaukee & St. Paul RR Co. v. Minnesota, 134 U.S. 418, 458 (1890). This doctrine was put in some doubt in Budd v. New York, 143 U.S. 517 (1892), when the Court went back to the Munn doctrine far enough to say that what it meant was that the legislature itself could set rates without court review. This distinction proved, however, to be a temporary aberration which was quickly set right: "The province of the courts is not changed," said the judges in 1894, "nor the limit of judicial inquiry altered, because the legislature instead of a carrier prescribes the rates." Reagan v. Farmers' Loan, p. 397.

order to reach this conclusion Peckham had to invent an involved chain of reasoning, which he did in the following words:

> [The liberty of the Fourteenth Amendment includes] not only the right of the citizen to be free from the mere physical restraint of his person, as by incarceration, but the term is deemed to embrace the right of the citizen to be free in the enjoyment of all his faculties; to be free to use them in all lawful ways; to live and work where he will; to earn his livelihood by any lawful calling; to pursue any livelihood or avocation, and for that purpose to enter into all contracts which may be proper, necessary, and essential to his carrying out to a successful conclusion the purposes above mentioned.[29]

A literal reading of Peckham's words would render the states even more powerless than Peckham apparently desired; but then, the purpose was probably largely hortatory and not intended to be taken literally. Certainly not all of the Court's later decisions indicated that the rest of the judges had done so! But he had constructed a doctrine that was convenient to use whenever the Court felt that a state had imposed an unreasonable regulation (whether or not it involved a contract). The scope of the doctrine will be briefly surveyed in a moment.

The important case of *Smyth* v. *Ames*, in 1898, marked the final entrance of substantive due process in the rate field.[30] Since the case also illustrates the economic thicket into which the Court was entering, it is worth fairly extended treatment. Nebraska had passed a law which set rates for intrastate rail shipment, and the Court held the rates to be unconstitutional; not, be it noted, because they were confiscatory, but because they would not allow a "fair return on a fair valuation of the investment." In other words, the rate schedule was not "reasonable."

Justice Harlan, who wrote the opinion, was no economist, nor were most of the other members of the Court. It is not surprising, in view of the complexities involved, that they wandered into a morass. There were several extremely difficult questions which had to be answered. The concept of "fair return" had to be defined; the way in which it was to be determined had to be discovered; and on top of all this some means had to be evolved for figuring out whether the state's rate schedule would permit a fair return. The question:

[29] Allgeyer *v.* Louisiana, 165 U.S. 578 (1897).
[30] Smyth *v.* Ames, 169 U.S. 466 (1898).

What is a fair return? was, in essence, neither legal nor economic, but ethical: how much ought an entrepreneur be entitled (in a public utility business) to earn on his investment? Courts have generally settled at something like 6 per cent, but there is obviously nothing except an arbitrary sense in this particular figure. It was, however, in the determination of how to figure the return that the courts ran into trouble. "Fair return on fair valuation" sounds fine, but how does one arrive at a fair valuation? Justice Harlan's contribution to this controversy was notable for its unwillingness to settle on any one measure:

. . . the original cost of construction, the amount expended in permanent improvements, the amount and market value of its bonds and stocks, the present as compared with the original cost of construction, the probable earning capacity of the property under particular rates prescribed by statute, and the sum required to meet operating expenses, are all matters for consideration, and are to be given such weight as may be just and right in each case.

This would seem to have been enough for the Court to worry about, but in case he had overlooked something of importance, Harlan added that "we do not say that there may not be other matters to be regarded in estimating the value of property."[31] Lawyers spent many years, as did utility commissions, trying to figure out which of these methods particular courts would favor, and trying to persuade judges to adopt the method which favored their interests. This kind of guessing game was at last abandoned, more or less, in the 1940's, in the meantime having caused countless hours of midnight oil to be burned both by lawyers and by judges.

Perhaps the most difficult aspect of judicial action in these rate cases, however, was the court's own guessing game revolving around the question: How would a particular rate schedule affect the returns of a company? One could (as Harlan did in Smyth) take the amount of business done by the company in recent years and project this into the future at the new rates imposed by the state. This involved, however, the making of at least two untenable assumptions: that the new rates would not affect the amount of business, and that the general level of business activity would remain the same. Since neither of these assumptions was even approximately correct, the

[31] *Ibid.*, p. 547.

Court was likely to make predictions which varied widely from what actually happened. Assuming that the state utilities commissions contained even a modicum of good will and expertise, they were likely to do better than the courts at making these rarefied economic calculations, and for the courts to substitute their own judgment was in reality an act of supreme supererogation. Nevertheless, even federal courts still cling to the power (no longer often exercised, however), while the state courts still actively use it.

Since its central concern is with fairness and reasonableness, *Smyth* v. *Ames* stands for the proposition that courts can and should be willing to substitute their judgment as to what is desirable for that of other agencies of the government. The concern for fairness is laudable, the lack of expertise to apply to the question is deplorable, and the view of the judicial function is at least questionable. For these reasons substantive due process marked in many ways the high point of judicial power in the United States. To the extent that it was used rather than merely threatened it had the effect of making judges into legislators in ways far different from the ways in which all judges must be. It is of some importance, then, to look at the ways and the degree to which it was used.

The difficulty of doing so can be measured by the breadth of possible state action, for anything that a state might do could conceivably be challenged in court on due process grounds. The actual cases are bewildering both in numbers and in variety. They can be classified broadly into those cases involving the police power and those involving public interest business.[32]

Among the police power cases, public health was a primary area of state regulation. The doctrines of substantive due process required, in this as in other matters, that the laws adopted by the state bear a reasonable relation to the evil sought to.be cured. Thus, the first question asked (considering the fact that the police power has become a limitation on power rather than a grant) is always: Is this actually a public health measure? If not, it lies, presumably, outside the power of the state. If so, another question arises, that of reasonableness. Justice Harlan (once more) illustrated the ambiguities of these considerations when, "in an orgy of double negatives," he upheld the Pennsylvania prohibition of oleomargarine.

---

[32] C. Herman Pritchett, *The American Constitution* (New York, 1959), pp. 559–591, is the source for the subclassification used here.

[A court] cannot adjudge that the defendants' rights of liberty and property . . . have been infringed by the statute of Pennsylvania without holding that, although it may have been enacted in good faith for the objects expressed in its title, namely, to protect the public health and to prevent the adulteration of dairy products and fraud in the sale thereof, it has, in fact, no real or substantial relation to those objects. . . . The court is unable to affirm that this legislation has no real or substantial relation to such objects.[33]

The Court here applied a presumption of validity which it made explicit in a Massachusetts vaccination law case. Again Harlan wrote the opinion upholding the law. He pointed out that there were conflicting medical theories as to the value or dangers of vaccination, and that in such a situation the legislature had to choose between conflicting theories; the Court's function was not to "determine which one of two modes was likely to be the most effective for the protection of the public"—that was a decision for the legislature.[34] It is true that in the same year the Court (over Harlan's violent objections) struck down a bakery regulation law which was also justified at least partly on health grounds, by doing exactly what Harlan said should not be done: second-guessing the legislature; the famous Lochner case will, however, be examined under another heading. With the exception of Lochner, it appears that no health regulation was struck down before 1917.[35]

The protection of public morals is another area of the police power; it covers such subjects as gambling, drinking, blasphemy, obscenity, and sexual "irregularities." In this field the courts were extremely reluctant to invalidate state actions, mostly because the judges agreed with the legislators that the evils were, indeed, evil.[36]

Safety regulations, likewise, were uniformly upheld, and probably for the same reasons. The purposes of such regulations are generally quite obvious, and the requirements themselves, while often expensive to the employer, are clearly related to that purpose.[37]

The problems of due process have usually come in areas in which the economic interests of business have been more intimately involved and the justifiability of the law less obvious. Municipal zon-

---

[33] Powell v. Pennsylvania, 127 U.S. 678 (1888).
[34] Jacobson v. Massachusetts, 197 U.S. 11 (1905).
[35] Lochner v. New York, 198 U.S. 45 (1905).
[36] See Pritchett, American Constitution, pp. 564–566.
[37] Ibid., pp. 566–567.

ing ordinances provided such doubts, and Los Angeles was blocked, in 1904, in its attempt to rezone an area in order to prevent the erection of a gas plant, because the Court felt that no change had occurred in the neighborhood since the enactment of the previous zoning regulations which would justify the change.[38] The Court seemingly did not think that the city had a right to change its mind, for there was little doubt that the ordinance would have been held constitutional had it been the first one rather than a change. Another instance, in which Richmond, Virginia, apparently attempted to standardize lot sizes by preventing building on substandard lots— a law which was adopted at the request of most (but not all) of the property owners in the neighborhood—was treated rather unceremoniously by the Court, which said that this amounted to the taking of private property for the convenience of other private persons rather than for public use.[39] Finally, in a case more often categorized under race relations, the Court struck down a Louisville housing segregation ordinance which provided that in any block in which the majority of houses was occupied by whites property could not be sold to Negroes. This decision, in effect, made segregation by zoning impossible and thus led to the practice of segregating through private restrictive covenants—which led to a constitutional question in its turn.[40]

But if the Court was disposed to be somewhat stricter in cases involving zoning ordinances, this did not mean that all of them were invalid; as a matter of fact, most were upheld, and the concept of zoning itself was specifically approved in 1926.[41]

The Court, in a long series of cases, developed substantive requirements for the procedures to be used by states in imposing taxes. These involved such questions as due notice, hearings, and appeals procedures, and while most state practices in these cases were upheld, there were a fair number which were found constitutionally deficient.[42] And finally, it held in an isolated case that a drainage

[38] Dobbins v. Los Angeles, 195 U.S. 223 (1904).
[39] Eubank v. Richmond, 226 U.S. 137 (1912).
[40] Buchanan v. Warley, 245 U.S. 60 (1917).
[41] Euclid v. Ambler Realty Co., 272 U.S. 365 (1926).
[42] See, for instance, Turpin v. Lemon, 187 U.S. 51 (1902); Glidden v. Harrington, 189 U.S. 255 (1903); St. Louis Land Co. v. Kansas City, 241 U.S. 419 (1916); Londoner v. Denver, 210 U.S. 373 (1908); Dewey v. Des Moines, 173 U.S. 193 (1899); Central of Georgia RR Co. v. Wright, 207 U.S. 127 (1907).

district tax could not be applied to a self-contained island, apart from the rest of the drainage district, which would not benefit from the drainage project.[43]

But the police powers received harsh treatment in the liberty of contract cases. Here, as in the commerce cases, the Court took a fairly strong and consistent stand against legislation which restricted employers in their dealings with workers. Although the Court started off fairly liberally in the first case following the evolution of the liberty of contract doctrine in the Allgeyer case, it soon reverted to its familiar pattern of favoring employers at the expense of employees. In 1898 the judges upheld a Utah statute providing for an eight-hour day for miners and smelters.[44] Justice Henry Billings Brown, who wrote the opinion, had some trouble getting around Peckham's overbroad generalizations; he did it by admitting that the liberty of contract was not unlimited. In some situations contracts may be void as against public policy declared through the police power. This doctrine was easy enough to apply in the Utah case, since the judges could easily visualize the law as falling within the traditional police power to protect life and health. The Court found that there were grounds for believing that these workers were subject to uncommon hazards in their work which long hours might well exacerbate. Justice Brown, apparently in a liberal mood, went further (it was this which drew the dissents of Peckham and that old laissez-faire advocate, David J. Brewer); he pointed out that the bargaining power of labor in making the employment contract was not equal to that of capital, and that therefore it was reasonable for the state to step in to redress the balance; he reserved ironic comments for the employers who were, in bringing the case to court, being so solicitous of the freedom of their employees to contract: "The argument would certainly come with better grace and greater cogency" from the employees themselves, he pointed out.[45]

Holden was a 7–2 decision; by the time of the Lochner decision in 1905 this solid majority had been converted to a 5–4 lineup in exactly the opposite direction. While three new judges joined the Court in the interim, one of these was Oliver Wendell Holmes, who was hardly likely to line up with Peckham; so that if all the other

[43] Myles Salt Co. v. Iberia Drainage District, 239 U.S. 478 (1916).
[44] Holden v. Hardy, 169 U.S. 366 (1898).
[45] Ibid., p. 397.

judges remained in the same camps there would still have been at worst a 5–4 majority for the state. Actually there were more shifts than this: for not only did Chief Justice Fuller swing over to the laissez-faire dogma, but he took Brown himself along, while another of the new justices (William R. Day) joined Holmes, Harlan, and Edward D. White in dissent. The shift of these two is not explained in the opinions. Fuller's biographer, indeed, points out that the case was originally decided in favor of the state, but was swayed by the argument of a baker who had studied law.[46] With an employee arguing, this perhaps had an effect on Justice Brown.

The Lochner case is often looked upon as the apogee of due process, perhaps not so much because of the decision itself as because of the uncompromising language in which Justice Peckham chose to phrase the majority's opinion.[47]

The state argued that the law—which prohibited bakery employees from working more than ten hours a day or sixty a week—was calculated to protect the health of the bakers. Justice Peckham was perfectly willing to substitute his judgment on this matter for that of the legislature of New York. He pointed out that most people did not regard baking as particularly unhealthful; and in answer to Harlan's dissent he cited statistics to show that the occupation was not especially out of line with others, from which he concluded that since hours could not be regulated in other lines of work there was nothing special about baking which would allow it; the regulation of hours for all workers was apparently out of the question. He refused to accept Brown's earlier argument that workers were in an unequal bargaining position, concluding that unless the occupation was dangerous, statutes regulating hours of work constituted "mere meddlesome interferences with the rights of the individual." Thus, leaving the bakers to the tender mercies of their employers, Peckham wrote into constitutional law one of the most drastic restrictions on the police power that our history knows.

Harlan's dissent had originally been intended as the opinion of the majority. It is of a good deal of historical significance since it investigated with some thoroughness the health conditions of bakers, concluding that there was sufficient evidence of health hazards to justify the legislature in passing the law, thus anticipating by a few

[46] King, *Fuller*, pp. 297–298.
[47] Lochner *v.* New York, 198 U.S. 45 (1905).

years Brandeis' use of the social facts which has become known as the "Brandeis brief."

Justice Holmes wrote a separate dissent, in which, refusing with vast Olympian detachment to discuss the health conditions existing in the baking industry, he instead attacked the whole concept of liberty of contract. Some of the most memorable Holmesianisms come from this dissent. He held that legislative majorities should have their way unless the statute could not be accepted by a rational and fair man, an argument that blinked the whole issue, since there is little doubt that most if not all of the majority thought that this was the very test they were applying. Holmes further accused the majority of using its economic predilections rather than the Constitution to decide the case: "The Fourteenth Amendment," he remarked, "does not enact Mr. Herbert Spencer's *Social Statics*." But, of course, there was also a legal theory involved—that the state's police power did not extend beyond the protection of health, safety, and morality; and basically, since baking was not considered unhealthy, the majority turned to the conclusion that the law was not a regulation of health but of labor; and as we have already seen, the Court's hostility to the protection of labor was pronounced.

By 1917 the Lochner decision was practically overruled—but on Harlan's grounds rather than those of Holmes. The process began in 1908, when, perhaps taking his cue from Harlan's Lochner dissent, Louis D. Brandeis argued a case from Oregon before the Supreme Court in which he presented only a few pages of strictly legal materials, devoting most of his space to the discussion of the social and medical facts justifying the law. The Oregon law involved was a ten-hour-day law for women in industry, and Brandeis had little difficulty in persuading the Court, even Peckham and Brewer, that "woman's physical structure, and functions she performs in consequence thereof, justify special legislation" regulating her working conditions.[48] The unanimous decision went back to Holden, using a "special circumstances" approach, and did not really undercut Lochner. Nevertheless, Brandeis' success with this new approach to legal argument before the Court soon was used by all lawyers, making the Lochner type of decision less likely if not impossible. The effect of the approach, it should be noted, was to accept the doctrine

[48] Muller *v.* Oregon, 208 U.S. 412 (1908).

of the limitation of the police power through the liberty of contract, but to try to prove in each individual instance that here was an exception which the Court should allow.

Oregon in 1917 provided a further test of the Lochner doctrine, which resulted in its practical reversal. This case involved a ten-hour law covering all male industrial workers (thus including bakers), with the provision that they could work up to three hours overtime at time-and-a-half rates. The Court avoided Lochner by regarding the law as a health regulation—apparently because company lawyers did not effectively present the case that it was not. Of course, by this time Peckham and Brewer were no longer on the Court, nor were Fuller or Brown, so that most of the Lochner majority had disappeared and there was less of a tendency for anyone to try to make a personal defense of his own previous record; it was a 5–3 decision with no significant dissenting opinions.[49]

Health thus proved to be a sufficient covering principle for hours limitations for workers. Another area of importance was the state's regulation of wages. Oregon—the apparent leader in this type of legislation—provided the first case, which came up in 1917.[50] The law was a minimum wage statute for women, and the Supreme Court split 4–4, Brandeis abstaining as he had in Bunting, apparently because he had, before becoming a Justice, advised in the preparation of the two cases. The tie vote had the effect of leaving the state supreme court's decision as the final one, and this had upheld the law. Since there was no doubt how Brandeis would have voted, most commentators regard this as being in reality a 5–4 ruling in favor of the law. This decision was, however, to be overturned a few years later.[51]

How about a state statute outlawing "yellow dog" contracts? It will be remembered that the Supreme Court, in 1908, disallowed a federal law on this subject. In 1915 it extended this prohibition to the states, when it invalidated a Kansas statute protecting the right of laborers to organize. The Court used, as it had in Adair, the idea that workers were equal bargainers who needed no help from labor unions in order to secure their desires from their employers. Holmes dissented on the familiar grounds that organization might "reason-

[49] Bunting v. Oregon, 243 U.S. 426 (1917).
[50] Stettler v. O'Hara, 243 U.S. 649 (1917).
[51] In Adkins v. Children's Hospital, 261 U.S. 525 (1923).

ably" be believed by workers (rightly or wrongly, he said) to be a device which would establish bargaining equality.[52]

One exception to this otherwise consistent pattern of hostility to labor occurred when the Court in 1917 did uphold the right of states to establish workmen's compensation laws, despite the fact that they put the entire financial liability for industrial accidents on the employer and that they interfered with the freedom to contract about work conditions.[53]

It will also be remembered that in the Munn case Chief Justice Waite had held that businesses "affected with a public interest" could be regulated in ways not possible for other business. This left open the question of definition, and there were frequent cases challenging state laws on the grounds that the businesses affected were not in fact of public interest. While Justice Field wanted to restrict this category to public utilities, this restrictive definition was never accepted by the Court as a whole; nevertheless, the question of what other types of business were included in the state's broader powers such as price regulation provided continuous difficulty. In the Munn case the grain elevators involved had almost a monopoly of the business in Chicago, and Waite had placed some emphasis on this fact. The question was therefore left open whether similar businesses without the monopoly feature could be regulated: in 1892 and 1894 the Court held that they could.[54] The regulation of insurance premiums was similarly upheld, because of the importance to the public of this business, as were stockyards and tobacco warehouses.[55] As a matter of fact, up to 1917 the Court did not strike down any price regulations on public interest grounds. That was to come later. But neither did it arrive at a satisfactory statement of what constituted the public interest in such cases. This was left as a process of gradual inclusion and exclusion by the time-honored common-law method. The closest the Court came to striking down a price-fixing law was when, in 1917, it invalidated a Washington statute which attempted to prevent employment agencies from charging anything at all for their services. This rather extreme measure was struck down by the somewhat unusual device of ruling that employ-

---

[52] Coppage v. Kansas, 236 U.S. 1 (1915).

[53] New York Central Ry. Co. v. White, 243 U.S. 188 (1917).

[54] Budd v. New York, 143 U.S. 573 (1892); Brass v. Stoeser, 153 U.S. 391 (1894).

[55] German Alliance Insurance Co. v. Lewis, 233 U.S. 389 (1914); Cotting v. Godard, 183 U.S. 79 (1901).

ment agencies are in the public interest and that therefore the state has no right to do away with them.[56]

Public utilities, such as railroads, were regarded universally as business affected with a public interest, of course, and we have seen that the Court in 1898 adopted the practice of reviewing those rate regulations which were challenged as being so unfair as to be violations of due process. Here again, as we pointed out earlier, the result was confusion, as the courts struggled to figure out ways of determining the fair value of the property involved. Generally, at least until 1917, Harlan's "reproduction cost" idea was used. It cannot be said that the Supreme Court struck down many rate schedules, although one may assume that the threat of such action influenced state regulatory agencies considerably, besides which the state courts were sometimes more enthusiastic about such matters than the nation's highest court. It appears that the Supreme Court itself found only one such schedule unconstitutional, in 1899.[57]

This review of the substantive due process cases, down to 1917, leads to two major conclusions: one is that the Court was not, despite some of its critics, wholeheartedly pro-business or pro-free enterprise at any time. Indeed, the cases are marked by hesitance, ambiguity, indecisiveness, and inconsistency, and in fact many more of the decisions favored the state than the other way around.

Second, whether intentionally or not, substantive due process had the effect of maximizing the Court's influence on the development of the American political system, and certainly on the policies adopted by American governments. It was with the adoption of this doctrine that the Court reached the high estate, the high-water mark of its power, which it has held with some variations ever since. While the Court has long ago given up most of its power in the field of economic regulation with which we have been so far primarily concerned, it has at the same time moved into other areas of equal importance, and despite the New Deal controversies in which it was involved, it has retained its "power position" in the American political system.

[56] Adams v. Tanner, 244 U.S. 590 (1917).

[57] Lake Shore &c. Ry. Co. v. Smith, 173 U.S. (1899). See also Northern Pacific Ry. v. North Dakota, 236 U.S. 585 (1915); Norfolk & Western Ry. v. West Virginia, 236 U.S. 605 (1915); Rowland v. St. Louis & San Francisco RR Co., 244 U.S. 106 (1917).

CHAPTER 7

Civil Liberties for Black and White

EVEN though Justice Miller, in the 1873 Slaughterhouse cases, intimated that the primary purpose of the Fourteenth Amendment was the protection of the freed Negro, any substantial protection flowing from the Reconstruction amendments was long in coming. The Supreme Court might be interested in protecting the rights of property, but this interest did not, seemingly, extend to other fields of rights. The paradoxical result was that the amendments meant more in an area which was almost certainly not intended by their framers than they did in the area which was, most certainly, uppermost in their minds. In this inversion of interest the judges were merely following (sharing might be the better term) the shift of interest of the American public and the American politician signalized by the "Compromise of 1877."

This unspoken formula called for an expansive interpretation of the amendment in the area of economic interests and a restrictive interpretation in the sphere of civil rights. That is exactly what the Court did, and we need not cry corruption or charge cynicism to explain its actions. We need only see it in its proper historical perspective as a court of men, predominantly successful corporation lawyers, conservative in outlook, predisposed to the businessman's point of view, tragically mistaken but patriotic within their lights, and convinced that the destiny of the nation lay in giving free reign to the doctrine of *laissez-faire* economics.[1]

[1] Loren Miller, *The Petitioners* (Cleveland, 1967), pp. 115–116.

The Court, in this respect, stayed close to one aspect of Mr. Justice Miller's Slaughterhouse opinion: it interpreted the amendments narrowly, so as to avoid any substantial change in the power relations of the federal system (except in the economic realm—a development against which Miller fought a long rear-guard action). The Court's purpose was, in other words, so far as possible, to restore and maintain the ante-bellum federal system, without slavery but with the other rights of the states kept intact. There might be certain procedural areas in which the Court had a lawyer-like interest, such as the protection of the integrity of juries, but outside these areas there was little disposition to extend the amendments' protections even to the people who most needed them.[2]

At the same time it was to the white Southerner's self-interest—at least as he perceived it—to frustrate the purposes of the amendments by denying the full rights of citizenship to the Negroes. Not only were the Negroes regarded as ignorant and incapable of intelligent political action, but the political situation within the white community was all too likely to end up by giving Negroes the balance of political power if they were allowed to have any power at all. The possibilities of this were well illustrated by the Populist movement, which succeeded, or came close to success, in those places where white Populists and Republicans were able to form coalitions with those Negroes still voting in the 1890's. And as we have seen, it was the realization of this danger which led the Bourbon Democrats to appeal to the poor whites against the Negro, but also to keep Negroes (and perhaps poor whites also) from taking part in politics. The major constitutional developments in this arena have already been surveyed.[3]

For present purposes the important part of the Constitution is the Fourteenth Amendment, especially the clause in Section 1 which prohibits the denial by any state of "the equal protection of the laws," and Section 5, which gives Congress the power to "enforce" the provisions of the rest of the Amendment by "appropriate legislation." So long as the Radicals dominated Congress (a period which was ended by 1877) this last section was important, for it could be used by Congress to pass affirmative legislation which protected the

[2] The jury cases are discussed pp. 202–204.
[3] See Chapter 4.

rights of Negroes and other minorities, and various such laws were actually passed, ending with the Enforcement Act of 1875. But the section also left many possible constitutional questions, as well as political ones. Politically, it proved to be impossible for Congress—after 1877—to adopt any kind of civil rights legislation, and this was especially true after the development of the filibuster in the Senate in the latter years of the century. Constitutionally, one obvious question arose, and one less obvious—indeed, some say it was manufactured out of whole cloth by the Supreme Court. The questions, which were answered by the Court in the Civil Rights cases and *U.S.* v. *Harris* in 1883, were: What does the Amendment mean when it says that no "state" shall deny rights to any person? What kinds of congressional actions are permitted by Section 5? The answers provided by the Court gave little hope that the Amendment would soon prove to be a charter of liberty for the freed slaves.

The Harris case grew out of the attempt of the government to apply provisions of the Enforcement Act of 1871.[4] Several Negroes had been taken from the custody of a Tennessee sheriff by a mob; one was killed and the others were beaten. The government's contention was that the state's failure to protect the Negroes constituted a denial of the equal protection of the laws, and that Congress had power to act to prevent such denial. The Court, however, ruled that sins of omission were not covered by the amendment; only if the state discriminated by some affirmative act did it violate the Constitution, and only then did the powers of Congress come into play. The mob constituted private action, and the failure of the state to prevent its formation, while regrettable, did not constitute constitutional culpability. Mr. Justice Harlan in this case began his long career of dissent from the majority's reading of the Fourteenth Amendment's attempts to provide equal treatment for minorities.

The Civil Rights cases carried the Court's denial of congressional power even further.[5] These cases arose under the Civil Rights Act of 1875, the last great Reconstruction statute, which included an early version of today's "public accommodations" law, with the difference that in 1875 no one thought of using the commerce clause as the constitutional hook upon which to hang it: the assumption was that Section 5 of the Fourteenth Amendment gave Congress

[4] U.S. *v.* Harris, 106 U.S. 629 (1883).
[5] Civil Rights Cases, 109 U.S. 3 (1883).

ample power. Five cases were combined for argument and decision: they involved the denial of a meal in a restaurant, a seat in a theater and also in New York's Grand Opera, hotel accommodations, and a seat in the "ladies' car" of a train. They thus did not all come from southern states. The government argued that the Thirteenth Amendment had conferred all the rights of free citizens on the Negro, and that the Fourteenth gave Congress the power to legislate to protect that freedom.

Justice Joseph P. Bradley, for the Court, disagreed with both contentions, and in so doing robbed Section 5 of all effect and the two amendments of most of their meaning. He argued that one could not interpret every act of discrimination as a renewal of slavery—here he was probably on firm enough ground—and that such acts as those involved in the case were thus not violations of the Thirteenth Amendment. But the Fourteenth Amendment arguments were the most serious.

The core of Bradley's opinion lay in his concept of "state action," but his view of the powers of Congress was also of great importance. He maintained that Congress had, indeed, no affirmative power of legislation at all: that its only power was remedial. In other words, in the absence of an affirmative action by the state, Congress had no power to legislate even against state action. It could not act prospectively but only correctively. In the 1875 law, Congress had attempted to cope with prospective evils and had thus gone beyond its constitutional power. This was an argument which at one stroke eliminated most of the power of Congress under the amendment and left the protection of Negroes to the courts, where it was largely to reside until the later expansion of the meaning of "interstate commerce" gave a Congress which had gained renewed incentive the constitutional basis for new legislation. After 1883 the question was no longer whether one was violating federal law, but whether one was violating the amendment directly, in such a way that court action could secure redress for the injured party.

Congress, said Bradley, was also out of bounds because the 1875 law was an attempt to reach what he regarded as "private," rather than "state," acts. In 1883 most states did not yet have Jim Crow laws, so it was presumed that all five cases involved denials of facilities without affirmative state commands that the facilities must be denied; had there been Jim Crow laws which commanded segregation Bradley would have had a much more difficult time, and would in fact have had to resort to the type of specious argument which was later to be used by Justice Brown in the Plessy case. Bradley's argument rested, in other words, on the fairly strong ground that the proprietor of a restaurant, theater, or hotel, or the management of a railroad, was indeed a private person running a private business and thus acting in a purely private capacity. Such acts might well be illegal, but if they were there was nothing in the Constitution which said so, and the only possible recourse for the injured citizen was state law and the state courts. (There was, indeed, the possible implication in Bradley's opinion that if the litigation had come through state courts which had ruled against them, these state decisions might constitute state action; but since all the cases had come directly through the federal courts under the provisions of the 1875 act, this was irrelevant. But such a concept would have been difficult in any case, for it made protection dependent upon the case-by-case procedures of courts rather than the blanket provisions of a statute, and thus the protection afforded was slow, uncertain, and individual rather than general.)

Justice Harlan, in a masterly but lonely dissent, took issue with most of Bradley's arguments. He maintained that Congress did have an affirmative power of legislation and that to deny this was to deprive Section 5 of any real meaning, especially since the Court had before the Civil War accorded Congress similar powers to prevent state action in cases involving fugitive slaves.[6] He accused Bradley of thus having sacrificed the purpose of the amendment "by a subtle and ingenious verbal criticism" which, when subjected to analysis, could not stand up. And, he said, Congress was to be the judge of what constituted "appropriate" legislation, not the courts.

But the more important part of Harlan's dissent focused upon the concept of state action. He made use of the concept of businesses "affected with a public interest," as developed in the Munn case, to argue that railroads and hotels, restaurants and theaters, had always been regarded as serving important public functions, and had been licensed and otherwise regulated by the states. Therefore, he continued, they serve in a sense as the state's agents, and what they do must be considered as having the consent of the state; for this reason their acts are state acts which can be reached by Congress acting un-

[6] He referred to Prigg v. Pennsylvania, 16 Pet. 539 (1842).

der the Fourteenth Amendment. Although Harlan did not make use of it, the commerce clause could also have been brought to bear, since the Court had only a few years earlier voided a Louisiana integration law on the grounds that it invaded the federal commerce power;[7] Harlan could have argued that Congress was merely using this power, at least in that one of the five cases which involved railroads.

The Civil Rights cases had the effect of nullifying the Fourteenth Amendment so far as segregation imposed "privately" was concerned, and those sections of the 1875 law which attempted to reach such acts were declared invalid. This left open one important question: What would happen to state *laws* imposing segregation? These were already beginning to appear by the time of the decision, but no cases involving them had yet come to the Court. As noted above, the Court *had* invalidated a law requiring *in*tegration, but on commerce grounds rather than under the Fourteenth Amendment. Nevertheless, this would seem to have placed segregation laws upon pretty infirm ground, at least in the transportation field. The railroad case in the Civil Rights litigation cut across this to some extent, but since no state law had been challenged it still left the matter doubtful.

The Court went some way toward eliminating the doubt in 1890. This case involved one of the earlier Jim Crow laws, which was applicable to railroads in Mississippi. The Court upheld the law against a commerce clause challenge, distinguishing it unconvincingly from the earlier Louisiana case by interpreting it as a law requiring segregation only in intrastate travel. Harlan again dissented, on the obvious grounds that the Louisiana integration law had been struck down by refusing to consider it as intrastate in effect. He was for commerce clause consistency: the rest of the Court, by 1890, was more interested in upholding segregation.[8]

The rest of the way toward abrogating the Fourteenth Amendment was traveled in the famous Plessy case—which is so well known that extended comment on it seems unnecessary.[9] By now Louisiana had eliminated its carpetbag regime and, like other southern states, imposed segregation by law in various fields. Plessy, who was only technically Negro, was refused seating in a car reserved

[7] Hall *v.* deCuir, 95 U.S. 485 (1878).
[8] Louisville, New Orleans & Texas Ry. Co. *v.* Mississippi, 133 U.S. 587 (1890).
[9] Plessy *v.* Ferguson, 163 U.S. 537 (1896).

for whites, under a Louisiana law requiring segregation in transportation. Since the commerce clause was not now available, he sued the state under the equal protection clause of the Fourteenth Amendment, claiming that forced segregation is by its very nature discriminatory action by the state. In an opinion notorious for its casuistry, Mr. Justice Henry Billings Brown for the eight-man majority wrote a short dissertation in sociology, claiming that since the law on its face does not speak of an inferior race but merely of separation of the races, it is only because the Negro race chooses to regard it as implying inferiority that it has such an effect. The states' police power was broad enough to allow laws which would prevent "a commingling of the two races upon terms unsatisfactory to either." Among his other thoughts was a disastrous excursion into legal philosophy: in an interesting anticipation of William Graham Sumner's dictum that "law ways cannot change folkways," he claimed, in one of those phrases that live in constitutional history largely because of their inaccuracy, that "legislation is powerless to eradicate racial instincts based upon physical differences, . . . [and] if one race be inferior to the other socially, the Constitution of the United States cannot put them upon the same plane." Since Jim Crow laws were in reality quite new, he was in effect claiming that law can bring into effect conditions which it is then powerless to change!

Harlan wrote his customary dissent—one which has become his greatest monument. He started from the proposition that the Constitution does not permit any public authority "to know the race of those entitled to be protected in the enjoyment" of the rights it grants. Segregation, he pointed out to his benighted brethren (who probably knew it, although they would not admit it), is in itself discriminatory. It implies Negro inferiority and in fact would not be used if it were not for the assumption of inferiority. Even though private persons may want segregation, the translation of their desires into law runs head on into the constitutional command "that the common government of all shall not permit the seeds of race hate to be planted under the sanction of law."

There was, as we now know, a catch in Brown's majority opinion. Discrimination by law, he admitted, was forbidden by the Fourteenth Amendment. But segregation is not discrimination (for reasons outlined above) and therefore does not violate the amendment unless—here is the catch—the separate facilities are unequal. Since Plessy's lawyers had not known that the Court would invent this doctrine—since become famous as "separate but equal"—they had not presented the Court with data regarding the equality or inequality of the car to which Plessy had been "assigned." Consequently the question was not discussed in the majority opinion. Harlan's dissent was based on the obvious proposition that *any* separation by law is inherently unequal and discriminatory, so he did not argue about the equality of the facilities either. But later cases would take up the point, if only because the South persisted in giving them the opportunity to do so by commonly providing unequal facilities. While not many of these cases came to the Court before 1917, one which did is a straw indicating a possible liberalization of Court opinion as well as the wedge technique that would eventually be used to destroy the separate but equal doctrine itself. In 1914 an Oklahoma law which required separation, but allowed railroads not to provide sleeping and dining cars for Negroes if there was little demand for them, was castigated as a violation of the equal part of separate but equal.[10] Much later, courts were to emphasize the equality so firmly that it became more and more difficult to achieve equal separateness, but this was far in the future. From 1896 to the 1940's little attention was paid anywhere to whether Jim Crow facilities were in any real sense even physically equal.

Other cases arising under the equal protection clause showed a somewhat similar pattern, although they did not all involve Negroes. Four may be mentioned. The first is important because it is exceptional for this period in that the Court seemed disposed to find some meaning in the clause. A San Francisco ordinance which allowed the city to apply its licensing power so as to discriminate against Chinese laundry owners was found to be a denial of equal protection, and by a unanimous Court.[11] Similarly, an Arizona law which attempted to require that 80 per cent of the workers in all establishments having more than five must be American citizens was found to run afoul of the Constitution.[12] But other cases during the period showed a Plessy-like insensitivity to the realities of discrim-

[10] McCabe v. Atchison, Topeka & Santa Fe, 235 U.S. 151 (1914); but relief was denied on technical grounds.
[11] Yick Wo v. Hopkins, 118 U.S. 356 (1886).
[12] Truax v. Raich, 239 U.S. 33 (1915).

ination. In an 1899 case even Justice Harlan went along—indeed, he wrote the opinion—with a decision which upheld the right of a local school district to close a Negro high school for financial reasons even while keeping the white school open. Even though there were private schools available at little or no greater cost, the idea that it was the state's duty to provide equal facilities seems not to have been pronounced.[13]

Finally, the Court upheld in 1908 a Kentucky statute prohibiting integration in privately incorporated educational institutions.[14] Here the Supreme Court performed a neat tactical exercise in evasion by interpreting the issue as merely one involving technical questions of whether Kentucky could change the terms of a corporate charter. It entirely avoided any real constitutional issue. In so doing it provided Harlan with the chance to write his last great dissent in a racial discrimination case. He pointed to the obvious fact that the Kentucky statute was not a mere corporate regulation, but an act of discrimination entirely beyond the state's reach under the equal protection clause. "Have we become so inoculated," he asked, "with prejudice of race that an American government . . . can make distinctions between . . . citizens in the matter of their voluntary meeting for innocent purposes, simply because of their respective races?" The Court's decision was mute evidence of the answer to his question. Corporations could not, perhaps, be regulated where their profits were concerned, but if only people were involved there was no bar to regulation.

Thus ends the sad catalogue entitled "Race and the Supreme Court, 1877–1917." It is not, apart from the memorable dissents of John Marshall Harlan, an inspiring part of the Court's history. The most that can be said for it is that most Americans of that period—white Americans, that is—had they given the matter a thought at all, would probably have agreed with the Court. For purposes of Negro rights the Supreme Court was following the election returns too closely.

In the area of procedural due process—what rights a person has when he falls afoul of the law—the Court had a better record, at least when federal cases were involved. But when cases came from

13 Cumming v. County Board of Education, 175 U.S. 528 (1899).
14 Berea College v. Kentucky, 211 U.S. 45 (1908).

the states, the judges returned to the ante-bellum federal system, usually ruling that the Fourteenth Amendment imposed no procedural requirements on the states. Here again Justice Harlan distinguished himself in dissent, and here as in the race cases he proved eventually to have history on his side, for most of what he asked has been provided by later courts, though not always in the ways that he suggested.

Of the hundreds of cases involving federal rights under the Bill of Rights, only a few can be mentioned here; to do all of them justice would take a treatise in itself. There were, however, several which had a significant formative impact on constitutional development. On the whole, the Supreme Court was engaged in a process of drawing fine lines between what the Constitution required and what it did not, and the precise location of these lines, while of tremendous importance to individual litigants, was not of great constitutional significance. The pair of cases which discussed the connection between the search and seizure provisions of the Fourth Amendment and the self-incrimination clause of the Fifth were, however, of great importance to the nature of criminal investigation and trial, and are worthy of discussion here. The courts early adopted a practice of looking at the right against search and seizure without a warrant as a part of the general right not to be forced to incriminate oneself, and thus there has been a tendency to construe the Fourth Amendment broadly. A congressional act requiring the production of records and other papers was thus invalidated in 1886, with Justice Bradley grounding the Court's action in very broad terms:

> The principles laid down in this opinion affect the very essence of constitutional liberty and security. They reach farther than the concrete form of the case . . . before the court, with its adventitious circumstances; they apply to all invasions on the part of the government and its employees of the sanctity of a man's home and the privacies of life. . . . It is not the breaking of his doors, and the rummaging of his drawers, that constitutes the essence of the offense; but it is the invasion of his indefeasible right of personal security, personal liberty and private property, where that right has never been forfeited by his conviction of some public offense. . . .[15]

Even earlier the Court had ruled that a sealed first-class letter could not be opened without a warrant.[16] As one commentator has

[15] Boyd v. U.S., 116 U.S. 616, 630 (1886).
[16] Ex parte Jackson, 96 U.S. 727 (1878).

remarked, these decisions meant that the Fourth Amendment protects even against action "that was not a search or seizure in the traditional sense," and that the Court was mainly interested in "the intrusion on privacy," as protected by the Fifth Amendment. But there still remained the problem of enforcement; for police could not be forced to desist from illegal searches except by difficult private suits coming only after the occurrence, while the evidence thus gained might in the meantime have been used to help convict the accused. This problem could be solved—given the obvious incentives for police thus to break the law—only by making it impossible for evidence gained illegally to be used in a person's trial. At common law it had always been held that evidence was admissible regardless of the manner in which it was obtained.

This step was taken, for federal courts, in 1914, when the Court ruled that evidence which had been found in a person's home as a result of an illegal search and seizure could not be used as evidence at his trial.[17] The Weeks case was a landmark decision, especially since such evidence is normally conclusive, and its exclusion may result in the freeing of a guilty man. Nevertheless, no easier means of protecting Fourth Amendment rights seemed available.

The limitations of this set of decisions may be seen from two circumstances: one, that even under the circumstances of the 1914 decision, it was conceded that if the search had been conducted by state rather than federal officials, and the information then handed over to the federal prosecutor, the evidence would have been admissible. This is known as the "silver platter" doctrine, and it had a long and inglorious history during which federal officials would often call in state investigators to conduct searches for them, thus being able to use the evidence at trial without challenge. Second, the decision applied, of course, only to federal courts. Under then prevailing interpretations of the reach of the Fourteenth Amendment, state courts were free (as indeed they remained until 1961) to admit illegally obtained evidence so long as their own state constitutions or laws permitted it, which most did.

These circumstances point to the importance of what the Fourteenth Amendment is adjudged to mean in terms of fair police and trial procedures. Here, in line with its general tendency—apart from cases involving social and economic regulations—to construe

[17] Weeks *v.* U.S., 232 U.S. 383 (1914).

the amendment narrowly so as to disturb the existing federal system as little as possible, the Supreme Court unvaryingly held that the states maintained plenary power over their own legal procedures, with the single important exception of jury trial when Negroes were involved. Since the exception was as uniform as the rule, and in fact was developed before the rule, it may be well to discuss it first.

Juries from which Negroes were excluded were universal in the South and common in the North; the various civil rights laws after the Civil War had provided that no one could be disqualified from jury service because of race, and that cases involving such questions could be transferred from the state to the federal courts. Whites, of course, would not normally complain of lack of Negro jurors, and the only way the right could be enforced was through individual actions coming as appeals after conviction. For these reasons only Negroes brought jury cases to court, and a sort of rough "separate but equal" rule grew up. Judges and lawyers were wedded perhaps excessively to the idea that "the individual defendant was solely concerned with the issue of whether or not a particular jury before which he appeared was composed of *his* peers." [18] So if Negroes were to serve on juries at all, it would be only after complaint by Negro defendants and after some kind of higher court action. The Supreme Court provided more protection in this area than in most others: it was conscious of the effects of the jury upon fair trial rights. Yet the actual protection afforded even here was imperfect.

Three cases decided simultaneously in 1879 will go far to illustrate these general observations. The Court struck down a West Virginia statute restricting jury service to whites; however, juries selected under the law continued to be valid unless they were individually challenged.[19] In a second case, the action of a state judge barring Negroes from juries in his court was ruled to be state action and thus to violate the federal statutes.[20] And in a third case, it was held, in effect, that the absence of Negroes from a *particular* jury is not decisive, and that therefore a trial could not be removed to federal court *before* the jury was chosen, even though (in this case) the jury commissioner had a record of excluding Negroes.[21] While the right

[18] Miller, *Petitioners,* p. 120.
[19] Strauder *v.* West Virginia, 100 U.S. 303 (1879).
[20] *Ex parte* Virginia, 100 U.S. 339 (1879).
[21] Virginia *v.* Rives, 100 U.S. 313 (1879).

of Negroes who were defendants to have jury systems from which Negroes were not excluded was definitely established in these cases, it was yet true that the right of Negroes to *serve* on juries was not; that absence of Negroes from any individual jury did not invalidate the trial; and that long and expensive litigation proving willful exclusion was necessary in each individual case before a ruling could be obtained.

Other cases did not make much advance on this front; one held that Delaware's 1831 constitutional provision, which restricted jury service to voters (and thus to whites), was abrogated by the Fifteenth Amendment, which made Negroes voters.[22] Another stressed the point that it was jury panels from which Negroes could not be excluded, not individual trial juries.[23] In effect, the Court proved unwilling to look behind the face of a state law or act, and if discrimination did not appear on the face, the state was upheld. An extreme example came when Mississippi, after having used every possible constitutional device to prevent Negroes from being voters, then restricted jury service to voters. The Supreme Court upheld this practice, holding that since the voting laws were constitutional under the Fifteenth Amendment, and did not show discrimination on their face, the jury provision must also be constitutional.[24]

Most of the jury cases did not involve the Fourteenth Amendment—they were decided under either the civil rights laws or the Fifteenth Amendment. Consequently they did not provide the Court with a chance to determine the reach of the Fourteenth in governing state trial procedures. In the other cases, which did not involve Negroes or anything as definitively commanded as jury equality, the Court was not willing to accord the amendment any force at all: in fact, it might almost as well never have been written, if the cases decided up to 1917 are any criterion. The basic question involved, from a constitutional point of view, is: What trial rights are included in due process? On this matter there have been (in principle) three points of view. One has found it difficult to find any affirmative meaning in the clause at all. A second has held that due process means the fundamentals of fair procedure—those rights which, as Justice Benjamin Cardozo once said, "are essential to a

[22] Neal *v.* Delaware, 103 U.S. 370 (1880).
[23] Bush *v.* Kentucky, 107 U.S. 110 (1883).
[24] Williams *v.* Mississippi, 179 U.S. 213 (1898).

scheme of ordered liberty," but which, since they can be determined by judges only in the course of case-to-case proceedings, are indefinite and (Justice Hugo L. Black has charged) can only be drawn out of natural law. The third viewpoint has been that due process includes the specific fair-trial provisions of the Bill of Rights: no more and no less.[25]

As remarked earlier, the Supreme Court was most concerned that states' rights be preserved except when property rights were also involved. Another way of putting this is to say that the Court as a whole showed a vast indifference to individual rights when state action was involved. Limitations of the state power occurred almost entirely in the commerce and economic regulation cases, while when purely individual rights came up, state power was still regarded as plenary—the principle of *Barron* v. *Baltimore* remained essentially if not verbally the determining rule.[26] The main exception in the cases to be considered here was, predictably, a case involving corporate property.

Lawyers first, using the pattern shown them by Campbell in the Slaughterhouse cases, argued that the privileges or immunities clause safeguarded trial procedures. But increasingly it became obvious that this argument would fail, and thus they resorted to the due process clause—in which, after all, the criminal lawyers were merely copying their betters, the corporate lawyers, who were pressing the same argument with increasing success. Putative criminals were, however, given short shrift by Supreme Court justices concerned with more lofty matters such as the preservation of the free enterprise system. The pattern was set in the first important case, which came to the Court in 1884.

In Hurtado and most of the rest of these cases, Justice John Marshall Harlan's dissents are more interesting and more important than the opinions for the majority. Their prophetic quality, as in the race cases, has gained them in effect the assent of the judges of more recent times, while the more pedestrian opinions for the majority increasingly gather dust on the shelves of constitutional lawyers. For this reason it may be more valuable to look at these cases from

[25] Cardozo's statement appears as the opinion of the Court in Palko v. Connecticut, 302 U.S. 319 (1937); Black's as a dissenting opinion in Adamson v. California, 332 U.S. 46 (1947).

[26] Barron v. Baltimore, 7 Pet. 243 (1833), held that the Bill of Rights applied only to the federal government, not the states.

Harlan's point of view. His position was, basically, that the privileges or immunities clause secured all the rights of the Bill of Rights against state action. But since cases arguing this point were monotonously rejected by the Court majority, he, like the lawyers, soon resorted to the due process clause in cases which concerned trial procedures.

The Hurtado case brought to the Court the question of whether the Fourteenth Amendment's due process clause meant that a state had to abide by the Fifth Amendment's command that capital cases can be brought to trial only after an indictment by a grand jury.[27] California law did not require this. Harlan wrote a long dissent to the Court's decision that neither the Fifth Amendment itself nor the due process clause on its own made any grand jury demands upon the state. He concluded that the due process clause "evidences a purpose to impose upon the states the same restrictions, in respect of proceedings involving life, liberty and property, which had [before its adoption] been imposed upon the general government." This was to become Harlan's persistent theme.

An 1892 case presented the Court with an opportunity to apply the cruel and unusual punishments clause of the Eighth Amendment; the majority refused the chance. Harlan again dissented: cumulative punishment on several counts of violation of a Vermont prohibition law mounted up to a total of $6,638.72 or 19,914 days in prison. Harlan regarded this as an extreme penalty for a relatively minor offense and used the due process argument again.

. . . since the adoption of the Fourteenth Amendment, no one of the fundamental rights of life, liberty, or property, recognized and guaranteed by the constitution of the United States, can be denied or abridged by a state in respect to any person within its jurisdiction. These rights are principally enumerated in the earlier amendments of the constitution. . . . Among these rights is immunity from cruel and unusual punishments secured by the Eighth Amendment against federal action, and by the Fourteenth Amendment against denial, or abridgement by the states.[28]

Since the case involved a business (liquor sales) and property (money), it is perhaps not surprising that Justice Field also dissented; he said specifically that the Eighth Amendment bars "all

---

[27] Hurtado v. California, 110 U.S. 516 (1884).
[28] O'Neal v. Vermont, 144 U.S. 323 (1892).

punishments which by their excessive length or severity are greatly disproportioned to the offenses charged." [29]

Harlan's most effective dissent came in a 1900 case which again raised the question of indictment without a grand jury, with the added issue of whether a state could use an eight-man trial jury. Routinely, the Court held that the due process clause did not affect state practices in either matter, and Harlan took the occasion to review the entire question of the application of the Fourteenth Amendment to the states. He first went back to the privileges or immunities clause and tried to convince his colleagues that it was an attempt to apply the Bill of Rights to the states. But since this argument was doomed to failure, he passed on to the due process clause. He strongly castigated the Court (this was soon after the final adoption of substantive due process) for being more interested in property rights than in the individual.

If, then, the "due process of law" required by the Fourteenth Amendment does not allow a state to take private property without just compensation, [this had been decided by the Court in 1879—CB & Q Rr Co. v. Chicago, 166 U.S. 226] . . . but does allow the life or liberty of the citizen to be taken in a mode that is repugnant to the settled usages and the modes of proceeding authorized at the time the Constitution was adopted and which was expressly forbidden in the national Bill of Rights, it would seem that the protection of private property is of more consequence than the protection of life and liberty of the citizen.[30]

Then, as he often did, Harlan invoked the argument *ad horrendum,* citing the possibilities of what a state might do without falling afoul of the Supreme Court. In an interesting anticipation of the type of question which has since come to the Court, he asked what would happen should the state of Utah establish Mormonism supported by taxation. "Could its right to do so, as far as the Constitution . . . is concerned, be gainsaid under the principles of the opinion just delivered?" He concluded by combating the "partial inclusion" principle which later became the established interpretation of due process in the Cardozo opinion in *Palko* v. *Connecticut.*[31] All the rights of the Bill of Rights, he maintained,

[29] See also the Chicago anarchist case, Spies v. Illinois, 123 U.S. 131 (1887).
[30] Maxwell v. Dow, 176 U.S. 581 (1900).
[31] 302 U.S. 319 (1937).

are equally protected by the Constitution. No judicial tribunal has authority to say that some of them may be abridged by the states while others may not be abridged. . . . There is no middle position, unless it be assumed to be one of the functions of the judiciary by an interpretation of the Constitution to mitigate or defeat what its members may deem the erroneous or unwise action of the people in adopting the Fourteenth Amendment. If some of the guaranties of life, liberty, and property, which at the time of the adoption of the national Constitution were regarded as fundamental and as absolutely essential to the enjoyment of freedom, have in the judgment of some ceased to be of practical value, it is for the people of the United States so to declare by an amendment of that instrument.[32]

Patterson v. *Colorado* was a free speech case: a newspaper writer had criticized the judges of a court, and was then found by them to be in contempt.[33] Among other arguments (the Court rejected the contentions on the basis of the First Amendment free press clause) his lawyers claimed that a contempt proceeding is a violation of due process since the judge who has been criticized presides and is an interested party. The Court held, in an opinion by Justice Holmes, that the state is free to adopt its own procedures: if it allows such actions, this violates no constitutional right.

The last great case on this subject before 1917 came in 1908. Two defendants in a misdemeanor case who did not testify in their own behalf claimed that the state law which allowed the judge to comment (in his charge to the jury) on their failure to take the stand constituted involuntary self-incrimination and thus was a violation of due process.[34] Justice William H. Moody, who wrote the opinion of the Court, seemed to feel that there might be some merit in the old privileges or immunities argument, which was also revived by the litigants; but he felt foreclosed by the previous decisions from considering this very seriously, concluding that it was "not profitable to examine the weighty arguments in its favor, for the question is no longer open in this court." As to the due process claim, he started out by defining it as that set of rights which were "settled usages and modes of proceeding in the common and statute law of England," but these, he said, had to be modified by the judges in the light of changes rendered desirable by new circumstances—thus claiming in

[32] Maxwell *v.* Dow, p. 616.
[33] Patterson *v.* Colorado, 205 U.S. 454 (1907).
[34] Twining *v.* New Jersey, 211 U.S. 78 (1908).

one sentence a vast, discretionary, natural-law-like power for the courts. The only restriction was whether the new practice "disregards those fundamental principles, to be ascertained from time to time by judicial action, . . . [which] protect the citizen in his private right, and guard him against the arbitrary action of government." [35] Moody concluded from a hasty survey of early American constitutions and court decisions that the privilege against self-incrimination was not fundamental. Moody's opinion hardly rises to the rank of a great state paper; nevertheless, its fundamental thesis was adopted later by Cardozo and it remains at least verbally the doctrine upon which cases are decided by the Court. What has changed in recent years is the willingness to find that specific rights are indeed fundamental, and accompanying this a greater willingness on the part of judges to nationalize individual rights even at the cost of producing great changes in the federal system: Moody had stressed that "in our peculiar dual form of government, nothing is more fundamental than the full power of the state to order its own affairs and govern its own people." [36]

Harlan was by now an old man, but the fires still burned, and he returned to the attack in another memorable dissent. Again in anticipation of the kind of question later to be so troublesome he spoke specifically of the First Amendment and went on to say that "as I read the opinion of the court, it will follow from the general principles underlying it . . . that the Fourteenth Amendment would be no obstacle whatever in the way of a state law" allowing the rack or thumbscrew, censorship, unreasonable search, or double jeopardy.[37]

Even this hasty review of these cases will demonstrate the extent to which the Supreme Court since 1937 has nationalized legal proceedings through the use of the due process clause, in contrast to the treatment accorded to them by the Court during the tenures of Waite, Fuller, and White as Chief Justices. While the Court still adheres today to Moody's idea that only "fundamental" rights are included in due process, "fundamental" has come more and more to include the major provisions of the Bill of Rights. And while the grand jury provision has never been extended to the states, the

[35] *Ibid.*, pp. 98, 100, 101.
[36] *Ibid.*, p. 106.
[37] *Ibid.*, p. 125.

privilege against self-incrimination, the search and seizure clause, and the right to counsel have been so applied, and the general tendency now is for the Court to assume an active supervisory power over the procedures of state police officials and courts quite in contrast to the assumptions of Moody and his brethren. Harlan has indeed been vindicated, if not explicitly, certainly in fact.

A final area in which the Fourteenth Amendment might have been thought to have some control is that of civil liberties—those rights of free expression which are mostly summarized in the First Amendment. Yet despite the importance of this field of constitutional law today, there was little that happened in the federal courts before 1917 that would have provided any basis at all for predicting its development. Even though John Roche has argued persuasively that civil liberties are better protected today than ever before in our history, American nostalgia for the simpler and freer society which supposedly existed before World War I still persists. When one searches federal court records one finds little that is enlightening, and the lack of cases must indicate either that there were no serious problems, that aggrieved persons did not take their problems to court, or perhaps that their problems were taken to state rather than federal courts. On the whole, the latter two seem the more probable, since the Court did not until 1925 actually admit that the liberty spoken of in the due process clause was a liberty including the rights of free expression and protecting individuals against state interference. (It is true, however, that there were a few cases even before 1917, and a few more before 1925, which—because the Court heard them at all—seemed to indicate such a conclusion.)

The number of federal cases before 1917 is also small; this is due, however, to a different reason. For the federal government before World War I had such narrow functions as compared to today that its legislation did not often conflict with the First Amendment even arguably. Modes of communication were less sophisticated, and Victorian morality made violation of such laws as there were somewhat less likely. Of course Victorianism had at the same time given rise to some laws, such as the famous "Comstock laws" of 1873, prohibiting the sending of obscene materials through the mail, and there were some cases involving the constitutionality and the interpretation of these statutes. On the whole, however, cases were both infrequent and insignificant in the total picture of developing constitutional law, and it is perhaps best to discuss them in terms of trends rather than individually.

In terms of trends, then, one can discern mainly a tendency for federal courts to allow more latitude, to both national and state governments, to interfere in matters of speech, press, and religion than is the case today. This may be demonstrated by pointing out that not a single federal or state law was found to be unconstitutional in these areas before 1917, but this is a superficial judgment, because one would need to know in detail what the laws were before he could be sure that the statement is correct. No one has apparently studied them thoroughly, and this is partly because most of the cases were decided in lower federal courts, which have not yet been the subjects of any great amount of historical scholarship.

A few instances may yet be cited. In the field of censorship, the courts upheld the constitutionality, without much serious question, of the Comstock laws; and in addition, they interpreted obscenity by the use of the English "Hicklin rule," which said in effect that obscenity is that which tends "to deprave and corrupt the morals of those whose minds are open to such influences, and into whose hands" the publication may fall; further, that even one or two isolated passages may corrupt an entire book.[38] The constitutionality of the laws was accepted without argument by the Supreme Court, which did not question the use of the Hicklin rule either. In one case, for instance, in which the Court was actually upholding the power of Congress to forbid the use of the mails for fraudulent purposes, it was remarked in passing that "for more than thirty years not only has the transmission of obscene matter been prohibited, but it has been made a crime . . . for a person to deposit such matter in the mails. The constitutionality of this law we believe has never been attacked." [39] This sort of statement could be found many times in the cases, and the same kind of remark was made about the power to exclude obscene matter from interstate commerce: in sustaining the Mann Act in 1913 the Court remarked that "surely the facility of interstate commerce can be taken away from . . . the debasement of obscene literature." [40]

[38] See U.S. v. Bennett, 24 Fed. 1093 (SDNY 1879).
[39] Public Clearing House v. Coyne, 194 U.S. 497, 508 (1904).
[40] Hoke v. U.S., 227 U.S. 308 (1913).

But such cases are not governing today except in the broadest constitutional sense; in other words, although the verbiage used would still be acceptable to modern judges, the types of materials to which it would be applied would be very different, since most of the books and other materials found obscene then (especially in state courts) would not be so regarded today; nor would the Hicklin test satisfy modern judges.[41] On the other hand, it is still believed by the courts that obscenity is not a variety of speech or press that is protected by the First Amendment.

The power of Congress to prohibit at least certain kinds of political activities by civil servants was early upheld; [42] and while the general power is still conceded to exist today, there is increasing dissatisfaction with rules which bar from politics several million persons— the volume of federal employment was not much of a problem in 1882.

Still another area in which second thoughts have been taking place concerns *where* speech takes place. The Supreme Court had no doubts at all about the absolute right of governments to regulate or completely prohibit speech in public places such as streets and parks: "For the legislature absolutely or conditionally to forbid public speaking in a highway or public park is no more an infringement of the rights of a member of the public than for the owner of a private house to forbid it in the house." [43] The words are those of Oliver Wendell Holmes; despite their august authorship, one must agree with the critic who said that under them "the right of natural speech is one that is of little value in the one forum that the individual without means possesses for the propagation of his ideas." [44] For these reasons the modern Court has receded from the Davis doctrine, although the matter still remains a controversial one.

Similar controversy has accompanied the general question of press comment about judges and trials. When an editor was punished for contempt for criticizing judges, the older doctrine was that no First Amendment issue was presented.[45] While the matter cannot be said

[41] Judge Learned Hand, indeed, expressed doubts as early as 1913: see U.S. *v.* Kennerley, 209 Fed. 119 (SDNY 1913).

[42] *Ex parte* Curtis, 106 U.S. 37 (1882).

[43] Davis *v.* Massachusetts, 167 U.S. 43, 47 (1897), quoting from Commonwealth *v.* Davis, 162 Mass. 510 (1895).

[44] Bernard Schwartz, *Rights of the Person* (2 vols., New York, 1968), I, 268.

[45] Patterson *v.* Colorado, 205 U.S. 454 (1907).

to be settled even today, there has been a tendency to allow somewhat more scope for press comment than the Patterson case found necessary—judges, in general, take the First Amendment more seriously. The Patterson, like the Davis, case came from a state and illustrated the Court's willingness to consider cases which raised the question whether the Fourteenth Amendment included protection against violations of First Amendment rights.

Of similar import in several other areas, the Court upheld the conviction of a person accused of having published an article encouraging a breach of a state law against indecent exposure; the Court felt that to advise disobedience to law is in itself a crime.[46] Here again the Court treated in an offhand, almost casual, fashion an issue which deserves extended consideration. Later cases demonstrate the complexities which the judges ducked; the whole civil rights movement, the anti-Vietnam protests, and many other instances could be cited. No present-day judge could treat serious issues so lightly.[47]

The Court also treated the first movie censorship case in a backhanded fashion. It refused even to consider movies as a form of speech, comparing them rather to such phenomena of the entertainment world as vaudeville or circuses. Films, it said, are "a business pure and simple, originated and conducted for profit," and "not to be regarded as part of the press of the country or as organs of public opinion." [48] The modern Court of course views movies as a most important form of speech; but in our more sophisticated world it is likely that even circuses might be regarded as something more than mere business: in a sense, one might say, all entertainment has been assimilated to speech and press, even though it may actually communicate little or nothing in the way of ideas. Censorship has thus become, not a matter of prescriptive right where entertainment is concerned, but rather a subject which must be justified constitutionally in the same manner as the censorship of ordinary speech.

The cases involving the religion clauses of the First Amendment stand, in one way, in sharp contrast to the speech and press cases: none of them came from a state. On the other hand, they exhibit the

[46] Fox v. Washington, 236 U.S. 273 (1915).

[47] For the Court's treatment of a similar issue—speech used to encourage illegal conduct (a boycott)—see Gompers v. Bucks Stove and Range Co., 221 U.S. 418 (1911).

[48] Mutual Film Corp. v. Ohio Industrial Commission, 236 U.S. 230 (1915).

same general tendency toward restricting the scope of First Amendment rights. The most famous of them involved the Mormon church; but possibly the more significant in the long run were those concerning federal aid to religion.

Does Congress have a police power in regard to the government of federal territories? And if so, can this power be exercised so as to prohibit polygamy when it is practiced as a religious belief? The first question is answered almost in the asking: of course any court would hold that in the government of territories Congress has the same powers that a state government would have. The second was not quite so easy, for it raised a serious issue as to the meaning of the free exercise of religion clause of the First Amendment. Of course in the nineteenth century—most likely today also, for that matter—a court could conveniently come to only one decision where polygamy was concerned. While paying due obeisance to the freedom implied by the amendment—he quoted approvingly Jefferson's dictum that it creates "a wall of separation between church and state"—Chief Justice Waite went on to point out that even Jefferson acknowledged that civil authority may interfere with religious practices when they "break out into overt acts against peace and good order." Polygamy, he felt, had always been considered "odious" in the Western world; it was punishable at common law and had always been considered an offense against society. Further, marriage as a civil contract may be regulated by government. Whether something which is merely "odious" is an act against peace and good order was not considered by the Court.[49] A modern court might have to treat such a question in a somewhat more sophisticated manner, but there is little doubt that its answer would be the same. The Court carried the analysis somewhat further in 1890, when in another Mormon case it held that "crime is not the less odious, because sanctioned by what any particular sect may designate as religion." Unfortunately, this obscures the main question, which is whether Congress can make anything it wishes into a crime.[50]

There is no doubt that in these cases the Court was in effect imposing Christian morality—as understood by non-Mormons—as if it were written into the Constitution. There may be no help for this in any polity, but here, as in the speech cases, the social conditions of

[49] Reynolds v. U.S., 98 U.S. 145 (1879).
[50] Davis v. Beason, 133 U.S. 333 (1890).

the day made the question seem easier to answer than it seems to us now, so that even if we can understand the decision the reasoning is likely to strike us as being very weak. The Court in those days, too, consisted mostly of God-fearing Christians who were no more averse to writing Christianity into the Constitution than Justice Field was to writing laissez-faire into it. The Court was incautious enough, indeed, to state officially that this is not only a religious nation but a Christian one, in a case, oddly enough, which ruled that under the First Amendment the immigration laws could not be used so as to prevent ministers (even Jewish ones) from being "imported" to serve local congregations.[51]

Two cases which held that certain forms of federal financial aid to religious bodies were constitutionally permissible are of some interest as precursors to the decision of Congress in 1965 to give general aid to parochial as well as public schools. The Supreme Court late in the last century found nothing wrong with a federal grant for the construction of a hospital to be run by a Catholic order. The Court ruled that a hospital is a secular institution no matter who runs it, and that there was thus no First Amendment issue presented.[52] Such aid to hospitals has become routine and has been approved in many court decisions. Financial aid to schools, because of the intimate relation between religious and secular knowledge, poses a more difficult problem, which the Court succeeded in evading until long after 1917. The only case decided was so exceptional in its circumstances that it is difficult to see it as a precedent or a trend. In it, the Court upheld a federal contract "made at the request of Indians to whom money was due as a matter of right, under a treaty, for the payment of such money by the Commissioner of Indian Affairs for the support of Indian Catholic schools."[53] Apparently the money was regarded as in reality belonging to the Indians rather than to the government, and thus again the First Amendment issue was averted.[54]

It cannot be said that the contributions of the federal courts to civil liberties law were markedly libertarian before 1917—nor that they were very numerous or significant. One is struck by the comparative unimportance of these cases, especially if they are judged

[51] Church of the Holy Trinity v. U.S., 143 U.S. 457 (1892).
[52] Bradfield v. Roberts, 175 U.S. 291 (1899).
[53] Corwin, *Constitution*, p. 862.
[54] Quick Bear v. Leupp, 210 U.S. 50 (1908).

from the standpoint of today. The courts are the children of history, however, and the questions they decide, no less than the way in which they decide them, are matters only to a partial extent governed by their preferences. This is a point which is reinforced by even a hasty survey of state constitutional law, to which we now turn.

CHAPTER 8

State Courts and the Constitution

S TATE courts have always, in total influence, bulked larger than the federal. Not only do they possess the power to review the constitutionality of state and federal acts, and to interpret state and local statutes, but they possess the power and status of the English common law courts. In common parlance we might call them America's courts of "general jurisdiction." This means that most law is made or enforced at the state level, since our federal Constitution leaves the broad areas of "the police power" to the states. The criminal law familiar to watchers and readers of Perry Mason is state law; the law governing birth, marriage, divorce, and death; the law regulating business incorporation, commercial transactions, the holding and use of property—all is state law. The Holy Trinity of the American civil lawyer—Property, Contract, Tort—is almost solely the province of the states.

Much of the work of the state courts, following from the above, is routine; and even much of that which rises above the routine is not normally of constitutional interest. Yet the fact remains that in the English tradition common-law courts have a creative function; they, indeed, despite what constitutions say about the separation of powers, make and have always made a good deal of law. The crusty Vermont judge who answered a questioner, "Do judges make law? 'Course they do. Made some myself," was merely remarking on a commonplace, especially during the formative periods in each state's early existence. William Plumer, lawyer and governor of New

Hampshire early in the nineteenth century, was more careful if not as succinct when he remarked, "It is our business to do justice between the parties, not by any quirks of the law out of Coke or Blackstone, books I never read and never will, but by common sense and common honesty between man and man." [1]

The frontier period of creativity so well epitomized in these statements was followed, in the latter part of the nineteenth century, by a period of relatively dry formalism based on a rigid adherence to the hardened categories of the English common law. This adherence was never complete, it is true, but it was pronounced enough to serve as a good illustration of the way in which law could be used, negatively rather than positively, to serve policy purposes. While it does not necessarily mean laissez-faire conservatism, it was historically conjoined with that doctrine. Formalism means, rather, the refusal to view the law and the functions of judges as means of adjusting to the needs of society, and the acceptance of the idea that law consists of rules strictly applied.

. . . the rules of law are to decide the cases; policy is for the legislature, not for the courts, and so is change even in pure common law. Opinions run in deductive form with an air or expression of single-line inevitability. "Principle" is a generalization producing order which can and should be used to prune away those "anomalous" cases or rules which do not fit. . . . Sense, the ways of men with words, the ways of businessmen in dealing, these are irrelevant and literally inadmissible. . . . Finally, even as the common law is thus moved with sweat toward a simpler and more peacefully life-remote structural system, the disturbing statute (inconsistently with "Policy for the Legislature") is dealt with as an enemy invader.[2]

Formalism failed to bar innovation because its premises were wrong: the common law did not consist of clear rules which could be applied by a slide-rule method; but it could drive conscious creation mostly underground, "make change and growth things to be ignored in opinions, and to be concealed not only from a public but from a self." [3] Even a great judge like Holmes could be a formalist, and it is of course equally true that formalism was a tendency which could be

---

[1] Quoted in John Philip Reid, *Chief Justice: The Judicial World of Charles Doe* (Cambridge, Mass., 1967), p. 94.

[2] Karl N. Llewellyn, *The Common Law Tradition: Deciding Appeals* (Boston, 1960), pp. 38–39.

[3] *Ibid.*, p. 40.

ignored by a strong judge such as Charles Doe, the chief justice of New Hampshire in the late nineteenth century. But to most, "a strong opinion was one in which by the employment of pure legal reasoning one arrived inescapably at a conclusion which no layman could possibly have foreseen." [4]

Nothing like a comprehensive treatment of the role of state courts in constitutional development exists, and what can be said must be suggestive rather than definitive. Since the state political systems are the same except in details (which does not mean that the details are not sometimes very important, especially those concerning political parties), certain commonalities may serve as a starting point. The most obvious is that all of the state court systems possess, as noted above, the power of judicial review. While this institution is basically the same everywhere as it is in the national government, there are again differences of detail. State constitutions are typically more lengthy and detailed, and cover more subjects, than does the national document. They will, for instance, specify exactly the time and length of legislative sessions, and they will need to deal with state-local relationships, with public education, with the organization of counties, and with many other matters which are not within the province of the national government. This attempt to specify details and the broader coverage mean that there can be much more frequent constitutional challenges of the acts of the innumerable units of government than of the single national government. And it does seem to be true that state courts are more often called upon to interpret their constitutions, even though this type of case is also a much smaller portion of their total burden.

An influence perhaps running in the opposite direction is that the state courts have usually been more "political" than the federal. Whether the judges are elected or appointed, they seem more likely to be active politicians at the time of selection and also more apt to retain their political interests while on the bench and to gravitate back into active politics rather than remaining on the bench for life. This means that they may be close to politicians in legislature, statehouse, county seat, or city hall, and consequently not very desirous of overturning governmental actions. One writer, speaking of Virginia, concludes that despite the many instances in which constitutional cases were brought to the Virginia Supreme Court, it over-

[4] *Ibid.*, p. 39, n. 31.

turned few acts, mostly in minor matters or in cases involving its own powers. Virginia courts apparently "did little to protect the rights of individuals and less to retard the development of social legislation." [5] And in New York the situation was not much different: "neither the hopes of its advocates that judicial review would be the cure for legislative misbehavior, nor the fears of its opponents that it would act as an insuperable obstacle to essential laws, have been realized." [6]

There is little reason to suppose that New York—a northern industrial state—and Virginia—a southern agrarian state beset with the problems stemming from the Civil War—were in any essential ways different from the rest. During the period 1877–1917 the two states showed much the same specific tendencies: to allow their legislatures relatively free hands in lawmaking for local governments; to allow encroachments on civil rights and liberties which would not be allowed today; to use the federal interstate commerce clause as a means to slow down state regulation of business and industry; in New York, to take an interest in legislative apportionment; to develop and use substantive due process, but seemingly not much more enthusiastically than the United States Supreme Court (indeed, in Virginia less so).

If the United States Supreme Court was ambivalent in its attitudes toward business and its regulation by government, the states were no less so. Allowing for differences among individual states, it yet is true that no court—not even that of Judge Rufus Peckham in New York before his elevation to the federal bench—was wholeheartedly laissez-faire in its decisions. And this seems to be true throughout the period 1877 to 1917.

One instance of this is the famous sequence in which the New York court first invalidated and then upheld the Workmen's Compensation law; and while this reversal came explicitly because the state constitution was amended so as to permit such laws, decisions in other states were such that it seems likely that a New York reversal was merely a matter of time in any case. The original deci-

[5] Margaret V. Nelson, *A Study of Judicial Review in Virginia, 1789–1928* (New York, 1947), pp. 221–222.

[6] Franklin A. Smith, *Judicial Review of Legislation in New York, 1906–1938* (New York, 1952), p. 225.

sion, in 1911, was based on the court's feeling that the common-law rule "no liability without fault" embodied a fundamental rule of justice which could not be changed even though, in general, legislation overrides common law. In this case the common-law rule, the court felt, was supported by the due process clauses of the state and federal constitutions.[7] After the consitution was amended, the court upheld a similar act,[8] which was then affirmed by the U.S. Supreme Court.[9]

State courts are often influenced, it should be noted, by the trend of decisions in other states, and so, perhaps, are the federal courts. In any case, it is of interest that New York was almost, if not quite, alone in treating workmen's compensation or employers' liability laws so unceremoniously. Connecticut and Indiana went along with New York, at least in part,[10] but apparently no other state did; Wisconsin, although not the first, is a good example: here the court held that the fact that the law was on its face noncompulsory was conclusive in the absence of evidence that it had a coercive effect in practice.[11] By 1917 the constitutionality of such laws was almost beyond challenge, and the Supreme Court decision of that year merely ratified an existing fact.

The antilabor proclivities of the U.S. Court were also duplicated to some extent by the states. Even though Massachusetts upheld a ten-hour law for women as early as 1876,[12] other such laws were often struck down,[13] as were laws prohibiting payment of workers in scrip instead of money, laws requiring weekly payment or prohibiting payment in goods, and coal "screening" laws (which tried to prevent mining companies from paying miners by the weight of coal produced after screening out the unusable part of the product).[14]

[7] Ives v. The South Buffalo Railway Co., 94 N.E. 431 (1911).

[8] Matter of Jensen v. Southern Pacific Co., 215 N.Y. 514 (1915).

[9] New York Central Railroad Co. v. White, 243 U.S. 188 (1917).

[10] Hoxie v. New York, New Haven and Hartford Railroad Co., 73 Atl. 754 (1909, Conn.); Bedford Quarries Co. v. Bough, 80 N.E. 529 (1907, Ind.).

[11] Borgnis v. Falk, 133 N.W. 209 (1911, Wis.).

[12] Commonwealth v. Hamilton Mfg. Co., 120 Mass. 383 (1876).

[13] Low v. Rees Printing Co., 41 Nebr. 127 (1894); Ritchie v. People, 155 Ill. 98 (1895); In re 8-Hour Bill, 21 Colo. 29 (1895); Ex parte Kuback, 85 Calif. 274 (1890).

[14] Ramsey v. People, 142 Ill. 380 (1892); State v. Fire Creek Coal & Coke Co., 33 W. Va. 188 (1889); State v. Goodwill, 33 W. Va. 179 (1889); Braceville Coal Co. v. People, 147 Ill. 66 (1893); Frorer v. People, 141 Ill. 171 (1892); Godcharles v. Wigeman, 113 Pa. St. 431 (1886); In re House Bill No. 203, 21 Colo. 27 (1895); State v. Loomis, 115 Mo. 307 (1893); Jordan v. State, 103 S.W. 633 (1907, Tex.).

Such decisions were ordinarily based on the doctrine of the liberty of contract, but the fact that they were based as much on emotion as on legal reason can be demonstrated by statements such as the following.

[It is inadmissible] to arbitrarily brand . . . one class . . . as too unscrupulous, and the other class as too imbecile or timid or weak, to exercise that freedom of contracting which is allowed to all others.[15]

[The state cannot prevent] persons who are *sui juris* from making their own contracts. [Such action constitutes] an insulting attempt to put the laborer under legislative tutelage.[16]

[Government is not authorized] to do for its people what they can do for themselves. . . . It is an attempt to degrade the intelligence, virtue and manhood of the American laborer . . ., it assumes that the employer is a knave, and the laborer an imbecile.[17]

Putting laborers "under legislative tutelage" so as to equalize bargaining power was, of course, precisely what was intended by such laws, but since they were new in concept (at least as applied to laborers) and since they were uniformly to the economic disadvantage of employers, it is surprising neither that management fought them or that courts accepted the freedom of contract arguments of corporation lawyers.

But even here there was no unanimity. Indiana upheld a "scrip law" as early as 1890 and West Virginia in 1892, and Rhode Island a weekly payment law in 1892.[18] And there were dissenters, like Holmes in Massachusetts objecting to the invalidation of a law preventing employers from withholding wages for imperfect work, and to the court's outlawing of picketing and other union practices.[19] Despite such objections, the state courts were more nearly unanimous in the labor area than in most others, and their resistance to laws protecting labor lasted until some time after 1917: while Washington upheld the limiting of hours of work for women in 1912,[20]

[15] Frorer *v.* People, 141 Ill. 171 (1892).

[16] Godcharles *v.* Wigeman, 113 Pa. St. 431 (1886).

[17] State *v.* Goodwill, 33 W. Va. 179 (1889).

[18] Hancock *v.* Yaden, 121 Ind. 366 (1890); State *v.* Brown & Sharpe Mfg. Co., 18 R.I. 16 (1892).

[19] Commonwealth *v.* Perry, 155 Mass. 117 (1893); Sherry *v.* Perkins, 147 Mass. 212 (1888).

[20] State *v.* Somerville, 122 Pac. 324 (1912, Wash.).

and North Carolina the outlawing of employment of children under twelve,[21] Illinois struck down a law prohibiting the assignment of wages,[22] Massachusetts the limiting of working hours in "steam railroad stations," [23] Missouri the limitation of bakers' hours,[24] and several states struck down statutes prohibiting employers from firing or threatening workers involved in union activities.[25] New York even found invalid a law prohibiting employers from working their female employees during the night, in an action which was possibly the high-water mark of the protection of management against such burdensome regulations.[26] All of these decisions came after 1905, when the influence of the Supreme Court's Lochner decision was at its height: when, indeed, the state judges may have felt that they were merely "obeying" the Supreme Court.

Labor violence in this period was widespread, and the solid citizens tended to blame it on "foreign radicals." Whoever was to blame, there is no doubt that the middle classes were frightened by the violence which appeared in strikes throughout the period, and that the courts when they issued labor injunctions were doing what not only management but most other Americans outside the working class felt was just and necessary. The public feeling aroused by the trial of "Big Bill" Haywood, the leader of the Western Federation of Miners (in 1907), demonstrates this feeling. Haywood was tried for complicity in the murder of Idaho's former governor, Frank Steunenberg, who had endeared himself to the miners by his response when they blew up several mines in the Coeur d'Alene area: he called for federal troops, herded the miners into "bullpens," and issued labor permits which prevented any union members from working. As usual in human affairs, violence begat violence. Haywood was finally, with the help of the great criminal lawyer Clarence Darrow, acquitted—which restored some of the faith of workers in the fairness of American justice and perhaps averted further violence.[27]

[21] Starnes v. Albion Mfg. Co., 61 S.E. 525 (1908, N.C.).
[22] Massie v. Cessna, 88 N.E. 152 (1909, Ill.).
[23] Commonwealth v. Boston & Maine RR Co., 110 N.E. 264 (1915, Mass.).
[24] State v. Miksicek, 125 S.W. 507 (1910, Mo.).
[25] Bemis v. State, 152 Pac. 456 (1915, Okla.); State v. Daniels, 136 N.W. 584 (1912, Minn.).
[26] People v. Williams, 101 N.Y.S. 562 (1906).
[27] This story is interestingly told in Walter Lord, *The Good Years, from 1900 to the First World War* (London, 1960), pp. 150–179.

In areas where businessmen were pitted against each other, of course, the courts were more likely to uphold state regulations, and the same was true where obvious public interests such as health were involved, or where "noxious articles" such as liquor were banned or controlled. There was also a rough distinction made between businesses in which the judges felt that the public had a legitimate interest and those which they regarded as essentially private.

These considerations provide at least some reasons why the regulation of railroads was accepted so readily by courts which were not in general favorable to the idea of government interference in economic affairs. Shippers constituted an interest of great importance, and most of their desires ran contrary to those of the railroads. Even "big" businesses, like steel, had no reason to wish to leave themselves to the tender mercies of E. H. Harriman or "Commodore" Vanderbilt, though they could, by reason of their size, probably get a better deal through rate rebates and bulk shipment rates than could individually small shippers like farmers. Then, too, railroads before the turn of the century had almost catastrophically high accident rates, especially in "minor" accidents in which there was no damage except to the life or limb of an employee: and the courts were not likely to pay much attention to railroad lawyers who argued against the imposition of safety devices which could cut down the injury rate. Finally, the influence of the common carriers on American economic life in the age of industry was so obviously great that no one could pretend that they were private industries except in some special sense.

Whatever the reasons, the state courts put few bars up against legislation regulating the public utilities. The general right to regulate was invariably upheld, even early in the period,[28] at least for railroads, and the use of regulatory commissions passed without much comment.[29] Specific regulations, especially of rates, were naturally not accepted as readily: but as early as the eighties and nineties regulations having to do with smoke, spark damage, and even the requirement of "on time" notices in railroad stations were

---

[28] Burlington, C. R. & N. Ry. Co. v. Dey, 48 N.W. 98 (1891, Iowa); Laurel Fork & S. H. RR Co. v. West Virginia Transp. Co., 25 W. Va. 324 (1884); Chicago, B. & Q. RR Co. v. Jones, 37 N.E. 247 (1894, Ill.).

[29] Gregg v. Laird, 87 Atl. III (1913, Md.); Southern Ry. Co. v. Hunt, 83 N.E. 721 (1908, Ind. App.).

upheld.[30] A great deal of this development proceeded under the idea, as stated by the Wisconsin court, that "the business of operating railroads differs from other business in its nature and is subject to special regulation to meet the conditions peculiar to it." [31]

The courts were, on the other hand, very careful to maintain their own right to review the regulations established by the states. Hundreds of cases stated the principle that no regulations were conclusive on the courts, nor could the states prevent court review.[32] Having thus maintained their own position in the power structure, the judges found considerably fewer cases in which the specific regulation under review was found invalid, but even these were quite frequent.[33] They were usually based on some variation of a rule of reason—such as the right to a reasonably fair rate of profit—or on the assumed unfairness of regulations which applied differentially to different industries (or in a few cases, which applied to corporations but not to other forms of business organization).[34]

Public utilities outside the transportation field—indeed, even within it when railroads were not involved—sometimes received greater protection against the state from the courts. This was partly because their great adversary was the general consuming public, which all too often had no bevy of lawyers to plead its cause or to apply political pressures on its behalf. Then, too, the other great utilities—telephone, gas, electricity—were quite new; their importance to the general public was not as obvious; and therefore the case for regulating them seemed weaker. Early in the period, for instance, a New Jersey decision held that the making and selling of gas is a private endeavor into which any person had a right to enter: the state had no power to regulate entrance into the business.[35] Several

---

[30] Harmon v. Chicago, 51 Am. Rep. 698 (1884, Ill.); Burrows v. Delta Transp. Co., 64 N.W. 501 (1895, Mich.); State v. Indianapolis & I. S. RR Co., 32 N.E. 817 (1892, Ind.); Smith v. Boston & Maine RR Co., 63 N.H. 25 (1884).

[31] Kiley v. Chicago, M. & St. P. Ry. Co., 119 N.W. 309 (1909, Wis.).

[32] Among the earlier such decisions were Priewe v. Wisconsin State Land & Improvement Co., 67 N.W. 918 (1896, Wis.); Stone v. Natchez, J. & C. RR Co., 62 Miss. 646 (1885).

[33] Munhall v. Pennsylvania RR Co., 92 Pa. St. 150 (1879); State v. Chicago & N. W. Ry. Co., 30 N.W. 398 (1886, Iowa), etc.

[34] State v. Donald, 153 N.W. 238 (1915, Wis.); Mt. Vernon Woodberry Cotton Duck Co. v. Frankfort Marine Accident & Plate Glass Ins. Co., 75 Atl. 105 (1909, Md.); Western Union Tel. Co. v. State, 121 Pac. 1069 (1912, Okla.); Bedford Quarries Co. v. Bough, 80 N.E. 529 (1907, Ind.).

[35] Jersey City Gas Co. v. Dwight, 29 N.J. Eq. 242 (1878).

states came to the same decision about the operation of ferryboats where the operator owned the river banks involved.[36] Out of such decisions came a sort of rule (imperfectly observed, to be sure) that, as stated by the Ohio court, the licensing power of the state can be exercised only "when a special benefit is conferred at the expense of the general public, or the business imposes a special burden on the public, or where the business is injurious to or involves danger to the public." [37] The interpretation of such a rule was, naturally, left to the courts themselves, and it left them a wide range of discretion. If South Dakota could not regulate entrance into the banking business,[38] this did not necessarily mean that other states operated under the same disability. And if several state courts held that cities could not grant monopolies,[39] this did not inevitably debar cities in other states, nor did it necessarily mean that the state could not do so. Indeed, the courts themselves often used the old common-law rule forbidding combinations in restraint of trade as an anti-monopoly device.[40] New Hampshire's Supreme Court, under the leadership of Charles Doe, perhaps the strongest state judge of his era, even attempted for a ten-year period to enforce the common law and ignore the railroad antitrust statutes passed by the legislature.[41]

Another perceptible tendency, especially after the U.S. Supreme Court's decisions upholding various types of regulatory activities under the interstate commerce clause, was for the state courts to use federal decisions or statutes as a pretext for limiting state action. Sometimes this meant a ruling that the state could not have different (*i.e.*, stricter) rules than were in existence federally; [42] sometimes a doctrine of federal supersession was used to block state legislation; [43] more often state statutes were struck down merely because

[36] Chenango Bridge Co. *v.* Paige, 38 Am. Rep. 407 (1880, N.Y.); Appeal of Braddock's Ferry Co., 3 Pa. 32 (1882).

[37] Marmet *v.* State, 12 N.E. 463 (1887, Ohio).

[38] State *v.* Scougal, 51 N.W. 858 (1892, S.D.).

[39] *In re* Lowe, 39 Pac. 710 (1895, Kans.); Davenport *v.* Kleinschmidt, 13 Pac. 249 (1887, Mont.).

[40] Among many, see Distilling & Cattle Feeding Co. *v.* People, 41 N.E. 188 (1895, Ill.); Anheuser-Busch Brewing Assoc. *v.* Houck, 27 S.W. 692 (1894, Tex.); People *v.* North River Sugar Refining Co., 5 L.R.A. 386 (1889, N.Y.).

[41] Reid, *Chief Justice,* pp. 267–281.

[42] State *v.* Texas & N. O. RR Co., 124 S.W. 984 (1910, Tex.); State *v.* Chicago, M. & St. P. Ry. Co., 117 N.W. 686 (1908, Wis.).

[43] Among many cases, see Vickery *v.* New London Northern RR Co., 89 Atl. 277 (1914, Conn.).

the state court felt that they involved the regulation of inter- rather than intra-state commerce,[44] or because they imposed a "burden" on interstate commerce.[45] One can never tell, in such cases, what the real reason for the court's action was: were they honestly trying to carry out the implications of the federal Constitution's commerce clause and the Supreme Court's decisions thereunder, or where they using this as a cover for hostility to the regulatory laws themselves? Probably the judges themselves didn't even know the answer to such a question, for the layers of rationalization and the lack of self-analysis combined to make it difficult to find the real motives.

Health and safety regulations were, as the railroad cases illustrate, generally upheld. For instance, it was not uncommon for state courts to allow administrative authorities the summary power (that is, without a hearing) to destroy diseased fruit or animals [46] (but not to take cruelly treated animals [47]) summarily. Regulation of the medical and dental professions was easily accepted,[48] as were quarantine and inoculation laws,[49] inspection and certification statutes,[50] requirement of the provision of safety devices in mines and factories as well as on railroads,[51] and laws requiring animals to be fenced in or otherwise prevented from roaming at large.[52] These results seem not unexpected, even from "conservative" courts, for the public interest is readily identifiable, and the needs posed by the closely packed urban centers and the widespread use of potentially dangerous machinery are clear.

There was a certain tendency for state judges to favor "settled" types of businesses at the expense of itinerant forms: regulation of

[44] Mississippi River Bridge Co. v. Lonergan, 91 Ill. 508 (1879); Bennett v. American Express Co., 22 Atl. 159 (1891, Md.).

[45] Circular Adv. Co. v. American Mercantile Co., 63 Sou. 3 (1913, Fla.); Lehigh Portland Cement Co. v. McLean, 92 N.E. 248 (1910, Ill.); Schmidt v. Indianapolis, 80 N.E. 632 (1907, Ind.); State v. U.S. Express Co., 145 N.W. 451 (1914, Iowa).

[46] People ex rel Lodes v. Dept. of Health, 82 N.E. 187 (1907, N.Y.); Colvill v. Fox, 149 Pac. 496 (1915, Mont.); Nelson v. Minneapolis, 127 N.W. 445 (1910, Minn.); Los Angeles Berry Growers Coop. Assoc. v. Huntley, 146 Pac. 373 (1915, Wash.).

[47] Jenks v. Stump, 93 Pac. 17 (1907, Colo.).

[48] Richardson v. State, 25 S.W. 187 (1886, Ark.); People v. Fulda, 4 N.Y. Supp. 945 (1889).

[49] Brown v. Murdock, 3 N.E. 208 (1885, Mass.).

[50] People v. Harper, 91 Ill. 357 (1878).

[51] Krueck v. Phoenix Chair Co., 147 N.W. 41 (1914, Wis.).

[52] But there were limits: a Texas court invalidated a law requiring fences to have a gate every 3 miles; Dilworth v. State, 36 S.W. 274 (1896, Tex.).

peddlers and auctioneers (mostly through license fees) was wide-spread and was usually accepted by the courts.[53] But courts were less willing to accept such regulations when they attempted to aid local business by putting onerous burdens on outsiders.[54]

A pronounced hesitancy to accept laws based on aesthetic considerations showed itself. Early zoning and building permit laws had rough sledding; [55] on the other hand—for reasons having little to do with rural beauty—game conservation laws were usually upheld.[56] The flavor of the courts' attitudes toward aesthetics may be shown by two illustrations: in Illinois an attempt to put a statutory limit on how close billboards could be placed to parks or boulevards was stigmatized as an attempt "to limit the proper use of private property for aesthetic reasons"; [57] the mere statement indicates that such considerations were of only minimal importance and thus the police power did not extend to them. And in Massachusetts, when the legislature tried to protect the view of the state capital by restricting the height of buildings near it, Judge Oliver Wendell Holmes himself led the court in condemning the law. While the decision was based on technical grounds, Holmes made it quite clear that he doubted whether the police power extended so far. While it may be argued, he said, that one object of the law "was to save the dignity and beauty of the city at its culminating point, for the pride of every Bostonian and for the pleasure of every member of the State," the fact remains that this is a purpose "which may be described as of luxury rather than necessity," and that "to sustain the restriction . . . under the police power would be a startling advance upon anything heretofore done." [58] So much for beauty.

The regulation of businesses or products regarded as harmful, as

[53] State v. St. Paul, 25 N.W. 449 (1885, Minn.); State v. Wheelock, 64 N.W. 620 (1895, Iowa); People v. Russell, 14 N.W. 568 (1883, Mich.); Commonwealth v. Gardner, 19 Atl. 550 (1890, Pa.).

[54] Carrollton v. Bazette, 42 N.E. 837 (1896, Ill.); Rash v. Holloway, 6 Ky. Law Rep. 710 (1885).

[55] City of Sioux Falls v. Kirby, 50 N.W. 156 (1894, S.D.); Willison v. Cooke, 130 Pac. 828 (1913, Colo.).

[56] Roth v. State, 37 N.E. 259 (1894, Ohio); State v. Norton, 45 Vt. 258 (1872); Stuttsman v. State, 57 Ind. 119 (1877); People v. Bridges, 31 N.E. 115 (1892, Ill.).

[57] Haller Sign Works v. Physical Culture Training School, 94 N.E. 920 (1911, Ill.).

[58] Parker v. Commonwealth, 178 Mass. 199 (1901). Holmes later changed: dissenting in Tyson v. Banton, 273 U.S. 418, 446 (1927), he said "the legislature may forbid or restrict any business when it has a sufficient force of public opinion behind it."

defined (or redefined) by judges, was acceptable. But courts reserved to themselves the right to make an independent judgment of what was, and what was not, harmful. It was thus to be expected that courts composed entirely of males should uphold laws designed to keep females out of saloons, or from working as barmaids.[59] Liquor being putatively harmful anyway (as we shall see), it was obviously even more harmful for women than for men. It is not quite so obvious why so many judges would contradict their legislators' judgment that trading stamps were bad enough to be prohibited; nevertheless, many courts did substitute their own ideas of wise public policy for those of the legislature in just such a way.[60] Colored oleomargarine was seen for some odd reason as harmful by both legislatures and the courts, and laws prohibiting its sale were uniformly upheld.[61]

Liquor, during this period at least, falls into a separate category. For one thing, it was big business—but beyond this, there was a startling consensus that it was so deleterious that it should be heavily regulated if not, indeed, forbidden completely. In addition, it was a socially acceptable source of prolific revenues through taxation. For these reasons the many and varied laws regarding the liquor business were almost unanimously accepted by the courts of the various states. There is little need to go into the details of this,[62] but it is interesting that one type of law which one might expect courts to resist, simply because it gives privileges to some people in the state while withholding them from others—the local option law—was also uniformly upheld.

Possibly such arrangements would not have survived constitutional challenge had they involved businesses other than liquor.[63] This was because courts felt that "unreasonable" classifications were unconstitutional, though what they might hold to be unreasonable was, as might be expected, unpredictable. Often, it was held that a regulation or tax was invalid because other businesses which were

[59] Laughlin v. Tillamook, 147 Pac. 547 (1915, Ore.); In re Carragher, 128 N.W. 352 (1910, Iowa); People v. Case, 116 N.W. 558 (1908, Mich.).

[60] State v. S & H Co., 144 N.W. 795 (1913, Nebr.); Leonard v. Bassindale, 89 Pac. 879 (1907, Wash.).

[61] People v. Freeman, 90 N.E. 366 (1909, Ill.).

[62] Some early cases are State v. Aiken, 20 S.E. 221 (1894, S.C.); Valverde v. Shattuck, 34 Pac. 947 (1893, Colo.).

[63] Saville v. Corless, 151 Pac. 51 (1915, Utah).

"similar" in some way (such as similarly harmless) were not also regulated.[64] For instance, one decision held that a tax on oil trucks was invalid because it did not apply to other trucks;[65] again, a license fee for peddlers of stoves, ranges, and wagons was held bad since it did not include other harmless items.[66] But other classifications would be upheld in the same states, and the same ones in different states, so that no patterns seem discernible except that the legislature guessed wrong. In an interesting reflection of Lochner, the Missouri lawmakers certainly guessed wrong when they enacted a sanitation law for "biscuit, bread or cake bakeries," only to be told by the state supreme court that they couldn't do this—because they had not included bakeries making "pie, pastry, crackers or confectionaries." [67] One state held that a wage law for skilled labor was invalid because it excluded unskilled workers;[68] while another abrogated laws prohibiting the selling of meat and groceries on Sunday because it did not prohibit other items.[69] Classifications imposing restrictions on Negroes, however, were usually upheld—but this is another story.

The court decisions so far surveyed, all in the field of business regulation, thus create an impression of overwhelming confusion. The bewildered reader might be pardoned for wondering whether the patterned nature of American law had completely broken down. Of course the confusion inherent in a hasty survey of forty-eight different jurisdictions makes this picture at least partially inaccurate, as does the fact that the cases cover a fifty-year period. If one were to look at a single state over a somewhat shorter length of time it is probable that more consistency would be revealed; and some color is lent to this possibility by the studies of New York and Virginia previously alluded to.

Nevertheless, to some extent the confusion was real. It was caused by the fact that the states, like the national government, were dur-

---

[64] State v. Donald, 153 N.W. 238 (1915, Wis.); Union Sawmill Co. v. Felsenthal, 108 S.W. 507 (1908, Ark.).

[65] Waters-Pierce Oil Co. v. Hot Springs, 109 S.W. 293 (1908, Ark.).

[66] State v. Wright, 100 Pac. 296 (1906, Ore.).

[67] State v. Miksicek, 125 S.W. 507 (1910, Mo.).

[68] Wright v. Hector, 145 N.W. 704 (1914, Nebr.).

[69] Mergen v. Denver, 104 Pac. 399 (1909, Colo.); City of Marengo v. Rowland, 105 N.E. 285 (1914, Ill.). Amusing is the case which struck down a law against the use of secondhand materials in bedding because it excluded pillows—see People v. Weiner, 110 N.E. 870 (1915, Ill.).

ing this period experimenting—sometimes wildly—with new types of regulations intended to meet the problems of the spreading industrial and communications revolutions. If the judges seemed inconsistent, this was merely an indication of the confused reactions in the entire governmental structure. Perhaps, given the nature of judicial review, one ought to be surprised at how much of the resulting (often experimental) legislation was found constitutional by the courts of the various states. Without going quite so far, it is nevertheless clear that the courts did not meet the regulatory age with anything like a solid phalanx of opposition. Nor is there much evidence that court decisions—taken singly or as a whole, possibly excepting the labor field—unduly restrained the states from meeting the problems of the day as their people wished.

In the area of human rights and liberties there was less confusion. In general, state courts did not distinguish themselves by their attachment to the spirit of their bills of rights; and patterns are more readily distinguishable. There were, of course, major differences among states: Massachusetts was famous for the strict application of its obscenity laws; [70] the southern states were in general less willing to accord rights to Negroes—one writer says of Virginia that "the Negro asked little and received less"; [71] and there were pronounced differences between the states in their approaches to the separation of church and state.

Lord Bryce found the significance attached to the state bills of rights somewhat surprising, "considering that all danger from the exercise of despotic power upon the people of the States by the executive has long since vanished, their executive authorities being the creatures of popular vote and nowadays rather too weak than too strong. . . ." [72] But Bryce seemed to have little conception of the possibility that popular majorities might wish to suppress certain liberties, nor that this would be done through the legislatures rather than the executives. In one of his less perceptive comments he remarks that "few complaints of practical evils . . . are heard," [73] de-

[70] See James R. Watson, "The Judicial Interpretation of 'Obscenity' in Massachusetts," unpub. M.A. thesis, University of Massachusetts, 1961.

[71] Nelson, *Judicial Review*, p. 201.

[72] James Bryce, *The American Commonwealth*, 2d ed., rev. (2 vols., London, 1891), I, 423.

[73] *Ibid.*

spite the fact that the courts were handling quite a few complaints; and the general lack of public dissatisfaction was probably due to the fact that popular majorities supported repressive legislation.

Popular majorities also revealed little tolerance for the alien immigrants crowded into our large cities; anti-Oriental laws were common, especially in the West, and even the Populists and Progressives revealed little active concern for the plight either of Negroes or of working people in general: both movements were strikingly rural-agrarian in their make-up and point of view, and their urban components were largely middle class. The courts tended strongly to reflect both the agrarian and the middle-class ends of this equation.

The area most prolific of court cases was probably that of church-state relations. This question, which has perennially bothered American politics, was largely centered on two specific concerns, as indeed it still is—Sunday laws and the status of religion in the public schools. In general Sunday laws were upheld, despite the general knowledge that Sunday is a Christian holiday and that observance of it as a day of rest was a favor to the Christian churches which was denied to all others.[74] In the Victorian era and in a country so overwhelmingly Christian (and with a strong Puritan background) this was only to be expected. But in view of the strong clauses which most state constitutions contained concerning the subject of church-state separation, courts had to construct nonreligious reasons for the observance of a religious holiday, and this was generally done by using the police power: the court would say that the state had the right to provide for a day of rest as a health or general welfare measure. The exceptions to this general policy are more interesting than the cases following it: one court held that a law prohibiting barbering after noon on Sunday was beyond the police power;[75] and in South Carolina the old Lord's Day law dating back to 1691 was invalidated, doubtless because of its archaic terms: as the court said, the act

for the better observance of the Lord's Day, commonly called "Sunday," which provides for punishing "the odious and loathsome sin of drunkenness, the root and foundation of many other enormous sins," is not of

[74] The cases are too numerous to be worth mentioning; they are summarized in Alvin W. Johnson and Frank H. Yost, *Separation of Church and State in the United States* (Minneapolis, 1948), pp. 219–255.

[75] *Ex parte* Jentzch, 44 Pac. 803 (1896, Calif.).

force. The act is not only inoperative for non-user, but the offender cannot now be punished publicly by sitting in the stocks as therein provided.[76]

One court held that those new phenomena, the movies, could be prohibited on Sunday, but not if they were shown as a part of a religious service,[77] and another that the state could not go beyond the prohibition of business—that is, it could not require the specifically *religious* observance of the day.[78]

Despite such exceptions, and despite many cases on the subject, it is fair to say that Sunday laws were taken for granted, by the general public, by politicians, and (consequently) by the courts. American courts have seldom set their faces against what they know to be an overwhelming public sentiment, and although they changed the rationale of these laws, they had neither the courage nor the desire to strike them down.

The kinds of religious experience that have been tried in American public schools are many and varied. During the period 1877–1917 they were mostly variants on the theme of Bible reading and recitation of the Lord's Prayer. State courts received these programs with widely differing attitudes. Since the First Amendment religious clauses were still assumed not to apply to the states, the question before the judges was whether their particular state constitutions permitted such practices, which were often commanded by legislation. In some states dissenting students were allowed to excuse themselves from the exercise, which by introducing the element of voluntariness changed somewhat the constitutional issue.

Some courts, in handling such cases, followed the line expressed by the Kentucky judges, which said that the Bible is not a sectarian book if read without comment, and that only sectarian exercises were forbidden by the state constitution.[79] The Kansas court carried this idea a little further when it pointed out that the Bible is the repository for our "noblest ideals of moral character. . . . To emulate these is the supreme conception of citizenship." [80] At times the courts practically contradicted themselves: the judges of Nebraska

[76] O'Hanlon v. Myers, 10 Rich. Law 128 (1878, S.C.).
[77] State v. Morris, 155 Pac. 296 (1916, Idaho).
[78] People v. C. Klinck Packing Co., 108 N.E. 278 (1915, N.Y.).
[79] Hackett v. Brooksville Graded School District, 87 S.W. 792 (1905, Ky.).
[80] Billard v. Bd. of Educ. of Topeka, 69 Kans. 53 (1904). Cf. Moore v. Monroe, 20 N.W. 475 (1884, Iowa); Church v. Bullock, 109 S.W. 115 (1908, Tex.); North v. Trustees, 27 N.E. 54 (1891, Ill.).

claimed that "the suggestion that it is the duty of government to teach religion has no basis whatever in the constitution or laws of this state, nor in the history of our people." But this ringing statement of the separation principle was followed by a decision upholding Bible reading, justified in the following terms: "Certainly the Iliad may be read in the schools without inculcating a belief in the Olympic deities, and the Koran may be read without preaching the Moslem faith. Why may not the Bible also be read without indoctrinating children . . . ?" [81] One may have reservations about how far the judges themselves would have accepted their own doctrine had the Koran, the Book of Mormon, or the speculations of Miss Mary Baker Eddy actually been involved in the case rather than the Bible.

And not all state courts followed this line of decisions. The Wisconsin court condemned religious instruction in state institutions even when those objecting were excused from class. The practice results, said the court, in a loss of caste and a subjection to "reproach and insult," as well as tending "to destroy the equality of the pupils which the constitution seeks to establish and protect." Justice Orton, in a separate opinion, stressed the rigidity of the wall of separation: he argued that the schools are godless, "in the same sense that the executive, legislative, and administrative departments are Godless." [82] And even a Bible Belt court agreed—the Louisiana court regarded the Bible as "a religious book" not suitable for use as a textbook "without regard to its religious character." [83]

Courts also struck down attempts to go further: in Washington it was ruled that credit could not be given for religion classes; [84] and various courts held that state funds could not be used for the support of sectarian schools [85] (although they could be given to other institutions such as orphan asylums or hospitals).[86] The question of

[81] Nebraska v. Scheve, 93 N.W. 169 (1903, Nebr.).

[82] Wisconsin v. Weiss, 44 N.W. 967 (1890, Wis.).

[83] Herold v. Parish Bd., 68 Sou. 116 (1915, La.). Cf. People ex rel Ring v. Bd. of Educ., 245 Ill. 334 (1910); Stevenson v. Hanyon, 4 Pa. Dist. Rep. 395 (1895).

[84] State ex rel Dearle v. Frazier, 102 Wash. 369 (1918).

[85] Otken v. Lamkin, 56 Miss. 758 (1879); State ex rel Nevada Orphan Asylum v. Hallock, 16 Nev. 373 (1882); Cook County v. Chicago Industrial School, 18 N.E. 183 (1888, Ill.); Dakota Synod v. State, 50 N.W. 632 (1891, S.D.); In re Opinion of the Justices, 102 N.E. 464 (1913, Mass.); Williams v. Bd. of Trustees, 191 S.W. 507 (1917, Ky.).

[86] Dunn v. Chicago Industrial School, 117 N.E. 735 (1917, Ill.); Sargent v. Bd. of Educ., 69 N.E. 722 (1904, N.Y.).

whether nuns could wear religious garb when they were functioning as public school teachers also came up. While at least one court held that to prohibit the wearing of the habit would be a violation of religious liberty,[87] there was a strong dissent, and in the following year the state legislated against such a practice, and the law was upheld by the court.[88] The court felt that the law was not directed at the religious sentiments of any person, but at "acts, not beliefs, and only against acts of the teacher while engaged in the performance" of her duties. Other states have commonly taken the same position.[89]

The fact that court decisions usually maintained a strict separation between church and state when support, in any form, of sectarian institutions was involved stands in sharp contrast to the Sunday law cases. The reason seems to lie in the narrowness with which courts (and the American people generally) interpreted the concept of "sectarian." As long as all Christians—or almost all—agree (as against non-Christian groups) the theory was that state support merely reflected the prevailing views of the population. But when Christian denominations disagreed with each other it was not regarded as proper for the state to support any one of them. The Bible-reading cases cut across this to some extent, perhaps a result of the sheer inability of judges, prevailingly Protestant as they were, to view the differences between the King James and Douay versions of the Bible as being of any importance. They would probably have been able to see it more easily had the schools been using the Catholic version.

There were two other interesting cases, both of which involved Mormons—a religious body which the American states have had great difficulty absorbing. In one case, Nevada had attempted to keep Mormons out of the state by passing a law denying them the right to vote: the state supreme court, however, struck down the law.[90] But the Idaho court upheld a law prohibiting polygamy, which was of course a common-law offense and the subject of a federal court ruling which we have already looked at, and denied polygamists the vote.[91]

[87] Hysong v. Gallitzin School Dist., 164 Pa. St. 629 (1894).
[88] Commonwealth v. Herr, 229 Pa. St. 132 (1910).
[89] O'Connor v. Hendrick, 184 N.Y. 421 (1906).
[90] State v. Findlay, 19 Pac. 241 (1888, Nev.).
[91] Innis v. Bolton, 17 Pac. 264 (1888, Idaho); Wolley v. Watkins, 22 Pac. 102 (1889, Idaho).

One would need to look no further than the volume of these cases regarding religion to come to the conclusion that Bryce was far off the mark in thinking that the state bills of rights were observed to the satisfaction of Americans. The discontent came from minorities in most cases, but it was nevertheless pronounced; and in other fields as well as that of religion the response of the courts was not such as would give an impartial observer any strong feeling that judicial review was a bulwark of American liberties. They were protected, for the most part, when clear majorities wanted it so. It has often been remarked that the Supreme Court is responsive to majority opinion, and the remark, though not meant for the state courts, was if anything more applicable to them. A glance at the treatment accorded to Negroes will bolster this conclusion.

No one now believes that the American Negro achieved, or was allowed to achieve, the promise implicit in the grant of citizenship, and as we have seen in earlier chapters, the courts played their role in this failure of democracy in the United States. While Negroes were accorded some legal protection—particularly in the area of jury trial (a matter on which judges could be expected to be sensitive) and that of labor contracts enforced by law—the larger social picture of the years 1877 to 1917 is one of spreading and legally enforced segregation at least in the South, a development which the courts abetted.

The United States Supreme Court led the way on the requirement that Negroes be allowed to serve on juries, a story which we have already surveyed. State courts for the most part accepted and followed, but did not extend, the decisions of the highest court of the nation. It is true that Nevada's exclusion of "Mongolians" from juries was upheld,[92] but otherwise state courts held to the rule that Negroes must be allowed on juries, but that they need not be present on any particular jury, even if the defendant was a Negro.[93]

The labor contract cases seem to be a little-known feature of state constitutional law. They were confined to the southern states where, after the "Black Codes" enacted immediately after the Civil War

[92] State v. Ah Chew, 40 Am. Rep. 488 (1881, Nev.).
[93] Haggard v. Commonwealth, 79 Ky. 366 (1881); State v. Casey, 11 Sou. 583 (1892, La.); State v. Joseph, 12 Sou. 934 (1893, La.); State v. Brown, 24 S.W. 1027 (1894, Mo.); Lawrence v. Commonwealth, 18 Va. 484 (1886).

were rendered invalid by the passage of the Thirteenth Amendment, many states tried to tie the freed slaves to their former owners by various types of labor contract arrangements which contained fines or criminal penalties for workers who jumped their contracts. These laws had the advantage, constitutionally, that they need not specifically mention Negroes, and there was thus some hope that they would pass muster when reviewed by courts, especially since the courts involved were manned by southern judges who could be presumed to be sympathetic with the purpose of the laws. However, even before the national Supreme Court outlawed such acts in 1911,[94] at least one state court had done so,[95] and other states naturally followed suit after 1911.[96] The South Carolina court which invalidated such a law in 1908 used both the Thirteenth Amendment and the state's constitution as grounds, holding (among other things) that it was a violation of the principle of equal protection, since it applied only to workers who had received advances (as most sharecroppers did), and also because there was no reciprocal obligation of the employer to observe the contract.[97] But discrimination on grounds of race was not explicitly mentioned.

Miscegenation laws were generally considered to be constitutionally proper. While the cases decided were mostly from southern states,[98] many northern ones had the same laws, and these were not struck down. One variant on the law, which was also upheld, was a prohibition of sexual intercourse between a white and a Negro, presumably whether or not married.[99]

Another interesting but apparently atypical law was a Maryland statute preventing Negroes from becoming lawyers. Again, the state courts could find no constitutional defect.[100]

But of course the subject most prolific of legislation was racial segregation. "Jim Crow" principles were applied to a wide variety of situations and generally upheld by southern courts, while northern judges tended to regard them askance. As noted above, segregation

[94] Bailey v. Alabama, 219 U.S. 219 (1911).

[95] Ex parte Hollman, 60 S.E. 19 (1908, S.C.).

[96] State v. Armstead, 60 Sou. 778 (1913, Miss.); Fortune v. Braswell, 77 S.E. 818 (1913, Ga.).

[97] Ex parte Hollman, 60 S.E. 19 (1908, S.C.).

[98] Green v. State, 29 Am. Rep. 739 (1877, Ala.); Dodson v. State, 31 S.W. 977 (1895, Ark.); State v. Jackson, 50 Am. Rep. 638 (1886, N.C.); Puitt v. Gaston City Comm., 55 Am. Rep. (1886, N.C.); Frasher v. State, 30 Am. Rep. 131 (1877, Tex.).

[99] Strauss v. State, 173 S.W. 663 (1915, Tex.).

[100] In re Taylor, 30 Am. Rep. 451 (1877, Md.).

by law reached into the area of sex relations, one court going so far as to hold that the state can punish adultery between races more severely than the more ordinary variety.[101]

In other cases, segregation in theaters,[102] schools (even some in the North),[103] railroads and their stations,[104] restaurants, soda fountains (Illinois regarded this as valid, since the antisegregation law there applied only to places of "accommodation and amusement," and the judges did not feel that soda fountains fell into this category),[105] skating rinks,[106] place of residence,[107] saloons,[108] cemeteries,[109] and many other areas of social and economic life were accepted. It was even held in one case that a prohibition of the playing of "craps," which the judges admitted to be typical among Negroes, could be upheld despite the fact that the law did not prohibit gambling in card games, which was typical of whites.[110]

But there were limits, especially in the North, where in any case the number of Negroes was usually too small for segregation to be economically feasible. A Kentucky homestead law was found unconstitutional because it excluded Negroes.[111] Some state courts felt that segregation in schools was unconstitutional,[112] even if separate schools were available.[113] California judges did not permit school segregation for Chinese children.[114] And several courts felt that local school segregation was impermissible unless it was specifically authorized by state law.[115] Texas found that the holding of a first-class

[101] Green v. State, 29 Am. Rep. 451 (1877, Ala.).

[102] Younger v. Judah, 19 S.W. 1109 (1892, Mo.).

[103] State v. Gray, 93 Ind. 303 (1883); Dawson v. Lee, 83 Ky. 49 (1884); Lehew v. Brummell, 15 S.W. 765 (1891, Mo.); People v. Gallagher, 45 Am. Rep. 232 (1886, N.C.).

[104] Central RR v. Green, 86 Pa. St. 421 (1878); Smith v. Chamberlain, 17 S.E. 371 (1893, S.C.); Chesapeake, Ohio & S. RR Co. v. Wells, 4 S.W. 5 (1887, Tenn.).

[105] Cecil v. Green, 4 N.E. 1105 (1896, Ill.).

[106] Bowlin v. Lyon, 25 N.W. 766 (1885, Iowa).

[107] Harris v. Louisville, 177 S.W. 472 (1915, Ky.); Hopkins v. Richmond, 86 S.E. 139 (1915, Va.).

[108] State ex rel Tax Collector v. Falkenheiner, 49 Sou. 214 (1909, La.).

[109] People v. Forest Home Cemetery Co., 101 N.E. 219 (1913, Ill.).

[110] Sparks v. State, 142 S.W. 1183 (1912, Tex.).

[111] Custard v. Poston, 1 S.W. 434 (1886, Ky.).

[112] Kaine v. Commonwealth, 101 Pa. St. 490 (1882).

[113] Wysinger v. Crookshank, 23 Pac. 54 (1890, Calif.).

[114] Tape v. Hurley, 6 Pac. 129 (1885, Calif.).

[115] People v. Quincy, 40 Am. Rep. 196 (1882, Ill.); Ottawa v. Tinnon, 26 Kans. 1 (1881); State v. Union Dist., 46 N.J. Law 76 (1884); State v. Bd. of Educ., 16 N.E. 373 (1887, Ohio).

rail ticket entitled a Negro to first-class accommodations even if (heaven forbid) this meant seating him among whites.[116] Some found restaurant segregation unconstitutional,[117] and the same was applied to theaters and skating rinks.[118] In at least one state, barbers were denied the right to refuse to serve Negro patrons.[119] Kentucky judges held that an industrial school for Negroes must be accorded the same legal rights as similar white institutions.[120]

Despite such decisions, the position of Negroes was nowhere even approximately equal to that of whites even in a legal sense. Even Northern states allowed their towns to enact "sunset to sunrise" laws which prohibited Negroes, in effect, from residing within the town limits. And it is well known that the various state laws prohibiting refusal of service to Negroes in hotels and restaurants were seldom observed; their enforcement was left to the few occasions upon which the individual who was refused had the courage to acquire witnesses and go to court, and such occasions were few indeed. The improvement of the status of Negroes was to depend to a great extent upon court action, but such action was not really either common or effective until long after 1917.

In view of the foregoing comments regarding religious liberty and race discrimination, one would not expect to approach the subject of individual rights before the police and the courts with the idea that state judges were any more liberal in their views. Nor were they. According to the rule developed by the national Supreme Court and affirmed as late as 1910 in the Twining decision,[121] the states were under no constitutional obligation to observe even the minimal rules contained in the Bill of Rights, since these limited only the federal authorities. For instance, the "Weeks rule," which prevented the introduction of illegally obtained evidence in trials, applied only in federal courts except in those few states which adopted their own versions of it.

It would be an error to regard this situation as an unmixed evil.

[116] Texas & Pacific Ry. Co. v. Johnson, 2 Willson, Civ. Cas. Ct. App. §186 (1884, Tex.).
[117] Fruchey v. Eagleson, 43 N.E. 146 (1896, Ind.); Ferguson v. Geis, 46 N.W. 718 (1890, Mich.).
[118] Baylies v. Curry, 21 N.E. 595 (1889, Ill.); People v. King, 18 N.E. 245 (1886, N.Y.).
[119] Messenger v. State, 41 N.W. 638 (1889, Nebr.).
[120] Columbia Trust Co. v. Lincoln Inst., 129 S.W. 113 (1910, Ky.).
[121] See above, p. 207.

The states had to handle the vast majority of all court cases and an even greater proportion of the police activity of the country. As the years wore on, this meant a tremendous and ever increasing case load, and a consequent need to experiment with methods by which they could cope with the volume of work thrust upon them. The federal Constitution, backed by federal court rules, would have been—at least in some areas—a disastrous strait jacket preventing the adaptation of method to need. It could not be assumed that all such experiments would produce injustice, nor that the framers of the Bill of Rights held all wisdom for all time on such subjects. Thus, though the federal courts were held to the rule that the only way a criminal case could be brought to court was on an indictment by a grand jury, the states were able to try a less manpower- and time-consuming method, in which the prosecuting attorney was allowed to bring cases through his own action in a document called a "criminal information," while grand juries were reserved for the relatively few really serious crimes.

The use of the criminal information procedure began, apparently, toward the end of the nineteenth century, and where it was challenged in the state courts, it was usually upheld.[122] In any case, by 1937 Justice Cardozo of the United States Supreme Court could regard the practice as so traditional as to provide him with a good example of a provision of the Bill of Rights which should not be applied to the states.[123]

In some fields there seem to have been no discernible trends; for if one state court invalidated a city ordinance permitting police to photograph and measure "such persons suspected of offenses as the officials of the department determine," [124] another set of judges upheld a similar practice.[125] But the new—and spreading—idea of enacting indeterminate sentence laws, which allowed the trial judge some latitude in sentencing, was generally found to be constitutional.[126] In at least one state an attempt to eliminate the practice of arraignment and plea was struck down,[127] and in another, the punishment without trial of a parent for the offense of a convicted child

---

[122] In re McNaught, 99 Pac. 241 (1909, Okla.); State v. Ju Nun, 97 Pac. 96 (1908, Ore.). There were exceptions; see Lewis v. State, 49 Sou. 753 (1909, Ala.).
[123] Palko v. Connecticut, 302 U.S. 319 (1937).
[124] Gow v. Bingham, 107 N.Y.S. 1011 (1907).
[125] Downs v. Swann, 73 Atl. 653 (1909, Md.).
[126] Woods v. State, 169 S.W. 558 (1914, Tenn.), and many others.
[127] Hack v. State, 124 N.W. 492 (1910, Wis.).

(a rather extreme early instance of attempts to reach the problem of juvenile delinquency) was found invalid.[128] There was some tendency for courts to permit the trial of minor offenses without juries.[129] And courts then as now were wrestling with the problem of how much and what kind of expert testimony should be permitted at trial: the Michigan Supreme Court ruled unconstitutional a state law permitting disinterested expert testimony when the issues involved expert knowledge; the court felt that this "changes the character of criminal procedure, and endangers the constitutional safeguards by giving undue weight" to the opinion of the expert.[130]

Plowing through a catalogue of cases is not very edifying, nor is it in the area of fair trial very informative either, since the scattered nature of the cases involving any one particular question makes "trend spotting" risky. It is as well, therefore, to pass on to other fields about which more can be said.

The freedom of expression was guaranteed in every state constitution. But as in other fields, there were frequent temptations for the legislatures or municipalities to limit it—a temptation which is seemingly timeless, since it still exists today. In most instances the final "protection" of the rights of speech and press lay with the courts; these were often found wanting. It cannot be said that there was wholesale suppression in any state, but in specific cases (and in the Victorian era) individuals often found that court protection was rather illusory.

Censorship was not unknown, and while it usually tended to concentrate on obscenity or indecency, this was not always true. Texas imposed a tax on specified newspapers only, which the courts upheld in 1884.[131] And Kansas prohibited the publication of papers which were "devoted largely to the publication of scandals, intrigues, and immoral conduct," with the courts again upholding the law, which may have been aimed at political criticism.[132] The right of peaceful picketing was often allowed by the courts,[133] but ap-

[128] Mill v. Brown, 88 Pac. 609 (1907, Utah).
[129] Marlow v. Comm., 133 S.W. 1137 (1911, Ky.).
[130] People v. Dickerson, 129 N.W. 199 (1910, Mich.).
[131] Thompson v. State, 17 Tex. App. 253 (1884).
[132] In re Banks, 42 Pac. 693 (1895, Kans.).
[133] St. Louis v. Gloner, 109 S.W. 30 (1908, Mo.); Ex parte Heffron, 162 S.W. 652 (1914, Mo.).

parently just as often denied,[134] but picketing was not necessarily regarded as a form of speech, so that these cases were decided on other grounds.

That new medium just becoming popular toward the end of the period, the movies, was already seen as a source of potential evil. Pennsylvania was allowed by its courts to create a state board of film censors in 1915,[135] and we have seen that in the same year the U.S. Supreme Court upheld a similar Ohio statute.[136] A few years earlier Chicago instituted a permit system under which city officials could deny a permit to show movies which in their judgment were immoral or obscene; the Illinois courts upheld this, also.[137] And Massachusetts upheld a similar licensing system for theatrical productions.[138]

The publication of deliberate falsehoods was held not to be protected by any constitutional provision; [139] Montana went further, ruling that even good-faith accounts of "infamous" acts may be punished if they are untrue.[140] One case going in the other direction occurred in Missouri, where the court, while conceding that the constitution did not protect "blasphemy, obscenity, sedition or defamation," went on to strike down a law which prohibited the publication of the results of investigations of candidates for political office without divulging in full the facts on which these were based and the names and addresses of the persons supplying it.[141] Similarly, it was held that court decisions may be criticized,[142] that a political party may comment on the records of candidates for judicial and educational offices,[143] and that the previous record of a publication cannot be used so as to prohibit its future publication.[144] But comment on judges and courts cannot descend to "mere scandalous abuse," nor can press comment on trials in progress assail the litigants, dictate the verdicts, or "spread before juries its opinion

[134] Hardie-Tynes Mfg. Co. v. Cruse, 66 Sou. 657 (1914, Ala.).
[135] Buffalo Branch, Mutual Film Corp. v. Breitinger, 95 Atl. 433 (1915, Pa.).
[136] See above, p. 212.
[137] Block v. Chicago, 87 N.E. 1011 (1909, Ill.).
[138] Commonwealth v. McGann, 100 N.E. 355 (1913, Mass.).
[139] McDougall v. Sheridan, 128 Pac. 954 (1913, Idaho).
[140] Kelly v. Independent Publishing Co., 122 Pac. 735 (1912, Mont.).
[141] Ex parte Harrison, 110 S.W. 709 (1908, Mo.).
[142] State v. District Court, 155 Pac. 278 (1916, Mont.).
[143] State v. Junkin, 122 N.W. 473 (1909, Nebr.).
[144] Ulster Square Dealer v. Fowler, 111 N.Y.S. 16 (1908).

of the merits of the case." [145] And a publisher cannot evade the liability for a libelous statement merely by publishing a retraction.[146]

The "Comstock laws" against obscenity in literature were a feature of the period, and Massachusetts gained a reputation for enforcing such laws strictly, partly because Comstockery led to the organization of the Boston Watch and Ward Society, which arrogated to itself the function of protecting the people of the state against immorality in literature. Even so, the Massachusetts courts, before 1917, sometimes used technicalities such as defective indictments to avoid ruling on the main question of whether obscenity was present.[147] After 1900, however, the attitude changed. In 1909 the Watch and Ward Society stimulated legal action against Elinor Glyn's novel *Three Weeks*, "an over-written romance about an exotic Russian noblewoman, the Tiger Queen, and a bourgeois Englishman." According to one commentator, "even the scenes of lovemaking have little, if any, realistic description and seem less erotic than exotic." [148] As evidence of obscenity the prosecution presented the following passage:

Then a madness of tender caressing seized her, she purred as a tiger might have done, while undulating like a snake. She touched him with her finger tips, she kissed his throat, his wrists, the palms of his hands, his eyelids, his hair, strong subtle kisses unlike the kisses of women and often between her purrings she murmured love-words in some strange fierce language of her own, brushing his ears and his eyes with her lips the while. And through it all Paul slept on, the eastern perfume in the air still drugging his senses.[149]

Judge J. Wilkes Hammond, who wrote the opinion for the Supreme Judicial Court, assumed that the book should be judged by the standards of general readers, possibly including impressionable youths. He wrote:

[145] *In re* Egan, 123 N.W. 478 (1909, S.D.).

[146] Byers *v.* Meridian Printing Co., 95 N.E. 917 (1911, Ohio).

[147] See Commonwealth *v.* DeJardin, 126 Mass. 46 (1878); Commonwealth *v.* Wright, 139 Mass. 382 (1885); Commonwealth *v.* McCance, 164 Mass. 162 (1895). In the last case the court held the indictment defective because it did not state the exact portions of *The Decameron* which were allegedly obscene.

[148] Watson, "Judicial Interpretation," pp. 31–32. The case referred to is Commonwealth *v.* Buckley, 200 Mass. 346 (1909).

[149] Quoted in Watson, "Judicial Interpretation," p. 33.

. . . an author who has disclosed so much of the details of the way to the adulterous bed . . . and has kept the curtains raised in the way that she has kept them can find no fault if the jury says that not the spiritual but the animal, not the pure but the impure is what the general reader will find as the most conspicuous thought suggested to him as he reads.[150]

Whether the impure and the animal are in themselves obscene the judge did not stop to argue. That such puerile stuff could be adjudged obscene by serious men seems from our present-day vantage point almost unbelievable: but perhaps the general change in moral standards accompanying the advancing years of the twentieth century have put us too far from them for us to be able to judge them fairly.

The last case to arise in Massachusetts before 1917 raised the question of whether pamphlets advocating and explaining birth control for the poor were obscene.[151] The state worried about the effects of the pamphlets on young girls, and the court held that "the details which are set forth in these pamphlets plainly would have warranted a jury in finding they promote wantonness." [152]

While there were similar cases in some other states, these will illustrate the tendencies of the times. Two aspects stand out: that a work need not be judged as a whole but may be condemned on the basis of individual passages; and that the standard to be used is the potential effect on the weakest or most susceptible probable reader. In general, the approach reminds one of the psychology questionnaire which asked a group of coeds what things aroused thoughts of sex; the most common answer was "boys." The courts did not go to the extreme of prohibiting boys, but the attitude was there.

A final important area of constitutional decision making by state courts concerned the control of the election process. This can be disposed of briefly. The state courts unanimously felt that they had the jurisdiction to decide apportionment cases—there was a spate of these, for unknown reasons, in 1892—but their decisions did not necessarily resemble the present "one man, one vote" rule, since they were governed by the specific provisions of state constitutions rather than the ambiguities characteristic of the federal document. Never-

[150] Commonwealth v. Buckley, p. 354.
[151] Commonwealth v. Allison, 227 Mass. 57 (1917).
[152] Ibid., p. 61.

theless, it is important that state courts did not regard apportionment as a "political" question which could not be handled by courts; instead they showed a marked lack of reluctance to enter what Justice Frankfurter later called a "political thicket." [153]

There was a good deal of concern about the qualifications for voting, which went along naturally with the election reforms noted in Chapter 4 such as the Australian ballot. Some states experimented with a literacy test not aimed against Negroes but, presumably, at the achievement of a more intelligent electorate. Such a test was upheld in Massachusetts in 1893.[154] And courts put up no barriers against the spread of compulsory registration laws.[155] Secret ballots were upheld; [156] courts acquiesced in state regulation of nominating procedures; [157] and the frequent decisions denying states the power to grant voting rights to women were, of course, negated by the passage of the Nineteenth Amendment in 1920, but had already been reversed in many states by their own constitutional amendments or by court decision.[158] Using the doctrine that voting is a privilege, not a right, southern judges were able to uphold the poll tax requirements that spread through the South in the 1890's.[159] And finally, the state experiments with campaign expenditure laws ran into no judicial obstacles.[160] Thus, aside from the issues of apportionment, it can be seen that state courts were not inclined to interfere with attempts to reform the political process: nor, in the South, with attempts to keep Negroes from the polls.

[153] Parker v. State, 32 N.E. 836 (1892, Ind.); Giddings v. Blacker, 52 N.W. 944 (1892, Mich.); People v. Monroe County Supervisors, 19 N.Y. Supp. 978 (1892); State v. Cunningham, 51 N.W. 724 (1892, Wis.); People v. Thompson, 40 N.E. 307 (1895, Ill.). Also see Ragland v. Anderson, 100 S.W. 865 (1907, Ky.); State ex rel Barrett v. Hitchcock, 146 S.W. 40 (1912, Mo.); Commonwealth v. Crow, 67 Atl. 355 (1907, Pa.).

[154] Stone v. Smith, 34 N.E. 521 (1893, Mass.).

[155] State v. Butts, 2 Pac. 618 (1884, Kans.); Commonwealth v. McClelland, 83 Ky. 686 (1886); Southerland v. Norris, 22 Atl. 137 (1891, Md.); Daggett v. Hudson, 3 N.E. 538 (1885, Ohio).

[156] Ellis v. May, 58 N.W. 483 (1894, Mich.); State v. Black, 24 Atl. 489 (1892, N.J.).

[157] In re County Treasurers, 21 Pac. 474 (1886, Colo.).

[158] For instance, women's rights were negated in People v. English, 29 N.E. 678 (1892, Ill.), only to be reversed the following year in Plummer v. Yost, 33 N.E. 191 (1893, Ill.).

[159] Frieszleben v. Shallcross, 19 Atl. 576 (1890, Del.); State v. Dillon, 14 Sou. 383 (1893, Fla.); McMahon v. Savannah, 42 Am. Rep. 62 (1880, Ga.).

[160] Adams v. Lansdon, 110 Pac. 280 (1910, Idaho).

Despite the great significance of constitutional law in the American system and its obvious relevance to a constitutional history, the work of the state courts was important far beyond the confines of cases interpreting the constitutional documents. As common-law courts of general jurisdiction, the state courts occupied a traditional "growth point" in American law, and in many respects substituted for the legislatures; for by changing and expanding the common law they were able to aid in the adaptation of our political system to the new conditions of an urban-industrial civilization. Pointing to the great growth in the roles of both legislatures and executives, as we have, should not obscure the continuing, but more quiet and perhaps gradual, work of the courts in this respect.

The equity power of the courts should also be kept in mind, for in some fields it was of crucial importance. In American conditions the common and equity jurisdictions are exercised by the same courts (with a few exceptions). Laymen can hardly be expected to distinguish between them, and no attempt to do so is made here beyond one brief example: "courts abused their equity powers to restrict strikes, picketing, and boycotts, often by *ex parte* injunction." [161]

The way in which courts could "legislate" may be illustrated by a rather simple example. The common law in general had always held that an owner is liable for damages caused by his animals if they are allowed to run loose. In American conditions this rule often seemed, however, not to make much sense; cattle were not kept in the neat enclosures envisioned by it. It is not surprising, then, to find that many state courts reversed the rule.[162] Like most such statements, there are exceptions to it,[163] and in later years the enactment of fence laws has restored the earlier rule, but by statute this time.

The emphasis of the common law on the essential privateness of human life presented a problem when questions of public interest arose. Property, contract, and tort, the three great areas of the com-

[161] James Willard Hurst, *Law and the Conditions of Freedom in the Nineteenth-Century United States* (Madison, Wis., 1956), p. 87. The following remarks follow closely the analysis of Hurst, who is our leading contemporary legal historian.

[162] Little Rock & F. S. RR Co. *v.* Finley, 37 Ark. 562 (1881); Hurd *v.* Lacy, 9 Sou. 378 (1891, Ala.); Woodward *v.* Griffith, 2 Willson, Civ. Cas. Ct. App. §360 (1884, Tex.); Savannah, F. & W. Ry. Co. *v.* Geiger, 58 Am. Rep. 697 (1886, Fla.).

[163] Pittsburgh, C. & St. L. Ry. Co. *v.* Stuart, 71 Ind. 500 (1900).

mon law, were all seen as private. Thus, as late as 1919, when Henry Ford in a burst of public spirit wanted to spread employment and wealth by cutting the prices of his cars, the supreme court of Michigan recalled him to his proper duty—the care and feeding of his stockholders: "A business organization is organized and carried on primarily for the profit of the stockholders . . . [I]t is not within the lawful powers of a board of directors to shape and conduct the affairs of a corporation for the merely incidental benefit of shareholders and for the primary purpose of benefiting others. . . ." [164]

While courts always reserved the power to refuse to enforce contracts which were against public policy, the power was not broadly used until the twentieth century, and even then was mostly confined to "the positive social harms that men might willfully do," [165] thus avoiding the more numerous instances in which damage arose because of indifference or lack of private power. Thus such obvious social values as public health and the conservation of natural resources could not be served by private endeavor. Indeed, the development of American land law by both courts and legislatures—a leading example of the adaptation of law to frontier conditions— instanced by the sale and grant of public lands without substantial controls, made conservation extremely difficult later on.

American law also operated to encourage the growth and concentration of capital. By 1890, however, it was becoming clear that this growth presented problems: "a pace of change which outran men's imagination, philosophy, and administrative competence." The abortive history of the antitrust laws indicates that "we neither realized nor had the capacity to affect our transformation until we were committed." [166] Mr. Dooley again posed the problem, if not the solution, when he wrote of Theodore Roosevelt's policies,

Iv all th' gr-reat evils now threatenin' th' body politic and th' pollytical bodies, these crool organizations an' combinations iv capital is perhaps th' best example iv what upright an' arnest businessmen can do whin they are let alone. They cannot be stamped out be laws or th' decisions iv coorts, or hos-tile ligislachion which is too frindly. Their destruction cannot be accomplished be dimagogues.

Th' thrusts are heejous monsthers built up be th' inlightened inther-

[164] Dodge v. Ford Motor Co., 170 N.W. 668 (1919, Mich.).
[165] Hurst, Law and the Conditions of Freedom, p. 76.
[166] Ibid., p. 83.

prise iv th' men that have done so much to advance pro-gress in our beloved counthry. On wan hand I wud stamp thim undher fut; on th' other hand not so fast.[167]

The common law, on the other hand, was helpful in the large freedom it gave for private association in an age when pressure groups became typical methods of influencing governmental action. While this had its role in the growth of the corporation, it also allowed counter-pressure groups, even labor unions, to exist. The courts often resisted various types of action by unions, but they did not deny their right to existence.[168] And further, while the state courts acquiesced in the development of licensing and legal quali-fications for entrance into various professions—law, medicine, den-tistry—they also accepted the common practice of turning over such regulation to private groups such as the state bar associations.[169]

But it was the area of corporate consolidation which provided the greatest problems. The Granger laws constituted an attempt to switch from a more or less pure competition approach, to legal regu-lation, and as we have seen, most states accepted such laws, at least when they involved "public interest" businesses. Some states tried their own antitrust laws: New Hampshire enacted a series of statutes which it was hoped would prevent the consolidation of the state's railroads; but both this attempt and Chief Justice Charles Doe's concurrent effort to achieve the same goal by court action proved to be abortive, as did the similar attempt of Chief Justice Ryan of Wisconsin.[170]

Another trend, to which we have already called attention, was toward the increasing use of legislation designed to enhance social solidarity and security by protecting groups and institutions which were so disadvantaged that they could not care for themselves. Ex-amples were the increasing use of institutional care (for such groups as the insane, dependent children, old people), and prevention, through health and sanitation measures and, later, through safety regulations for mine and factory, which included shifting the com-mon-law liability from the employee to his employer. While cour s

[167] Quoted in *ibid.*, p. 84.
[168] *Ibid.*, pp. 86–87.
[169] *Ibid.*, p. 87.
[170] For Wisconsin, see *ibid.*, pp. 88–90; for New Hampshire, see Reid, *Ch Justice*, pp. 267–281.

resisted such shifts, the resistance was slowly overborne by legislation. A last example, which was hardly begun by 1917, was the protection of the consumer. Food purity laws began to appear in the 1880's, and other measures later. Here again, the courts slowed the process by their hostility to shifting common-law liability to the producer instead of relying on the old and no longer practicable rule of *caveat emptor*. The development of standard insurance controls was not resisted as strongly, nor was conservation legislation.[171]

None of these trends, one should point out, have yet reached their terminal points; up to 1917 the states had made only beginnings; the federal government had hardly begun. The path to the future was clear, however—more social regulation, in which a greater share of the burden would be borne by the national government.

The role that the courts played in all these developments was everywhere large, but it varied from state to state and within states from time to time depending on who the judges were. These ranged from a Holmes, with his tendency to defer to the legislature, to New Hampshire's Charles Doe, with his free-wheeling judicial activism. Doe went so far, and was so successful, that his sometime friend and party colleague, Senator William E. Chandler, was able to warn, with some pardonable exaggeration, that "no law can be devised by the ablest and most astute legislators that cannot be defied and nullified by the chief justice"—a situation which, according to Chandler, made Doe "the uncontrolled and mighty ruler and governor of New Hampshire; superior to the executive and legislative branches of the government; and high above any laws that can be conceived, drafted, or passed by the legislature of the people." [172]

Neither Holmes nor Doe was typical; nor was either, despite his stature, able to turn aside the course of events. In the long run Massachusetts ended up in the same position as New Hampshire. American history is an illustration of the increasing inability of the states to control the forces of economic and social development. If this could be done, it must be done by the national government.

[171] Hurst, *Law and the Conditions of Freedom,* pp. 91–108.
[172] Quoted in Reid, *Chief Justice,* p. 265.

CHAPTER 9

1877-1917: An Overview

THE alert man who reached his majority in 1877 would, if he were of a reflective turn of mind, have realized in 1917 that he had in forty years lived through a revolution—perhaps, in fact, several of them. It would be difficult to say which was the more important; but the average man was more likely to be conscious of the social and economic changes than of the political. Even perceptive observers were not always aware—in 1917—of how different their constitutional system was from that described at the beginning of Chapter 1. Political change tends to follow rather than to lead the larger social shifts, and then (as now?) observers tended to think of it as almost glacial in its slowness to respond to the needs of the day. Hindsight is helpful here, and may make us more optimistic about the capacities of our contemporary system to adapt to new conditions. For if it teaches us anything, history tells us that American constitutional change, at least from 1877 to 1917, was anything but glacial; in some respects it more nearly resembled an avalanche.

Despite some permanent accretions of power resulting from the Civil War, the national government in 1877 was still thought of as—and largely was—a caretaker agency. Its duties were mainly those one would expect in a geographically large but primarily agrarian society: the control of foreign relations and of trade with other countries, and a minimal control of such domestic matters as postal service, interstate commerce, and the "vanishing Red man." Even such activity was based on day-to-day response to events rather than on planning or continuous supervision; in matters of commerce especially, there was a strong tendency to leave things to God or to the states until something occurred which seemed to make national regulation necessary. It was, in essence, a system based on decentralized power.

If there was a locus of constitutional power in 1877 it resided in the state governments. They were, after all, the repositories of the "reserved powers," and they also were regarded (at least in theory) as dominant over the local governments.

By 1917 one could no longer make such a statement with any certainty. True enough, the states by that time were even more powerful than they had been in 1877; but also by then the national government had begun to assume the vast control over the economy with which we are now so familiar. The regulation symbolized by laws such as the Interstate Commerce Act, the Sherman and Clayton Anti-Trust Acts, the Pure Food and Drug Act, the Federal Reserve Act, and the wartime legislation enacted in 1917–1918 had created a whole new government, for which the administrative apparatus was still being built.

The states and cities were at the same time undergoing much the same transformation—sometimes leading and sometimes following the national government. For every new national function two or three appeared at the state or local level. Increased control of banking and insurance, tremendous expansion of public school systems and of higher education, the beginnings of state park development, and utilities and franchise regulation are examples. Centralization, at every level, was the theme.

At the national level such expansion of function was accomplished almost without formal constitutional changes. The national Constitution's useful ambiguity enabled Congress and the President to assume new tasks without the necessity of going through the difficulties of the amendment process; and these tasks could then be constitutionally sanctified by any Supreme Court which was willing to use the implied powers so conveniently placed to hand by the Founding Fathers as interpreted by John Marshall. State constitutions, most of which were not so flexible, needed constant revision and re-enactment in the process of which new provisions were also made for the local governments, allowing "home rule," manager government, and other reforms.

But the adoption of such great new tasks required also a re-structuring of the governments themselves. Nineteenth-century government in the United States was fundamentally based on legislative supremacy. Executives were everywhere weak and "administration" almost nonexistent. In addition, however, the legislatures were either literally leaderless, like Congress, or if they were "boss-ridden," as some of the states and cities were, the bosses were not interested in general policy. Either way the effects were the same. The separation of powers theories on which these governments were founded did not make it easy for executives to assume the tasks of legislative leadership, nor did the federal system make easy the development of national policy-oriented parties which could do so. But it seemed unlikely that leadership could maintain itself within the legislatures, as the reaction to Czar Reed and Uncle Joe Cannon demonstrated. The political hallmark of Progressivism was the growth of personal leadership from the executive mansion à la Governor and then President Woodrow Wilson of New Jersey, whose personal role was duplicated by Theodore Roosevelt of New York and Washington; by Charles Evans Hughes of New York, Hazen L. Pingree of Michigan, Fighting Bob La Follette of Wisconsin, John Peter Altgeld of Illinois, Hiram Johnson of California; and by Tom L. Johnson of Toledo, Golden Rule Jones of Cleveland, Joseph M. Folk of Missouri, and many more. All of these men were successful to the degree that they had the willingness to exert legislative leadership and the ability either to subordinate existing party organizations or to build their own.

The system also had some resistance to the adoption of new functions built into it. The courts with their power of judicial review became significant shareholders in the constitutional system because they could be used as resistance mechanisms. This, more than anything, explains why Louis Boudin's charge that we had "government by judiciary" was more true after 1890 than it had ever been earlier. Boudin was thinking mostly of the United States Supreme Court, but little of his charge was inapplicable to the state courts. This resistance was never, it is true, wholehearted or consistent; but it did make the courts more powerful than they had ever been before.

The great growth of "interest groups" after 1877 was another instance of a "resistance mechanism," for many groups, like the American Bar Association and the Iron and Steel Institute, were formed to combat the threat of government regulation. It is, of course, also true that interest groups often *wanted* more government action—favorable to them. The various farm groups, labor, even the NAACP, were organized to push for protective legislation. Arthur F. Bentley felt that the "push-and-shove" of such groups was responsible almost solely for the substance of American governmental policy; even if one does not wish to go so far, they undoubtedly play a large constitutional role.

Despite everything, American constitutionalism remained invincibly middle class. The middle class ran the country, even if it was by 1917 a much different middle class than it had been in 1877. The gentleman farmer or professional (lawyer, preacher) had given way first to the exigent entrepreneur, who had in his turn by 1917 given way to the big corporate institution. In some sense the business of America had always been business, and even such democratic innovations as the popular election of Senators, the initiative and referendum, and nomination through the direct primary did little to dilute this.

With increasing size and complexity, and their concomitant, a permanent bureaucracy, government became inevitably more remote from the average man. One result was a decline in the proportion of those who took the trouble to vote. The alienated voter probably has existed at least since 1900.

This is but to say that in its attempts to cope with one set of problems—the nationalization of the economy, the wage economy, the growth and corruption of the cities, the communications revolution—the constitution makers of the day built new political institutions which, whatever their virtues, contained their own problems. The dangerous aggrandizement of the popular executive, the failure to develop internal legislative leadership or policy-oriented parties, the inability to look very far beyond the needs of the middle classes (or the needs of other groups as seen benevolently by the middle classes)—all these, and more, were emergent problems by 1917. The low level of voting was an early symptom of trouble which was, however, largely ignored. Even in the 1930's, when the problems of the poor became too noticeable to ignore, legislation by middle-class bureaucrats was the answer rather than institutional reform which could make government more responsive to all the people. The New

Deal was, in effect, like a doctor prescribing pills without seeing the patient.

It would be too much, nevertheless, to expect that our man of 1877–1917 could see either these changes in proper perspective or the problems to which they would give rise. Even had he seen them, the solutions might well have eluded him even as they seem today to elude us. Human beings have great capacities for solving technical problems; but despite great effort and astonishing ingenuity, the solution of social and political ones remains beyond our grasp. We of all generations should be charitable with the Theodore Roosevelts and Woodrow Wilsons of our history. We have not even succeeded in ridding ourselves of their unpleasant moral righteousness, and in fact we see it reborn in our own children.

Our contemporary constitutional crisis was, then, foreshadowed by the evolution of the constitution from 1877 to 1917. The decisions made then are to a surprising degree the problems we face now. The nature of societies is, however, too complex for us to accuse our forebears casually of being wrong. Circumstances may have closed off desirable alternatives; hindsight is available only to those who come later; and even hindsight does not induce infallibility. It should, indeed, induce humility.

Bibliographical Essay

General Works

There are not many general studies of the American political system which concentrate on the period from Reconstruction to the First World War. Those which do exist were written during the period itself and suffer from the twin defects of being too close to the subject to view it properly and of being written primarily out of experience without real historical research. Undoubtedly the most useful are the works of Bryce and Wilson. James Bryce brought an English detachment to the only work worthy of comparison with de Tocqueville, in his *The American Commonwealth* (published in many editions; the one used by the author was the second edition, revised, London, 2 volumes, 1891). Wilson did not cover nearly as much ground, since his interests were largely confined to national politics; nevertheless, *Congressional Government* (New York, 1885) and *Constitutional Government in the United States* (New York, 1908) are classics, especially valuable in their illustration of the shift in Wilson's (and the nation's) conceptions of the role of the President. Henry Jones Ford's *Rise and Growth of American Politics* (New York, 1898) is stimulating but biased.

The studies of the Constitution are in general both excessively legalistic and narrow; they tend strongly to deal with the Constitution as though the Supreme Court's decisions were its entire content. The most influential were undoubtedly Thomas M. Cooley, *A Treatise on the Constitutional Limitations Which Rest Upon the Legislative Power of the States of the American Union* (Boston, 1868), and Christopher G. Tiedeman, *A Treatise on the Limitations of Police Power in the United States* (St. Louis, 1886); both emphasized the laissez-faire implications of substantive due process.

Developments in the political and social thought of the period have received more attention, since both Populism and Progressivism had their contemporary scholarly advocates and have attracted historians. Advocates are of course partisan, but may reflect developing trends very well. Both Wilson and Ford, cited above, illustrate this. Excellent also are Herbert Croly, *The Promise of American Life* (New York, 1909); Walter Lippmann, *Drift and Mastery* (New York, 1914); Walter Weyl, *The New Democracy* (New York, 1914); and Brooks Adams, *The Law of Civilization and Decay* (New York, 1896)—the last a gloomy forecast of the end of civilization.

Most of the historians who have dealt with the intellectual trends of the period have done so with more or less of a Progressive slant. This was especially true of Vernon L. Parrington, whose brilliant *Main Currents of American Thought* (3 volumes, New York, 1927–30) influenced the writing of history until the fifties, when a revisionist trend set in, led by Richard Hofstadter, whose *The Age of Reform* (New York, 1955) stimulated, in its turn, both agreement and opposition. A most suggestive and well-written work is Henry Steele Commager, *The American Mind* (New Haven, 1950). Also valuable are the following: Matthew Josephson, *The Politicos* (New York, 1938) and *The Robber Barons* (New York, 1934); Ralph Henry Gabriel, *The Course of American Democratic Thought* (New York, 1940); Morton G. White, *Social Thought in America* (New York, 1949); R. H. Wiebe, *The Search for Order, 1877–1920* (New York, 1965); John D. Hicks, *The Populist Revolt* (Minneapolis, 1931); and Eric Goldman, *Rendezvous with Destiny* (New York, 1952).

One should also use the other volumes in The New American Nation series dealing with the period: John A. Garraty, *The New Commonwealth, 1877–1890* (New York, 1968); Harold U. Faulkner, *Politics, Reform and Expansion, 1890–1900* (New York, 1959); George E. Mowry, *The Era of Theodore Roosevelt, 1900–1912* (New York, 1958); Arthur S. Link, *Woodrow Wilson and the Progressive Era, 1910–1917* (New York, 1954); and Foster Rhea Dulles, *America's Rise to World Power, 1898–1954* (New York, 1954).

The National Government

Congress

Many of the works already cited deal at least in part with the role of Congress in the constitutional system. Bryce and Wilson are the most important of these. There are in addition more specialized works. Wilfred E. Binkley, *President and Congress* (New York, 1947), is old but still useful. Perhaps the best work in this field is David J. Rothman, *Politics and Power: The United States Senate, 1869–1901* (Cambridge, 1966), which documents the rise and fall of the Senate oligarchy. There is no really comparable book on the House, but George B. Galloway, *History of the House of Representatives* (New York, 1961), is useful. For special topics, see Mary Parker Follett, *The Speaker of the House of Representatives* (New York, 1896), and its sequel, Chang-Wei Chiu, *The Speakers of the House of Representatives Since 1896* (New York, 1928), and Charles R. Atkinson, *The Committee on Rules and the Overthrow of Speaker Cannon* (New York, 1911). In a class by itself stands the work of Robert Luce, whose three volumes together show a remarkable grasp of the workings of Congress: *Legislative Procedure* (Boston, 1922), *Legislative Assemblies* (Boston, 1924), and *Congress—an Explanation* (Cambridge, 1926). Interesting but frothy is Robert and Leona Train Rienow, *Of Snuff, Sin and the Senate* (Chicago, 1965). Aspects of politics are treated in J. Rogers Hollingsworth, *The Whirligig of Politics* (Chicago, 1963), and S. Walter Poulshock, *The Two Parties and the Tariff in the 1880's* (Syracuse, 1965).

Works by and about prominent legislators are also of value. Some of the best are L. J. Lang (ed.), *Autobiography of Thomas Collier Platt* (New York, 1910); John Sherman, *Recollections of Forty Years in the House, Senate, and Cabinet* (Chicago, 1895); N. W. Stephenson, *Nelson W. Aldrich* (New York, 1930); D. S. Muzzey, *James G. Blaine* (New York, 1934); A. R. Conkling, *The Life and Letters of Roscoe Conkling* (New York, 1889); Herbert Croly, *Marcus Alonzo Hanna* (New York, 1912); John A. Garraty, *Henry Cabot Lodge* (New York, 1953); W. A. Robinson, *Thomas B. Reed* (New York, 1930); Blair Bolles, *Tyrant from Illinois: Uncle Joe Cannon's Experiment with Personal Power* (New York, 1951); and Claude Bowers, *Beveridge and the Progressive Era* (Boston, 1932). There are unfortunately no adequate biographies of William Jennings Bryan or Robert M. La Follette.

The Presidency

Works dealing with the presidency during the period under review are not plentiful. The best histories which include this period are Edward S. Corwin, *The President: Office and Powers,* second edition, revised (New York, 1941), and Rexford G. Tugwell, *The Enlargement of the Presidency* (Garden City, 1960), both of which are quite valuable. Also of value, although in a different way, since it includes comparison with the state governors, is Joseph E. Kallenbach, *The American Chief Executive* (New York, 1966). Interesting because of their "old-fashioned" views of the presidency are Henry Campbell Black, *The Relation of the Executive Power to Legislation* (Princeton, 1919), and William Howard Taft, *The Presidency: Its Duties, its Powers, its Opportunities and its Limitations* (New York, 1916).

Useful also are the biographies of the Presidents, although they vary greatly in general quality and also in the attention they pay to the nature of the office and to the contributions of each President to that office. The following seem most useful. Harry Barnard, *Rutherford B. Hayes and His America* (Indianapolis, 1954); R. G. Caldwell, *James A. Garfield: Party Chieftain* (New York, 1931); G. F. Howe, *Chester A. Arthur* (New York, 1934); and H. J. Sievers, *Benjamin Harrison* (Chicago and New York, 1952–68), are inadequate to their subjects but of some use. Better treatments of the more significant Presidents include Allan Nevins, *Grover Cleveland: A Study in Courage* (New York, 1932); H. Wayne Morgan, *William McKinley and His America* (Syracuse, 1963); Henry F. Pringle, *Theodore Roosevelt, A Biography* (New York, 1931), and perhaps better, John M. Blum, *The Republican Roosevelt* (Boston, 1954); Henry F. Pringle, *The Life and Times of William Howard Taft* (2 volumes, New York, 1939); the definitive work on Wilson by Arthur S. Link is in multivolume form and still unfinished (Princeton, 1947, 1956, 1960, etc.), but there are also several excellent one-volume treatments: John A. Garraty, *Woodrow Wilson* (New York, 1956), and J. M. Blum, *Woodrow Wilson and the Politics of Morality,* are both good. Roosevelt, Taft, and Wilson, of course, each spoke and wrote for himself, although Roosevelt's *Autobiography* (New York, 1921) and Taft's work on the presidency cited above both constitute apologia written after the fact and cannot be taken too seriously, while Wilson's works cited above were written long before his presidency and may lose in value because they do not reflect scholarship refined by experience.

The Administration

American administrative history—at least before 1900—is known to us largely through the seminal works of Leonard D. White, whose final volume, *The Republican Era: 1869–1901* (New York, 1958), is an exceptional study. The new institutional developments of constitutional importance have not on the whole been adequately treated by historians. On civil service reform, see Ari Hoogenboom, *Outlawing the Spoils: A History of the Civil Service Reform Movement, 1865–1883* (Urbana, 1961), and Paul P. Van Riper, *History of the United States Civil Service* (Evanston, 1958). The development of economic regulation through the regulatory commission device is surveyed in Carter Goodrich, *Government Regulation of American Canals and Railroads: 1800–1890* (New York, 1960), Robert E. Cushman, *The Independent Regulatory Commissions* (New York, 1941), and Marver H. Bernstein, *Regulating Business by Independent Commission* (Princeton, 1955); except for Goodrich, these are not historically oriented. On antitrust law see the able summary of nineteenth-century attitudes in Sidney B. Fine, *Laissez-faire and the General Welfare State* (Ann Arbor, 1956).

The Courts

The material on the Supreme Court is abundant and good—so much so that to list a few works is by implication to denigrate others. One might mention the Progressivist work of Louis Boudin, *Government by Judiciary* (2 volumes, New York, 1931), and the conservative equivalent by Charles Warren, *The Supreme Court in United States History* (3 volumes, Boston, 1923). Four excellent books which concentrate upon the period, and especially on the laissez-faire attitudes of the judges, are Robert G. McCloskey, *American Conservatism in the Age of Enterprise* (Cambridge, 1951); Benjamin R. Twiss, *Lawyers and the Constitution: How Laissez-faire Came to the Supreme Court* (Princeton, 1942); Arnold M. Paul, *Conservative Crisis and the Rule of Law* (New York, 1969); and Arthur Selwyn Miller, *The Supreme Court and American Capitalism* (New York, 1968). There are many more; the various works of Edward S. Corwin will be cited below.

Legal writings of importance include the obvious: Oliver Wendell Holmes, Jr., *The Common Law* (Boston, 1881), which strongly influenced liberal trends in legal thought; and the seminal essay by Roscoe Pound, "The Scope and Purpose of Sociological Jurisprudence," *Harvard Law Review,* XXV (1911), 591.

The Federal System

Of the many general works on American federalism the following seem the most valuable. Morton Grodzins, *The American System: A New View of Government in the United States,* ed. by Daniel J. Elazar (Chicago, 1966), and the work of Daniel J: Elazar—*American Federalism: A View from the States* (New York, 1966) and especially *The American Partnership* (Chicago, 1962)—have been influential in leading to an emphasis on the interrelationships of constitutional power, forcing a reanalysis of nineteenth-century federalism. Other works of importance are M. J. C. Vile, *The Structure of American Federalism* (London, 1961), which, however, is largely concerned with the contemporary situation, and Jane Perry Clark, *The Rise of a New Federalism* (New York, 1938). The Supreme Court's development of the doctrines of dual federalism was well portrayed in Edward S. Corwin, *The Twilight of the Supreme Court* (New Haven, 1934). Also good is John R. Schmidhauser, *The Supreme Court as Final Arbiter in Federal-State Relations, 1789–1957* (Chapel Hill, 1958).

The biographies of the men who sat on the Court during the development of dual federalism are many and some of them excellent, although most of them have given in to the natural tendency to try to exonerate "the hero" from any complicity in the Court's acceptance of laissez-faire doctrines. Carl Brent Swisher, *Stephen J. Field, Craftsman of the Law* (Washington, 1930), is standard, but a new treatment is badly needed. Excellent are Alpheus T. Mason, *Brandeis, a Free Man's Life* (New York, 1946); Mark deWolfe Howe, *Justice Oliver Wendell Holmes* (2 volumes, Cambridge, 1957, 1963), is brilliant, but the author died before reaching Holmes' judicial years; Francis Biddle, *Justice Holmes, Natural Law and the Supreme Court* (New York, 1961) and *Mr. Justice Holmes* (New York, 1942), are not as encyclopedic but are finished. Merlo J. Pusey, *Charles Evans Hughes* (2 volumes, New York, 1961), is "official" but somewhat biased. Charles Fairman, *Mr. Justice Miller and the Supreme Court* (Cambridge, 1939); C. Peter Magrath, *Morrison R. Waite: The Triumph of Character* (New York, 1963); and Willard L. King, *Melville Weston Fuller* (New York, 1950), are all excellent. Mason's *William Howard Taft: Chief Justice* (New York, 1965) has some valuable material even though Taft's tenure came after 1917. There are no biographies of two very important Justices, Harlan and White. Less valuable are W. A. Cate, *Lucius Q. C. Lamar* (Chapel Hill, 1935); M. McDevitt, *Joseph McKenna* (Washington, 1946); J. E. McLean, *William Rufus Day* (Baltimore, 1947); H. L. Warner, *The Life of Mr. Justice Clarke* (Cleveland, 1959).

State and Local Government

The literature on state and local government is tremendous, but little that is reliable relates directly to the late nineteenth and early twentieth centuries. Much of what exists is in the form of controversial writing and must be used with caution. Bryce is important, of course. On the state governors Leslie Lipson, *The American Governor from Figurehead to Leader* (Chicago, 1939); and Joseph E. Kallenbach, *The American Chief Executive* (New York, 1966), are the best. Material on state legislatures is fugitive; Arthur N. Holcombe's relevant chapters in *State Government in the United States* (New York, 1916) are one source. Only scattered sources exist on state courts, and these are seldom interested in portraying the role of these courts in the constitutional systems of the states.

Several good treatments of the impact of political movements in various states have been written. See particularly Geoffrey Blodgett, *The Gentle Reformers: Massachusetts Democrats in the Cleveland Era* (Cambridge, 1966); George E. Mowry, *The California Progressives* (Berkeley, 1951); Hoyt Landon Warner, *Progressivism in Ohio, 1897–1917* (Columbus, 1964); Richard M. Abrams, *Conservatism in a Progressive Era: Massachusetts Poli-*

tics, 1900–1912 (Cambridge, 1964). Useful for the South is C. Vann Wood-ward's excellent *Origins of the New South* (Baton Rouge, 1951). Also good is Paul Kleppner, *The Cross of Culture: A Social Analysis of Midwestern Politics, 1850–1900* (New York, 1970). Also see William D. Miller, *Memphis During the Progressive Era* (Memphis, 1958); Robert S. Maxwell, *La Follette and the Rise of the Progressives in Wisconsin* (Madison, 1956); and Ransom E. Noble, *New Jersey Progressivism before Wilson* (Princeton, 1946).

The position in the constitutional framework of local governments, and the theories surrounding it, is ably surveyed in Anwar H. Syed, *The Political Theory of American Local Government* (New York, 1966). One aspect of the development of state regulation of business is treated in Lee S. Benson's influential *Merchants, Farmers, and Railroads: Railroad Regulation and New York Politics, 1850–1887* (Cambridge, 1955). And the reform of the cities, the need for which was so ably documented by the muck-rakers, especially Lincoln Steffens, *The Shame of the Cities* (New York, 1904), is surveyed partially both in coverage and in attitude in Frank Mann Stewart, *A Half Century of Municipal Reform: The History of the National Municipal League* (Berkeley, 1950).

The Public and Its Government

There are various works on Negro voting: among the best are Wood-ward, cited above, Richard Claude, *The Supreme Court and the Electoral Process* (Baltimore, 1970); Loren Miller, *The Petitioners* (Cleveland, 1966); and Perry H. Howard, *Political Tendencies in Louisiana, 1812–1952* (Baton Rouge, 1957). Kirk H. Porter, *A History of Suffrage in the United States* (Chicago, 1918), deals with the development of the voting rights of women; there appears to be no really adequate treatment of the women's suffrage movement. Woodward and Howard both treat in detail the disfran-chisement of the poor in the South; there is no such adequate treat-ment for the urban poor. Useful in general is Harold F. Gosnell, *Democracy: The Threshold of Freedom* (New York, 1948). The adoption of the secret ballot is well portrayed in L. E. Fredman, *The Australian Ballot* (East Lansing, 1968). Charles E. Merriam's old book *Primary Elections* (Chicago, 1907) is still useful, as is Merriam and Louise Overacker, *Primary Elections* (Chicago, 1928); but these should be considered along with the critical comments of authors like V. O. Key, *American State Politics* (New York, 1965). An excellent recent history is Richard Claude, *The Supreme Court and the Electoral Process* (Baltimore, 1970). Eulogies of the American two-party system such as Herbert Agar's *The Price of Union* (Boston, 1950) should be similarly balanced, perhaps by the Report of a committee of the American Political Science Association, *Toward a More Responsible Two Party System* (New York, 1950). The most challenging recent interpretations of American party history appear in William Nisbet Chambers and Walter Dean Burnham, *The American Party Systems: Stages of Political Development* (New York, 1967); for 1877–1917 the most important chapters in this book are those by Burnham and by Samuel P. Hays. Of writers during the period, M. Ostrogorski, *Democracy and the Organization of Political Parties*, Volume II, *The United States* (Chicago, 1964), remains a classic; the introduction to this edition by Seymour Martin Lipset is also valuable. The material on pressure groups is scattered; Arthur F. Bentley's *The Process of Government* (Chicago, 1908) was the first book to deal with them explicitly and in detail; as a theory of group political action it is, however, exaggerated and oversimplified. As a study of a particular group, Arnold Paul's work cited earlier is valuable for its discussion of the American Bar Association, as is Twiss for its emphasis on the nature of pressures on the Supreme Court. See also Robert Horn, *Groups and the Constitution* (Stanford, 1956).

The Supreme Court and National Business Regulation

All of the judicial biographies mentioned above survey developments in the field of national business regulation. In addition, the following are valuable. Edward S. Corwin's writings were among the most influential; see especially *The Commerce Power v. States Rights* (Princeton, 1936) and *Total War and the Constitution* (New York, 1947). Also influential was Felix Frankfurter's *The Commerce Clause under Marshall, Taney and Waite* (Chapel Hill, 1937). The story of the Supreme Court's response to regulation has been told many times, and many of the works have already been mentioned in other connections. Others which may be valuable are Henry Rottschaefer, *The Constitution and Socio-Economic Change* (Ann Arbor, 1948); Thomas Reed Powell, *Vagaries and Varieties in Constitutional Interpretation* (New York, 1956); Walton H. Hamilton and D. Adair, *The Power to Govern* (New York, 1937); Robert H. Jackson, *The Struggle for Judicial Supremacy* (New York, 1941); and Robert L. Hale, *Freedom Through Law* (New York, 1952).

The Supreme Court and State Business Regulation

Much of the legal controversy surrounding state business regulation concerned the meaning of the Fourteenth Amendment, a subject about which a great deal of ink has been spilled. The most useful works are Howard Jay Graham, *Everyman's Constitution* (Madison, 1968), a collection of the author's influential writings on the subject; Horace B. Flack, *The Adoption of the Fourteenth Amendment* (Baltimore, 1908), old but still useful; J. B. James, *The Framing of the Fourteenth Amendment* (Urbana, 1956); A. J. Lien, *Concurring Opinion* (St. Louis, 1957); and Jacobus ten Broek, *The Anti-Slavery Origins of the Fourteenth Amendment* (Berkeley, 1951), probably the dominant work in the field. Most of the works cited in the previous section are also relevant.

On more specific aspects of state regulation as treated by the Supreme Court a few of the more important works are Benjamin F. Wright, *The Contract Clause of the Constitution* (Cambridge, 1938); Clyde D. Jacobs, *Law Writers and the Courts: The Influence of Thomas M. Cooley, Christopher G. Tiedeman, and John F. Dillon upon American Constitutional Law* (Berkeley, 1954); Charles Fairman, "The So-called Granger Cases, Lord Hale, and Justice Bradley," *Stanford Law Review*, 5 (July, 1953), 587–679; J. A. C. Grant, "The Natural Law Background of Due Process," *Columbia Law Review*, 31 (January, 1931), 56–81; Walton H. Hamilton, "The Path of Due Process," in Conyers Read (ed.), *The Constitution Reconsidered* (New York, 1938); Rodney L. Mott, *Due Process of Law* (Indianapolis, 1926); and Roscoe Pound, "Liberty of Contract," *Yale Law Journal*, 18 (May, 1909), 454–487.

Civil Liberties for Black and White

The literature touching upon the history of the Supreme Court's handling of civil liberties questions is literally endless, and no point would here be served by attempting more than a "short list." One should probably start with the seminal article by Charles Fairman and Stanley Morrison, "Does the Fourteenth Amendment Incorporate the Bill of Rights," *Stanford Law Review*, 2 (December, 1949), 5, 140, which constitutes a powerful if not conclusive vote against incorporation. Loren P. Beth, "The Slaughterhouse Cases," *Louisiana Law Review*, 23 (April, 1963), 487–505, presents a somewhat different view. While there was little Supreme Court concern with civil liberties questions in general during this period—though James C. N. Paul and Murray L. Schwartz, *Federal Censorship* (New York, 1961), is valuable—the literature stimulated by its handling of racial discrimination cases is both plentiful and, regrettably, often too partisan to be reliable. A good treatment, presenting the Negro view, and including much information not easily available elsewhere, is Loren Miller, *The Petitioners* (Cleveland, 1966), which covers the entire period. Less wide ranging but very valuable is Robert J. Harris, *The Quest for Equality* (Baton Rouge, 1960). Other works are valuable as well, but repetitive.

State Courts and the Constitution

It is distressing that almost nothing has been written which does more than scratch the surface of state court activities, important though they obviously were. Good pictures of state supreme courts in action are given in John Philip Reid, *Chief Justice: The Judicial World of Charles Doe* (Cambridge, 1967), and *An American Judge: Marmaduke Dent of West Virginia* (New York, 1968). J. W. Hurst's work on the legal responses to changing conditions are fundamental; see his *Law and the Conditions of Freedom in the Nineteenth Century* (Madison, 1956) and *Law and Economic Growth: The Legal History of the Lumber Industry in Wisconsin, 1836–1915* (Cambridge, 1964). Studies of a different type, useful but not exciting, are Margaret V. Nelson, *A Study of Judicial Review in Virginia, 1789–1928* (New York, 1947), and Franklin A. Smith, *Judicial Review of Legislation in New York, 1906–1938* (New York, 1952). State cases on the church-state controversy are usefully surveyed in Alvin W. Johnson and Frank H. Yost, *Separation of Church and State in the United States* (Minneapolis, 1948). A mine of material, much but not all of which deals with the Wisconsin workmen's compensation laws, is Carl A. Auerbach *et al., The Legal Process* (San Francisco, 1961).

Index

Referendum, adoption of, 123–124
and legislative power, 80
Regulatory commissions, attitudes of
state courts toward, 223
development of, federal, 26–27
growth of, in states, 76–77
Reid v. *Cole*, 152
Religion in public schools, state court
treatment of, 232–234
Rent controls, wartime, 164
Representation, 135
Republican party, and laissez-faire, xix
Senate caucus of, 36–37
Reserved powers of the states, 167–172
Reynolds v. *U.S.*, 213–214
Richardson v. *State*, 226
Ritchie v. *People*, 220
Roche, John P., cited, 209
Roelofs, H. Mark, quoted, xii n.
Roosevelt, Theodore, and foreign policy leadership, 39–40
and growth of presidential power, 14
and labor, 10
and Negroes, 110
and Panama Canal, 39
and Spanish-American War, xxiv
and veto power, 13
and weakness of governors, 73–74
as an "issue" candidate, 122
as foreign policy leader, 20
as legislative leader, 19–20
as pragmatist, xxi
conception of presidency of, 10
estrangement from Cannon of, 35
on trust-busting, 44
opposes Senate oligarchy, 37
stewardship theory of, 20
viewed as unsound by Republicans,
xix
mentioned, 115
Roth v. *State*, 227
Rousseau, Jean-Jacques, xviii
Rule of reason, in rate cases, 178–179
use of, by state courts, 84–85
Russell, William E., and weakness of
governors, 74
Russo-Japanese War, Roosevelt's settlement of, 39
Ryan, Chief Justice, 247

Safety regulation, under police power,
183
upheld by state courts, 226

Saville v. *Corless*, 228
St. Louis v. *Gloner*, 240
St. Louis Land Co. v. *Kansas City*, 184
San Mateo County v. *Southern Pacific
Ry. Co.*, 173
Santa Clara County v. *Southern Pacific
Ry. Co.*, 173
Sargent v. *Board of Education*, 233
Savannah, F. & W. Ry. Co. v. *Geiger*,
245
Schmidt v. *Indianapolis*, 226
Schools, sectarian, public support of,
233
Schurz, Carl, and civil service reform, 24
mentioned, 5
Schwartz, Bernard, quoted on free
speech, 211
Search and seizure, 200–201
Segregation, in schools, 237
on railroads, 145
on steamboats, 145
residential, 237
treatment of, by state courts, 236–
238
See also Negroes
Selective Draft Law Cases, 163–164
Self-incrimination, in federal courts,
200–201
prohibition of, not applicable to
states, 207–208
Senate, direct election of, 123
leadership in, 35–37
party organization in, 35–37
Sentences, indeterminate, development
of, 239
Separation of powers, effects of administrative adjudication on, 87
Seventeenth Amendment, and decline
of Senate power, 37
mentioned, 123
Shannon, Jasper B., quoted on nature
of rural politics, 99–100
Sherman Anti-Trust Act of 1890, en-
actment of, 27–28
Sherman, John, 5
Sherry v. *Perkins*, 221
Shiras, Justice George, Jr., and income
tax cases, 158
Short ballot, adoption of, 118
Shreveport Rate Case, 150
Silver platter doctrine, 201
Sixteenth Amendment, as reversal of
income tax decision, 157

71 72 73 74   12 11 10 9 8 7 6 5 4 3 2 1